# THE STATUS OF ANIMALS

## Ethics, Education and Welfare

Edited by

David Paterson and Mary Palmer

D0169931

Published on behalf of the
Humane Education Foundation by

C·A·B INTERNATIONAL

Published on behalf of the Humane Education Foundation by

CAB International
Wallingford
Oxon OX10 8DE
UK

Tel: Wallingford (0491) 32111
Telex: 847964 (COMAGG G)
Telecom Gold/Dialcom: 84: CAU001
Fax: (0491) 33508


British Library Cataloguing in Publication Data

The Status of animals: ethics, education and welfare
    1. Animals. Relationships with man. Ethical aspects
    I. Paterson, David  II. Palmer, Mary  III. Humane Education Foundation
    179'.3

    ISBN 0-85198-650-1

Printed in the UK by BPCC Wheatons Ltd, Exeter

## RESOLUTION

(See page 224)

"This conference, being aware of the urgent need for humane education in its widest sense, calls upon individuals and organisations to make an educational contribution in whatever way they consider relevant to bring this subject to the attention of all levels of society".

# LIST OF CONTENTS

## PREFACE

David Paterson

Logically, this Symposium is one of a series. The first, Animal Rights - a Symposium (Paterson & Ryder, 1979), held at Cambridge University in the summer of 1978, opened up the whole question of the position of animals in our society. It was followed by several conferences and various publications on the issues raised, ranging from the use of animals in education (Bishop; Godwin; Paterson, 1979), to the ethics of animal usage (Carpenter, 1980).

The second, Humane Education - a Symposium (Paterson, 1981), was held at Sussex University and concentrated largely on a broad spectrum of educational issues in relation to animal usage and welfare. This triggered several in-depth investigations and surveys into our children's attitudes towards animals (Paterson, 1986; BBC/BVA, 1988).

In the meantime, parallel developments were taking place in America, Australia, Canada and New Zealand. Several one-day symposia on particular issues followed in this country - notably Andrew Linzey's on Ethics at Essex University during 1987, which sparked off this, the third major symposium, held at Nottingham University in the summer of 1988.

The value of these symposia is inestimable. Not only do they provide a useful "snapshot" of current positions on animal welfare, but they increasingly inspire significant forward leaps in theory and practice. Who, for instance, could have thought in 1978 that prominent members of the veterinary profession would play such a major part in our 1988 meeting?

It is also now obvious that regular and international reviews are needed to up-date and inspire all who are concerned with the welfare of animals and their humane treatment. It is with the hope that readers will find these proceedings equally enlightening and inspiring that we offer them to you - members of the "caring community".

## Bibliography and References

Bishop, G: Godwin, A: Paterson, D. (1979) Animals in Schools: a Practical Approach to their Educational Value and Welfare (Horsham, RSPCA).

Carpenter, E, editor. (1980) Animals and Ethics - a report of the Working Party convened by Edward Carpenter (London: Watkins).

Kellert, S: Westervelt, M. (1981) Trends in Animal Use and Perception in Twentieth Century America (Phase IV) (US Dept. of the Interior, Fish and Wildlife Service).

Kellert, S: Westervelt, M. Children's Attitudes, Knowledge and Behaviours Towards Animals (Phase V) (US Dept. of the Interior, Fish and Wildlife Service).

Paterson, D: Ryder, R, editors. (1979) Animal Rights - A Symposium (Fontwell: Centaur Press).

Paterson, D. (1986) Children's Ideas on Animals - A Developmental Study (MPhil Thesis: Sussex University).

Paterson, D. (1981) Humane Education - A Symposium (Burgess Hill: Humane Education Council).

Shaw, I. (1988) Children's Attitudes Towards Animals (BBC Special Projects Research Report).

The views expressed in individual papers and the reasoning proposed therein are those of the individual authors and not necessarily those of their fellow participants.

# ABBREVIATIONS USED IN THE TEXT INCLUDE:

| | |
|---|---|
| ATB | Agricultural Training Board |
| AWF | BVA Animal Welfare Foundation |
| BVA | British Veterinary Association |
| CIWF | Compassion in World Farming |
| CRAE | Committee for the Reform of Animal Experiments |
| DHSS | Dept of Health & Social Security |
| EEC | European Economic Community |
| FAWC | Farm Animal Welfare Committee |
| FRAME | Fund for the Replacement of Animals in Medical Experiments. |
| HMSO | Her Majesty's Stationery Office |
| HSUS | Humane Society of the United States |
| MAFF | Ministry of Agriculture Food & Fisheries |
| NFU | National Farmer's Union |
| PG | Post Graduate |
| RSPCA | Royal Soc for the Prevention of Cruelty to Animals |
| SCAW | Society for Companion Animal Welfare North Africa |
| SPCK | Society for the Promotion of Christian Knowledge |
| UFAW | Universities Federation for Animal Welfare |
| WSPA | World Society for the Protection of Animals |

# INTRODUCTION

## Lord Douglas Houghton

While some sceptics may doubt the value of the House of Lords as an institution, the fact remains that it is an essential part of the parliamentary process and it is still the place where all legislation has to end on its way to receiving the Royal Assent. Law-making takes place in Parliament and nowhere else. To achieve an end, therefore, of necessity all roads lead to Westminster. With three Sessions of this Parliament before us, and the next Parliament heading for the turn of the century, what do we seek to achieve?

In reaching 90 years of age I have had to consider what my future role should be in the Movement for the Welfare of Animals and in achieving a better understanding and harmony between the human species and the animal kingdom.

First of all, we must seek to lay the foundations for real progress through the education of the young in the full significance of human life and indeed all life; in the conservation of our environment and in the very survival of the human race. Animal welfare societies cannot by themselves obtrude into the educational system, but they can provide the philosophy for a better understanding by young people of the wonders of the natural world and our responsibility for it.

Several attempts were made during the debate on the recent Education Bill to get particular topics included in the obligatory curriculum. An appreciation of nature and the part of mankind in it was one of them. All, however, were refused on the grounds that the obligatory curriculum should be confined to what is described as "Core" subjects basic to the traditional educational system.

It is therefore up to local education authorities to choose other subjects for inclusion in the curriculum, and in this selection representatives of the parties as well as teachers and local authorities will necessarily be involved. We have to bring steady pressure to bear on them all if we are to achieve our objectives.

Personally, I fully support this and other efforts that are being made to build up our knowledge of the planet, and to teach the care and concern needed to save it from despoilation and destruction. As far as Parliament is concerned, I think that we should embark on a stock-taking exercise to try to get a balanced programme of reform to take through Parliament in the next five years.

We have to bear in mind that if we need changes in the law and if we need new Acts of Parliament, we shall need the support of the parliamentarians to deliver them. This means yet again concentrating on the place of animals in politics. That is to say in party politics and in back-bench endeavour.

1

Back-benchers are of great importance, but a condition of getting stronger parliamentary support is that we use the influence of professional bodies. Those who form public opinion must be on our side. To see our purpose prosper we must depend upon the weight of their opinion behind us and the influence of other major interests in society. We have experience of this. Those who formed the triple alliance to get the Animals (Scientific Procedures) Act, 1986, onto the Statute Book paved the way to getting what no-one had secured before, a Government Bill of reform negotiated through ministerial channels. The honour for that goes to the BVA, CRAE and FRAME.

My conclusions are -

(1) I believe that British politics must be much greener. If animals are to come second every time, and be sacrificed and exploited wholly to human ends, this may well lead to grievous consequences for mankind. Yet ours is now the only Parliament in Europe without some directly elected members to act as catalysts for ecological matters: and, due to our present electoral system, our Ecology Party can only lose its deposit every time.

(2) We should revive the idea of a Standing Commission or Committee on Animal Protection.

This Commission was to be a major part of the Labour Party's programme and Jim Callaghan, when Prime Minister in March 1979, said that an incoming Labour government would bring it into existence. Lord Whitelaw, then Chairman of the Conservative Party Policy Committee, considered that departmentalism would be more effective than umbrellaism. But he missed the point of what the Standing Commission or Council would do. What is needed is to look at our relations with the animal kingdom as a whole. What fundamental rights are to prevail? Is cruelty an evil capable of being identified and defined? It is certainly a matter of public concern. The Protection of Animal Acts, 1911 (1912), was an attempt to solve the cruelty problem to some extent, but wildlife was excluded, and look at the mess we are in over things like dog control for example.

The principal pre-condition of success in reforms of substance is to remove fear of extremists and extremism. The professionals can start with well-thought-out overtures, but Parliamentarians and especially the government fear the antics and vandalism of the young.

So long as I am around my services will be available and I am ready to help, but only for constructive work. Time is running against me and I have none to spare for things such as demonstrations. My base is Parliament. We must know our Parliament and use the system.

Two bodies hold the key to this enterprise and probably the whole future of the cause we all seek to promote: the BVA and the RSPCA. The BVA must have the courage and purpose to follow through its professional conclusions. The RSPCA should live boldly up to the charitable limits of its name; it must make up its mind to be committed to reform. Its members have nothing to fear from combating the evil of cruelty and going as far as their influence will take them.

Finally, the people who influence Parliament most are those in the field who remind M.P.s of their constituency, and those lobbies at the centre who need Parliamentary interest and support. Commercial lobbies are on the increase. Animals should be brought further into this area of activity. That requires constant effort and regular contact.

# PART ONE

# ETHICS – OUR MORAL OBLIGATION TO ANIMALS

Professor Stephen R L Clark

ETHICAL PROBLEMS IN ANIMAL WELFARE


1    WHAT PHILOSOPHERS CAN´T DO

I take it that no-one here believes that philosophical
enquiry is sheerly irrelevant to the problems that we
face.  Such enquiry, after all, is only an attempt to
think through those problems without taking too much for
granted.  People who won´t do this are usually, though
they fail to realise it, acting out the theories of some
earlier philosopher:  the sort of self-styled "practical
person" who is ignorant of the principles upon which she
acts and careless of the long-term consequences of what
she does.

> "The need for philosophy is just the ultimate form of
> the need for knowledge... The only choice we have is
> between a conscious metaphysics and an unconscious
> one, between hypotheses which we have examined and
> whose limitations we know, and hypotheses which rule
> us from behind, as pure prejudices do". (Jones 1891,
> p36).

No-one here, I am sure, thinks it improper or pointless to
treat issues "philosophically" when the alternative is to
treat them dogmatically, conceitedly, over-emotionally, or
without serious effort to consider other arguments and
points of view. But experience suggests at least two other
misunderstandings of the philosophic life which may cause
trouble.

Firstly, philosophers, and especially moral philosophers,
are sometimes thought to be expert moral casuists, with
straight-forward and rationally grounded solutions only
needing to be propounded to be believed. That is how we
conceive of experts in the physical sciences and in the
law, even if they do not in fact always have simple
answers to give us.  When it becomes clear that
philosophers disagree among themselves about even the
simplest and clearest matter, it may seem pointless to
invoke their aid.  If there are no agreed solutions, and
not even agreed methods, what sort of expertise have we?

Secondly, philosophers as individuals are popularly held
to have "philosophies", systems, favourite opinions
carefully rehearsed and ordered. Societies inviting me to
speak have sometimes, I suspect, been faintly
disappointed, or even annoyed, that I did not come across
as a whole-hearted advocate of whatever philosophic creed
it was that they had identified me with.

So it turns out that philosophers don´t only disagree with
each other:  they may well disagree with themselves:

> "Just as parents have affection for the offspring of
> their bodies, so also is the mind naturally attached

to its own reasonings. And just as to their parents who are emotionally attached the children appeal as the fairest and handsomest of all even though they might be the most hideous of all, so it is with the foolish mind.... However this is not the case with the wise man and his reasonings. Rather, when it seems convincing that they are true and correct, then especially does he distrust his own judgement but makes use of other wise men as judges of his own reasonings, and from them believes assurance" (Maximus, 1985 p69).

Philosophers, no more than poets, "believe" in what they say: we are not citizens of any single community of ideas; our philosophy rests rather on our wish to go a little further, trusting not in any single doctrine but in the mere capacity of rational imagination not to let us down.

In brief: if the presence of philosophers is valuable, it is not because we are likely to offer unanimous or clear solutions to practical or theoretical puzzles, and certainly not ones that all our absent colleagues would agree upon, nor yet because you can always count on a philosopher for a rousing piece of rhetoric in defence of your favoured programme. Our value is not that we have answers, but that we have questions, and some knowledge of the puzzles created by attempted answers of the past.

In saying all this I may, of course, have given rise to yet a third misunderstanding, namely that philosophers are professional sceptics of the tedious kind who ask questions but will not stay for an answer. That too is not quite right: few of us believe that there is any hope of founding all our serious beliefs on logically incontrovertible principle. There will always be room for debate, and rational disagreement. It does not follow that we can do without beliefs, or that we need to be much shaken by the mere fact that we could logically think the opposite of what we rationally do.


## 2    ABSTRACT PROBLEMS: CONCRETE CASES

So what are the problems of Animal Welfare? When Socrates asked his friends such questions as "what is Justice, Courage, Happiness?", their usual reply was to give instances of just or courageous actions, or happy people. That was not, he said, what he was after. If you give me a list of courageous actions, or of occasions when "animal welfare" was preserved or defended, it is usually possible to devise some superficially similar occasion which you would not be easily persuaded was of the same kind. What Socrates wanted to be told was what that kind was, what is it that an act must be to be truly courageous, what must be preserved if "animal welfare" is to be preserved? Is courage so-defined always a good thing? Suppose we decide that courage is the disposition to carry on doing what one had decided to do despite the personal danger: we might well wish that some people were less "courageous", for

6

their own and everyone else's good. A little cowardice should be admired! Justice itself, if it requires us to tell no lies and to repay our debts, might involve us in doing what is obviously the wrong thing (returning the Gestapo agent's gun and telling him where to find his prey). So my problem is not solved by a list of "animal welfare organisations", nor stories about abandoned dogs, or terrified cattle or dying seals. What I want to know is: what counts as "animal welfare", and how far does it count as something that is worth defending, preserving or increasing? These problems are abstract ones, and may seem cold and irrelevant to the genuine heartfelt concerns of veterinarians, or RSPCA officers, or animal lovers or conservationists. But those same "heartfelt concerns" may conflict, and the "welfare" that each tribe seeks to preserve may not be what others had in mind any more than "Liberty" or "Democracy" means quite the same thing to western liberals, or Communists or (the late) Khomeni.


## 3    SO WHAT COUNTS AS ANIMAL WELFARE?

So what is animal welfare? Broadly, it must be that state or condition or habitual activity in which animals are "well-off": but what does that amount to? A condition without positive pain, whatever that is? But would a creature in a coma be well-off? Or a creature unable to feel pain, and so in constant danger from sharp edges, fires and rotten food? Presumably not - unless the alternative, in that particular case, were even worse. So a concern for animal welfare is not identical with a wish to prevent animal pain - or else animal welfarists would be wholly dedicated to a policy of genocide. If pain were the only thing that mattered, all deaths, and not just some, would be a merciful release.

So shall we add that animal pleasures count? an animal is well-off not only if it is spared the major pains of life, but if it can and does enjoy its major or minor pleasures. So animals that are well-fed, well-housed and well-tended are well-off, even if they are soon going to be killed, or even if they have no chance to do the things peculiar to their kind which they would do if "free".

Human beings so treated are not regarded as well-off, even if they are better off in some prisons than others. Prisons are recognised as punitive, because they deprive the prisoner of "freedom", and particularly freedom to engage in ordinary human actions: playing, courting, parenting, investigating other possibilities, etc. A Prisoners' Aid Society might aim to make them "better off", but would not think them "well-off": they are in a state where they have reason to want change. Our human welfare is not well served by keeping us in jail.

These activities count as part of human well-being because they matter to human beings and we would count ourselves as badly off if we had no chance to engage in them. So shall we identify animal welfare as that condition in

7

which animals can do what matters to them - not only eat, drink and sleep, but also have dust-baths, groom each other, gallop over the grass and sing? Would such extras matter if a prisoner had been reared as a "happy slave", ignorant of human possibility or of the outside world? Would such a prisoner be well-off because she did not know what she was missing, or even felt no lack? We sense that there are worthwhile human activities that can be engaged in only as free men (whatever freedom is), such that to be denied them is a loss even if the victim does not know what she is missing, or if she is missing anything at all.

Does the same thing apply, analogously, to animals? Is a "stall-fed ox", brought out to be masturbated for a farmer's gain, "well-off"? He hasn't been killed, or maimed, or "badly treated" (in the sense of being burned, beaten, castrated, starved or even "spoken harshly to"). Perhaps he has never, since his calfhood, seen a cow, and certainly has never served a herd in the way his wild ancestors and cousins do. But is he living a life well-lived according to his kind, doing what admirable and enviable creatures of that kind would do? Could one not suspect or feel that the more he seems contented with his lot, the more distant he is from his species-good? Rabbits kept in rabbit hutches for so long that they have no concept of escape even when they have the chance to, may be, in one sense, well-off; in another, they are "deleporized", dead rabbits before their body dies!

Finally, does animal welfare include life itself? Suppose a deer, or baboon, or seal that has lived "freely" and in good fortune for its life so far, and has years to live if all goes "well", is killed "untimely"? We reckon humans who die young, who don't fulfil their promise, are to be pitied even if they never knew their end. Even if they have lived happy lives, perhaps, we think them injured by their early deaths. We grieve for octogenarians, no doubt, but who would think them badly-off because they're dead? Not all deaths are an equal evil, whether because death may be slow, agonising and untimely or may not, or because not all those who die are equally to be missed. So clearly we have less reason to protect some animals against imaginable deaths than others. The death of diseased seals is something that counts against the welfare of the seals in a way that the death of ageing seals, or even healthy seals by normal hazards of the sea (the price they pay for liberty) is not.

What counts as an animal's being "well-off", though difficult to specify in any particular case, is not all that obscure. We know what sort of things count as good for creatures of this kind or that. Maybe there is a case to argue about domestic dogs: are they well-off in principle, supposing them to be well-fed, well-cared for, well-befriended, without any wish to leave? Or is there a case for saying that they are as slavish, as far from canine well-being, as any "mindless", unrebellious slave?

Perhaps Rover would be no better off if sent to join a

feral pack of dogs? Rover, of course, would soon be dead, but is it obvious that dogs should be domestic? Are household pets a different case to zoo or laboratory animals: sometimes well-cared for, in a sense, yet unable ever to lead the lives their species would, and for that very reason not "well-off".

## 4    WHY DOES IT MATTER?

Animal welfare organisations are presumably formed by people who suppose that animal welfare does "matter", absolutely, and they think themselves entitled to bring it to other people's attention. It matters that "animals" be well-off - though perhaps that category of "animal" needs more careful scrutiny. If there are no "beetle welfare societies" as such, this may be because no-one much supposes that beetles are ever well-off or badly-off, or because we think that beetles will be well enough off anyway (and will probably be the only non-microscopic creatures to survive the nuclear winter), or because the well-being of beetles, slugs, mosquitoes and water boatmen (not to mention rats, sharks and vultures) does not engage our sympathy even when they are doing "us" no particular harm. Notoriously, cuddly and photogenic creatures, preferably ones that are not competitors, get more attention than creepy, slimy, ugly, or just boring ones.

Sometimes a concern for animal welfare is simply a concern that natural beauty, somewhat parochially defined, be preserved. We object to dying seals in much the same spirit as we object to dying elms: that there be healthy, glossy, jolly looking seals around our coasts matters to "us" who don't have to bother about our fishing nets - just as it matters that there be healthy, long-established elms around our countryside. If seals or elms became too inconvenient or expensive, we would transfer our affections and our cash. It is because we want a "beautiful" landscape that we want healthy animals across it: we feed squirrels (with a particular nostalgic affection for red squirrels, and not grey) and poison rats, unless we realise that squirrels are just fluffier than rodents, and do damage to our trees. To maintain that lovely landscape we are prepared to cull the animals who live in it, without regard for their individual welfare, and not always very much even for the welfare of the mass of creatures of that kind. Conservationists, game-wardens and cattle farmers have a lot in common, even if the end-product they are seeking differs.

I do not mean to denigrate these motives, nor to deny the good that proper conservation does: people who attend to the whole ecosystem we inhabit would think twice before introducing sheep to eat up men and countryside together. A sound conservation policy seeks to maintain a sustainable ecology, a world within which creatures of many kinds find a place, even though many of them, individually, will not do well, a point I shall return to.

These aesthetic, discriminatory or conservational motives for wishing animals well, largely because a world of "well-off" animals, or one in which the "ill-off" are out of sight is nicer for "us" to live in, are not usually "moral" reasons.

I have a "moral" reason for my action if it is done for the sake of someone's good, not mine, and irrespective of any special, accidental ties between me and the beneficiary. If I help my aged aunt because (a) she means to leave me money, or (b) she looks so sweet when (fairly) well, that is no moral action. If I help her because I like her, and therefore like her to be well because she likes herself to be well, many moralists would say that that was also no true moral action. Most of us would disagree.

We owe loyal affection to those close to us in ways not easily captured by moralising dicta. Such moralists have tended to suggest that any help I give my aunt is only moral if I would, for just the same reason, help any old lady, or any human being in distress, or any creature similarly situated. That is why good realists sneer a little at "British sentiment" as being hypocritical: Why do we despise Koreans for killing dogs to eat, while munching lamb chops? What difference is there between eating dogs and eating sheep? It cannot be simply that sheep do not enter our society as "pets": often enough they did - witness the poor man's lamb in the prophet Nathan's parable.

By way of riposte to the realist, what non-sentimental reason is offered for the differences between roast pig and roast baby? In the last half-century good liberals have done their best to show that any concern for human embryos, or even for human babies, is a sentimental attachment not to be enforced on others. If it is all right to procreate embryos for experimental purposes, or to provide spare organs for the needy, it does not seem entirely easy to insist that cannibalism is intolerable. And now you know why philosophers are unpopular!

There are perhaps two ways to go from here. The first is to admit that many of our actions rest on sentiment, on personal and unreflective attachments. We mind about those close to us, about those like us, about those who embody qualities our evolutionary and historic past have taught us to admire and love. People who entirely lack such sentiments are not rational sages, but psychopaths. To ask such questions as "Why should we mind what happens to our future selves, parents, spouses, children, friends and fellow professionals, family pets or farmyard cattle?" is very odd. Of course we mind about such things: maybe there are, somewhere in outer space, such creatures as the supermantis, who have no special friends, nor any soft affections. To a supermantis, any other supermantis of the requisite class and station serves as well: any concern for other things' well-being is so alien a thought

as never to occur at all. Such creatures would probably
have no conception of themselves as individuals, nor any
way of thinking even about their own interior states. If
they are "rational", it is not as we are. For us to be
like that would not be wicked, but insane.

Moral discourse is not divorced from sentiments like this,
and there is no reason to be ashamed of them. Animal
welfare, as far as it is a goal for us, will be the
welfare of those creatures with whom we share our lives,
towards whom we feel affection, with whose troubles we can
sympathise. It is worth remembering that our natural
sympathies, affections and understandings do not extend
only or even chiefly to members of our own species. We
are motivated to mind about our fellow human beings as
much as we are motivated to mind about our fellow mammals
or higher vertebrates, and may mind more about the latter
because we know more about them. There is a real sense in
which the average human male can sympathise more easily
with a randy bull than with a fellow (female) human being
with period pains. "I know just how you feel", addressed
by a would-be sympathetic male to such a female, is
neither true nor helpful. For similar reasons, I know more
about what our domestic cats require from life than I know
about Brazilian Indians.

But there is a second response available. Sentiment is
not enough. Once we have begun to enter into the feelings
and purposes of another so as to be concerned for her
well-being, not as an adjunct to oneself, but in her own
being, we can hardly avoid the questions posed by those
who are, in relevant ways, like our friend. Precisely
because I mind what happens to my wife irrespective of any
further consequences for my present self, the fact that
she is my wife becomes at least in part irrelevant. It
may be what first caught my attention, but what I am
attending to is something that would not be essentially
different if she were not (or even never had been) just my
wife. If I don´t want my wife to be mugged, raped,
robbed, defrauded, debauched or killed because all these
things would injure her (not merely me), how can I be
indifferent to the mugging, raping, robbing and so on, of
other people who might easily have been her? If I show
that I would not mind such crimes at all, my claim to mind
about her is suspect: apparently I only mind because such
acts reflect on me, or damage what I think is mine.
Similarly, if I genuinely care what happened to other
members of my species, how can I not mind at all what
happens to creatures of like kind, but not of my own
species? In the days when species were considered natural
kinds, distinguished by having specific, radically
different natures, I might have held that much of what can
happen to a human being can no more happen to a dog or a
chimp than to a stone, or to the number seven bus. If
species are instead mere sets of interbreeding
populations, and our natures are not wholly different from
theirs, then we are stuck with minding about other
creatures than just the ones immediately close to us,
simply because they are susceptible to the same injuries.

Minding about animal welfare is a function partly of sentimental attachment, partly of rational discovery that "they" are a lot more like "us" than we thought, and that to mind about "us" commits us to minding also about "them" on pain of being hypocrites.

But the question still remains: how much do they matter, and how do we deal with them? A proper concern with human welfare, after all, does not require us to make human beings as "well-off" as they as individuals could be. I acknowledge no duty nor desire to provide everyone in the world, or everyone in Britain, with a video recorder, Jacuzzi, free access to the international computer network and a holiday home in the Bahamas, nor even a duty to ensure that everyone could have as many of the world's goodies as they happen to desire, or even a "fair" share of these goodies. Would a fair share be an equal share, or a share commensurate with need, or one commensurate with merit, or one obtained without violence, fraud or other wickedness? How could I possibly make it a goal of mine to ensure such (quite different) ideals were realised?

Simone Weil insisted on eating only what would be available to prisoners of the Reich: that, I suspect, is in some sense also our fair share, "what we would be assigned if every living human were assigned an equal share of all the goods there are". But most of us suspect that this was almost suicide, or martyrdom: suicide would usually be wrong, and martyrdom is not obligatory.

I have no obligation, least of all in law, to care equally for every human being. Even those of us who attempt to do without personal friends and special clients only pay equal attention to the people that they meet, the down-and-outs who turn up on the doorstep. We don't deny our aid to them merely because on a "fair share" basis they aren't entitled to more than we could give to everyone. Robbers may have a special obligation to assist those whom they have beggared. The rest of us may feel in some sense obliged to help, but how much we help, and when, is our decision, and the beneficiary has no case against us.

Analogously, we have no necessary obligation to assist "animals" with whom we have no direct contact. We may do them good (say, by rescuing them from flood or fire), but only <u>have</u> to do so if we caused the flood or fire. Wild or distant animals have no right of support, unless it is our fault that they are beggared, but animals within our household, or wider society, may have that right. Pet owners who neglect their animals are in breach of an implicit contract, and of the law. We respect the claims of "owners" on condition that they care for the animals in their charge, and if they neglect those duties we may (and must) condemn them, and take on the burden of care ourselves. Veterinary practitioners are obviously at the workface here: what duties do they have to patients and to clients and to the wider community? If the patient's

12

welfare must be paramount, as the Royal College says
(without defining what that welfare is), how do you deal
with clients who will not or cannot care for the patient
as you, the veterinary practitioner, would wish? When do
you have recourse to law? Only some animals, in other
words, like some human beings, have positive rights of
assistance against us when the assistance is required only
to remedy natural failings. Enforcement of the duties of
animal-ownership is another matter, as is recompense for
past injustice.

Such positive welfare rights, and rights of defence
against particular injustices, are not the only sort of
rights there are. Negative rights of liberty are much
more wide-spread. I may have no duty to feed, clothe or
even protect a Philippine tribesman. In international law
I have no right, let alone a duty, even to protect such
tribesmen against genocide if the only way to protect them
is to invade the Philippines. But although I have no
positive duties here, I plainly have many negative ones -
notably not to rob, maim or kill. Positive duties to
strangers are rarely assignable, enforceable or
significant. Negative duties are quite easy. If someone
else is already looking after Jo, I have no need to. If
someone else is doing her negative duty by Jo (not to
molest), my duty not to molest Jo remains the same.
Analogously, I may rightly be forbidden to molest, maim or
kill an animal whom I have no special duty to care for. I
may be required to assist some animals against such
molestation. I am required to care for some animals with
whom I have some special tie.

And what about Rover? Obviously I have an enforceable
duty to look after him and attend to his well-being. If I
abandon him, my claims of ownership will lapse just as my
parental rights will lapse if I abuse them. But how do I
attend to his well-being? Should I release him on a
startled world? The argument reflects the ancient dispute
over civilisation; is civilisation a good thing or not?
Are we distorting our children′s happy natures by bringing
them up in chains, or are we enabling them to achieve such
goals as would be quite impossible for solitary savages or
feral apes? My suspicion is that those who think dogs,
real dogs, are better off without us share these false
perceptions of society that have dominated recent history.
If the social order is only a human one, and includes only
such obligations as individuals have freely incurred, then
dogs and children alike need liberation, and social order
collapses. If on the other hand the social order is a
historical community of many races, ages, sexes and
species, such that we come to life by learning obligations
that we freely choose, there is a strong case for
acknowledging dogs, horses, cats and sheep and other
commensal species as part of a civilised order that is
open to improvement.

What obligations of care and courtesy do we owe animals?
The ones that must be paid them if the social order is to
be one worth living; they have a claim on us for services

13

rendered throughout history, and still offer us the chance of forming new friendly relations that will be their own reward.

So perhaps you can count on a philosopher for a rousing piece of rhetoric after all!

# Mary Midgley

## PRACTICAL SOLUTIONS

First, a few remarks about what "practicality" is in general, then a note about its special difficulties in the field of animal welfare. And finally, some points about the various conflicting ways in which the ideal of "science" is conceived to affect these issues.

## 1    DREAM AND REALITY.

What is it to be practical? The regular, familiar answer to this question, is that a practical person is the opposite of an idealist. Idealists are supposed to be ineffectual because they are dreamers. Practical people are realists, accepting the present state of things because they recognise that it is unchangeable.

This stereotyping is extraordinarily foolish in a world which changes continually, as ours does today. Looking round us, we can see at once that dreams are immensely powerful things, because some of them are visibly changing that world. These effective dreams are sometimes bad and foolish (for instance, those that centre on weapons). But some, of course, are good dreams. And obviously, in the past, some very startling good dreams have produced vast reforms, generating institutions which everybody now accepts as right and necessary. Bernard Shaw said that, if you want to get the wheels turning, what you need is a crank: history supports his prescription. But the psychological machinery by which these cranks have to work is complicated, and calls for a bit of attention.

If people are to bring serious changes about, they need to combine two very different tempers. There must be real red-hot indignation and outrage about the existing conditions which are to be changed. But there must also be the spirit that we usually call practical - a readiness to work out the immediate, detailed first steps in change, and to discuss them calmly with people who have experience in the field. These people, in general, will not yet be indignant, because they take present conditions for granted. So unless some miracle suddenly augments the reformers´ power, these first steps must be relatively small, leaving a great deal of the present outrageousness untouched. The psychological difficulty is somehow to face the immediate problems realistically without losing the large-scale indignation that is one´s source of power.

In general, we deal with this difficulty by a tribal division of labour, forming separate groups. Some people act as prophetic extremists while others - the ones often called "practical" - pocket their fury and work with existing institutions. Up to a point this rôle-playing does work. The prophets provide the steam and hound on the moderates, making themselves troublesome enough to

educate the general public about their cause, so that
eventually some action does follow.

All the same, this system has real drawbacks. Outsiders
sometimes become so confused and irritated by extremism
that they turn their backs on the whole cause. And the
tribal division always produces friction, wasting precious
energy on those internal disputes that are notoriously the
bane of all reforming movements. (Marx, even in the
Communist Manifesto, displays almost as much fury against
rival theorists with different diagnoses as he does
against the ruling class.) There is also an unlucky
tendency for both parties to exaggerate their rôles.
Extremists are led to a kind of absolutism which tends to
become increasingly abstract and negative - concentrating
on the abolition of some practice without attending to
what will replace it. That (for instance) has been the
characteristic weakness of many anti-slavery movements,
whose slogan has been simply the abolition of slavery.
This negative, wholesale angle led them to pay little
attention to making arrangements for the ex-slaves once
abolition was officially reached, and the consequences of
that neglect have been grave. As for the moderates, they
are of course in constant danger of finding themselves
lunching with civil servants - particularly with "Sir
Humphrey" - and of agreeing with their hosts that the
objections to existing practices have been much
exaggerated.

What I want to stress here is something really very
obvious but surprisingly often neglected - namely, that
both these conditions are equally far from a proper
practical attitude. Neither of them is a permissible
option for anybody who actually does mean to make the
changes that they are demanding - and that intention is
surely a part of the proper meaning of being practical.
Extremists who pay no attention to finding the first steps
by which what they are demanding can be set in motion, or
to the likely side-effects of actually achieving it,
really do deserve the name of "impractical dreamers". But
equally, nominal reformers who have become totally
paralysed by respectability are now no longer practical,
because they no longer want to produce change. There is
some confusion about this last point, because the second
party (Sir Humphrey´s party) is of course the one that has
traditionally hijacked terms like "practical" and
"realistic". As has been nicely said, these are people
"whose knowledge is almost confined to what they see
passing around them, and who, on account of their
ignorance, are termed practical men" (Buckle, History of
Civilisation).


## 2    SPECIAL EMBARRASSMENTS ABOUT ANIMALS

So much for practicality in general; now for the extra
twists that arise when the topic of non-human animals
comes up. Because our central moral tradition has, till
lately, grossly neglected this issue, the conflicts here

are unusually raw and sharp. They have not had their corners properly knocked off by repeated controversy. This is a matter (like the position of women) about which people find it easy to dogmatize and very hard to _think_. They tend to find their own opinions about this particularly obvious and their opponents´ views particularly grotesque. For a long time, the main Christian tradition avoided paying any serious attention to it, suspecting all concern for animals was somehow pagan. Some Protestant theologians have gone even further than Catholic ones in declaring that the whole purpose of the divine Creation was to provide a stage for interactions between Man and God, so that all other creatures existed merely as tools for this. And many modern secular humanists too have followed this lead, confining all value and all serious attention to the human race.

Yet at the same time there has grown up, in the last two centuries, a moral attitude with a very different message - namely compassion, the humanitarian determination to control and minimise suffering simply as such, whoever feels it. In the words of the Hindu prayer quoted by Schopenhauer, "may all living beings remain free from pain". This way of thinking has gradually given form and conceptual clarity to the much less articulate ancient tradition of protesting against atrocious human treatment of animals, and has forced some public attention to the matter. Unofficial compassion has in this way gradually begun to become an official part of our culture. In English-speaking philosophy, Utilitarianism has been the main philosophic expression of this temper. But the attitude itself is far wider than any particular intellectual formulation, and it is surely something central to the morality by which we live today.

This compassionate, humanitarian thinking is, however, still very fitful. People who want to resist it can still often do so without argument, merely by dismissing it as weird, absurd and eccentric, the kind of thing to be expected from what are significantly called "old ladies". This dismissive strategy has, I think, retained more public respectability in the USA than it has in Britain. Over here, defenders of inhumane practices more often operate now by claiming to be actually very humane, and asserting that the practices they favour are really quite harmless. But the alternative, dismissive strategy is still available, because the theoretical issue of the proper bounds of compassion has not yet been sufficiently clearly faced and publicly settled. Exclusive humanism, attending only to MAN, and inclusive, compassionate humanitarianism have remained separate strands in our current morality, not properly brought together. This is easy because they are often treated as if they were the mores of two distinct tribes - extreme "Animal Rightists" and normal people - instead of complementary elements in the morality of each one of us. Battles between these tribes accordingly paralyse action. That is why it is so necessary to detribalise these rifts within the animal welfare movement itself. We need to be clearly aware that these partial attitudes are both thoroughly impractical. Within each extremist, there is - or ought to be - a moderate trying to get out, and within each moderate an equally restless extremist.


## 3    THE POSITION OF SCIENCE

The ideal of science has been, and still is, invoked strongly on both sides of this tribal conflict.  On the one hand, the mere fact that some branches of science use experiments on animals has sometimes been taken to imply that any concern for the welfare of these or other animals is itself anti-scientific.  This was the position taken by the great physiologist Claude Bernard in the last century, and it seems often still to be that of wholesale campaigners in his tradition today.  On the other hand, the Darwinian theory of evolution makes this attitude puzzling.  It shows us that we ourselves have had ancestors at every level of the animal kingdom, are akin to them all, and are especially closely allied to those primates who are now the most coveted of experimental subjects.  This theory radically shakes the massive traditional picture of ourselves as irresponsible alien colonists, directed by a despotic ruler to use the whole range of other life-forms merely as material for satisfying our wishes.

The Darwinian picture, by emphasising our likeness to our nearest relatives, raises two very uncomfortable questions about the possibility that their experiences may in some ways be quite like our own.  The question "would you like this done to you?" begins to seem increasingly relevant, not on sentimental but on scientific grounds.  If we are to dismiss it, we seem now to need much better reasons than those that satisfied some of our ancestors.  Vets, who find themselves situated at the cross-roads of these conflicting tendencies, with ample chance to notice the strange anomalies of public consciousness, are surely also particularly well-placed to work out how we are to deal with them.

All these difficulties arise out of the temper of our age. They are serious, and are not going to go away, but rather to become more pressing.  The consequent dilemmas are necessarily painful, because the institutions involved are ancient, entrenched and well-respected.  Meat-eating has had considerable ceremonial importance in our culture as a symbol of prosperity and hospitality, and this symbolism has traditionally been linked to ways of treating farm-animals which were much more defensible than today's intensive systems.

Similarly, wearing fur has been a traditional mark of rank.  Symbolic meanings of this kind are, no doubt, subject to historical change, but that change probably cannot be made very easily or quickly.

Scientific experimentation is a rather different matter, having claims to a much more ambitious place in the value-hierarchy. But it also, at present, seems to threaten much more extraordinary changes, centring on genetic engineering and the patenting of new life-forms. Deciding what is the general duty of all of us, and the peculiar duty of scientists in these matters is exceedingly hard. We shall rightly be dealing at this conference with some very detailed issues of particular facts and particular practical policies. My business in this opening session has been simply to point out how much we shall need to alter the impractical set of stereotypes which have so often been allowed to decide these questions in the past.

**The Revd Dr Andrew Linzey**

## REVERENCE, RESPONSIBILITY AND RIGHTS

In order to give some account of the status of animals within the Christian tradition, I propose to discuss three questions:

(1) Should we show reverence towards animals?
(2) Do we have responsibility to animals?
(3) Do animals have rights?

## (1)  REVERENCE FOR LIFE

The idea that the animal creation should be the subject of honour and respect  because it is created by God, however fundamental that idea may appear to us, is not one that has been endorsed throughout centuries of Christian thought.  Whilst it can be claimed to have some grounding in scripture in, for example, the Psalmist´s sense of the wonder and beauty of God´s creation and in the regard that Jesus claimed even for sparrows (Linzey & Regan, 1989) these intimations have never been developed into systematic theological thought, still less considered doctrine.  Again while it is true that many saints, sages, divines and poets (Linzey & Regan, 1988) within the tradition have shown or asserted respect for animals, the concept remains largely vague and unfocussed.

In order to define this issue, I intend to examine the opposing views of two significant, but very different, thinkers:   Albert Schweitzer and Karl Barth.

## (a)  **Schweitzer´s Concept**

It is Schweitzer who is most well-known for his development of this concept.  In his Civilisation and Ethics (1987) he surveys successive Western world-views and finds them wanting.

> "Our philosophising has become more and more involved in the discussion of secondary issues," argues Schweitzer.  "It has lost touch with the elemental questions regarding life and the world which it is man´s task to pose and solve, and has found satisfaction more and more in discussing problems of a purely academic nature and in a mere virtuosity of philosophical technique". (Schweitzer, 1987, preface).

The answer to the "spiritual crisis" of our civilisation, maintains Schweitzer, is the development of ethical thought which must seek to conceive life-affirmation as "a manifestation of an inward, spiritual relation to the world" which does not "lapse into abstract thinking" but remains, as Schweitzer calls it, "elemental", that is, understanding self-devotion of human life to every form of living being with which it can come into relation".

(Schweitzer, 1987, preface). From this, Schweitzer deduces
a classic definition:

> "Ethics consists, therefore, in my experiencing the
> compulsion to show to all [who] will-to-live the same
> reverence as I do to my own. There we have given us
> that basic principle of the moral which is a necessity
> of thought. It is good to maintain and encourage
> life; it is bad to destroy life or to obstruct it".
> (Schweitzer, from CT Campion, 1987 p118).

Three characteristics of this basic principle of reverence
can be noted.

First, the principle is comprehensive. Schweitzer does
not posit reverence as one principle among many, even as
the most satisfying or coherent principle, but as the sole
principle of the moral. Love and compassion, for example,
while important notions for Schweitzer, are entirely
subsumed under the concept of reverence. Compassion,
which suggests only "interest in the suffering will-to-
live", is regarded as "too narrow to rank as the total
essence of the ethical". Whereas the ethics of reverence,
"includes also feeling as one´s own, all the circumstances
and all the aspirations of the will-to-live, its
pleasures, too, and its longing to live itself out to the
full, as well as its urge to self-perfecting" (Schweitzer,
from CT Campion, 1987 p119).

Second, the principle is universal. Schweitzer sees
reverence as applying to all life forms, human or animal,
insect or vegetable. The ethical man "does not ask how
far this or that life deserves one´s sympathy as being
valuable, nor, beyond that, whether and to what degree it
is capable of feeling". "Life as such is sacred to him,"
maintains Schweitzer. In order to grasp the ramifications
of reverence-in-practice, it is worth enumerating some of
the examples given. "The ethical man" writes Schweitzer,

> "tears no leaf from a tree, plucks no flower, and
> takes care to crush no insect. If in summer he is
> working by lamplight, he prefers to keep the window
> shut and breathe a stuffy atmosphere rather than see
> one insect after another fall with singed wings upon
> his table.
>
> If he walks on the road after a shower and sees an
> earthworm which has strayed onto it he bethinks
> himself that it must get dried up in the sun, if it
> does not return soon enough to the ground into which
> it can burrow, so he lifts it from the deadly stone
> surface, and puts it on the grass. If he comes across
> an insect which has fallen into a puddle, he stops a
> moment in order to hold out a leaf or a stalk on which
> it can save itself". (Schweitzer, from CT Campion,
> 1987 p118)

As if to anticipate the mirth, even incredulity, of his
readers, Schweitzer continues: "He is not afraid of being

laughed at as sentimental". "It is the fate of every truth," he reminds us, "to be a subject for laughter until it is generally recognised".

Third, the principle is limitless. Schweitzer is no exponent of casuistry. Apart from one possible exception, namely animal experimentation (Schweitzer, from CT Campion, 1987, p120), he enters into no discussion about the relative rights and wrongs of this or any action when confronted with a particular dilemma. "Ethics," he insists with stark, perhaps unreasonable, simplicity, "are responsibility without limit to all that lives" (Schweitzer, from CT Campion, 1987 p119).

To understand Schweitzer at this point, we must clear our minds of two common, but deeply erroneous, perceptions of his position. The first is that he is advocating an absolutist stance, that he was an absolutist in practice, and second an absolutist in principle and inconsistent in practice. For, in the first place, as much as Schweitzer speaks of the limitless demand of reverence, he prefaces this claim with the significant statement that there will come a time when "people will be astonished that mankind needed so long a time to regard thoughtless injury to life as incompatible with ethics" (Schweitzer, from CT Campion, 1987 p119). In other words, Schweitzer did not regard all forms of life as inviolable under all circumstances. The very word "reverence" indicates to us that Schweitzer is not depicting obedience to law but the promotion of the good, which in turn requires an holistic response of the individual including attitude, disposition and motive as well as action. Some individuals have simply read Schweitzer´s examples and been taken with the sheer practical impossibility of their implementation. But such a reading is to mistake Schweitzer´s intention. What he gives us are examples of what reverence requires, without the pressure of necessity. "Whenever I injure life of any sort, I must be quite clear whether it is necessary," argues Schweitzer. "Beyond the unavoidable I must never go, not even with what seems insignificant" (Schweitzer, from CT Campion, 1987 p120).

In his personal life, Schweitzer was no absolutist in practice, as he was not in principle. He was no thorough-going vegetarian, vegan or anti-vivisectionist, for example. At least on one occasion, his biographer reminds us, he was involved in a pre-emptive strike against poisonous spiders (Brabazon, 1976 p255).

Nevertheless, Schweitzer does open himself up to the charge of absolutism by his apparent claim that reverence for life knows "nothing of a relative ethic". "Only the most universal and absolute purposiveness in the maintenance and furtherance of life is ethical, anything less than that is only a more or less necessary necessity, or a more or less expedient expediency" (Schweitzer, 1987 p227). This does not mean, however, that we do not sometimes have to make the choice between more or less necessary necessity or more or less expedient expediency.

The vital point to grasp is that when we have to do so, as we all surely do, we are not acting ethically as Schweitzer understands this term. In other words, even if we do our best most of the time, we are guilty, and guilty most of the time - a point that Schweitzer never tires of reminding us. "The good conscience," he warns, "is an invention of the devil" (Schweitzer, 1987 p209).

To place into perspective Schweitzer´s thought, it is necessary to recognise that reverence for life - far from being a new moral law - is more like a religious experience. He says almost as much. "The surmisings and the longings of all deep religiousness is contained in the ethic of reverence for life" (Schweitzer, 1987 p212). Philosophers, like Peter Singer (1979), immersed in utilitarian calculations, simply miss this point entirely when they debate Schweitzer´s apparent inconsistencies as do some religious commentators (Singer, 1979 117-125). It was Paul Tillich in his penetrating study on Morality and Beyond (1969), who held that "a moral act is not an act in obedience to an external law, human or divine," rather it is "the inner law of our true being, of our essential and created nature, which demands that we actualise what follows from it". Moreover: "the religious dimension of the moral imperative is its unconditional character" (Tillich, 1969 p12) Now if this is true, we may say that reverence has a religious dimension. "True philosophy," maintains Schweitzer, "must start from the most immediate and comprehensive fact of consciousness, which says ´I am life which wills to live, in the midst of life which wills to live´. This for Schweitzer is not an ingenious dogmatic formula. He speaks personally as one who has encountered revelation:

> "Day by day, hour by hour, I live and move in it. At every moment of reflection it stands fresh before me. There bursts forth from it again and again, as roots that can never dry up, a living world - and life-view - which can deal with all the facts of Being. A mysticism of ethical union with Being grows out of it" (Joy, 1952 p231)

It is this experiential, mystical identification of individual life with life, and through life with Being itself, which lies at the heart of Schweitzer´s philosophy. It is not so much a new law, code or maxim, but essentially an unconditional religious experience of great power. The insight that lies at its heart is quite simple, namely an apprehension of the value of other life-forms as given by God. Life is sacred or holy.

## (b) Karl Barth´s Reply

Although Schweitzer´s concept has received commentary of various kinds, only one theologian, namely Karl Barth, has - to my knowledge - given it detailed and critical attention. Before we address his criticisms, anticipating that these two great Germanic thinkers could hardly agree

on any theology, it is worth noting that Barth´s
discussion of Schweitzer is initially and to some degree
throughout, sympathetic, even irenical.  Barth (see,
Bromiley & Torrance, 1961) begins by accepting that
theological and naturalistic ethics have suffered from a
certain narrowness of ethical concern.  He quotes with
some approval Schweitzer´s well-known comparison of the
place of animals in European philosophy with that of a
kitchen floor scrubbed clean by a housewife who is
"careful to see that the door is shut lest the dog should
come in and ruin the finished job with its footprints"
(Bromiley & Torrance, 1961 p349). Barth then recounts some
of Schweitzer´s examples concerning the compassion to be
shown to worms and insects and even to the wayside flower.
Barth´s response does not fail to show the essential
seriousness which Schweitzer´s thought elicits.   "Those
who can only smile at this point," he writes, "are
themselves subjects for tears" (Bromiley & Torrance, 1961
p349).Such thought, Barth concludes, is certainly not
"sentimental".   Nor, according to Barth, can we justify
taking "the easy course of questioning the practicability
of the instruction given".  In short:  "whatever the
solutions proposed, the problem itself is important"
(Bromiley & Torrance, 1961 p350).

Barth develops three criticisms.  First, he is unhappy
about the grouping together of both vegetables and
animals, as though what was owed to vegetables was of the
same order as that owed to the higher mammals.  The
destruction of a plant and the destruction of an animal
are not comparable.  An animal is "a single being, a
unique creature existing in an individuality which we
cannot fathom but also cannot deny," whereas the using of
vegetable life does not constitute its destruction but
rather involves "sensible use of its superfluity"
(Bromiley & Torrance, 1961 p352). Barth comes to this
conclusion because respect for life only arises in "a
primary sense" in the relationship between human beings.
The concept of reverence may apply "analogically" to
animals who are distinct individuals but dissolves
entirely when it comes to vegetables.

Second, and relatedly, reverence and responsibility - for
he uses these two words almost interchangeably - properly
belong to the world of human-to-human relationships.
Barth accepts that the care of animals may constitute "a
serious secondary responsibility" but he is clearly
troubled by the universality and unconditional nature of
Schweitzer´s ethic.  Although Schweitzer is right to
protest at our "astonishing indifference and
thoughtlessness," what he proposes cannot be understood as
"doctrine, principle and precept" (Bromiley & Torrance,
1961 p350).   Why Barth is so adamant on this issue,
despite the clearly humanitarian sympathies displayed,
constitutes his third - and by far the most important -
theological criticism.

This third criticism runs as follows:  Schweitzer does not
appreciate the moral distinction between animals and

humans because he fails to grasp the meaning of the doctrine of the Incarnation. According to this doctrine, Barth expounds:

"(man) is the animal creature (sic) to whom God reveals, entrusts and binds Himself within the rest of creation, with whom He makes common cause in the course of a particular history which is neither that of an animal nor of a plant, and in whose life-activity He expects a conscious and deliberate recognition of His honour, mercy and power".

What follows is the "higher necessity" of human life and hence the right to "lordship and control" (Barth, 1960 p351). The one pivotal assumption throughout the twelve chapter-volumes of Barth's magisterial Church Dogmatics (1960) is precisely this: "that God's eternal Son and Logos did not will to be an angel or animal but man" (Bromiley & Torrance, 1960 p18). For Barth, humans are a cherished creature.


(c)  **Reverence:  Schweitzer v Barth**

How then are we to begin an assessment of Schweitzer's reverence and Barth's criticism of it? At least one of Barth's criticisms is well made. There are morally relevant distinctions between one kind of creature and another. It may not be sufficient, but it is at least relevant, to ask whether a being on which one is to bestow reverence has some consciousness of what reverence, or lack of it, might mean. Barth may be right or wrong about whether plants are ethical individuals (see, for example, Clark, 1977), but he is not wrong in supposing that what is done to a beast is - in his own words - "something which is at least very similar to homicide" (Barth, 1961 p352). There are good biblical as well as biological reasons for sensing a continuity in living agents, but also for positing greater capacities in spiritual self-awareness in humans and mammals (Linzey, 1987 p77-86).


That accepted, what is difficult in Barth is not that he proposes a fundamental theological distinction between humans and animals, but rather what he wants to deduce from such a distinction. What is so problematic is the way in which God's "yes" to humankind in the Incarnation becomes a "no" to creation as a whole. There are three Christological relationships which seem strangely absent, not just from Barth's own discussion of Schweitzer, but also throughout his four volumes on creation doctrine as a whole (Linzey, 1986) First, according to orthodox doctrine, the same Christ incarnate is also the Logos through whom all things come to be. The Logos is the source and destiny of all that is. St. Athanasius writes of how the Word "orders and contains the universe," illuminating "all things visible and invisible, containing and enclosing them in himself" (Thomson, 1971 p119). In this sense Christ is the key to the theological

understanding not only of humankind, but also the whole
creation. And neither is Athanasius a lone voice among
the Church Fathers.

"For God who made and brought into existence all things by
his infinite power contains, gathers, and limits them and
in his Providence binds both intelligible and sensible
beings to himself and to one another," maintains St.
Maximus (see Berthold, 1985). "As beings which are by
nature distinct from one another, he makes them converge
in each other by the singular force of their relationship
to him as origin" (Berthold, 1985 p186)  If this is true,
we should abandon our sharp, sometimes arrogant,
separation of humankind from nature, often buttressed by
non-theological considerations. With Eric Mascall (1986),
we shall reject the misconception that "Jesus Christ is of
immense significance for human beings, but of no
importance whatever to the rest of creation" (Mascall,
1986).

Second, we need to bring to light the ancient Patristic
principle that what is not assumed in the Incarnation is
not healed in the Redemption. The Barthian view that
there is a specifically human nature, absolutely
differentiated from all other natures or nature itself, is
untenable if Christ is also the Logos, the co-creator
through whom all things come to be.

> "When the Word visited the holy Virgin Mary, the
> Spirit came to her with him, and the Word in the
> Spirit moulded the body and conformed it to himself,"
> writes Athanasius, "desiring to join and present all
> creation to the Father, through himself, and in it to
> reconcile all things, having made peace, whether
> things in heaven or things upon earth" (see Torrance,
> 1969).

Again, Athanasius is not a lone voice.  "(I)n uniting
himself with man," writes St. John of the Cross, God
"united Himself with the nature" of all creatures. The
"yes" of God the Creator extends to all living beings:
the ousia assumed in the Incarnation is not only
specifically human, it is also creaturely. "The sheer
profundity of St. John´s thought is expressed in this
line: ´To behold (all creatures) and find them very good
was to make them very good in the Word, His Son.´" (see
Peers 1974 p48-49; Linzey 1987 p62).

Third, the same Christ who is the co-creator, the Logos,
the one who incarnates himself into the very nature of
being, is also the reconciler of all things. Indeed the
work of creation, incarnation and reconciliation are three
sides of the one mysterious divine activity accomplished
in Christ. Far too many interpreters have held that the
cosmic strands in the New Testament belong to a past age
and represent transient cosmological wrapping. For us in
our own time, their significance could not be greater.
God´s purpose " which he set forth" is, as Ephesians
(1:10) puts it, "a plan in the fullness of time to unite

all things in him, things in heaven and things in earth".
In Romans (8:28ff) the non-human creation "groans and
travails awaiting the redemption promised by the one who
subjected it in hope". Athanasius speaks of Christ as the
"Saviour of the Universe (tou panto)" (Linzey & Regan,
1989 p97). Once again, Athanasius is not alone in his
interpretation of the New Testament. In the well-known
passage from Against Heresies, St. Irenaeus insists that:

> "(T)his is our Lord, who in the last times was made
> man, existing in this world, and who in an invisible
> manner contains all things created, and is inherent in
> the entire creation, since the Word governs and
> arranges all things; and therefore He came to his own,
> in a visible manner, and was made flesh, and hung upon
> the tree, that He might sum up all things in Himself"
> (Roberts & Rambaut, undated, and Linzey & Regan,
> 1989).

Enough has been said to question Barth´s Christological
argument. It may appear presumptuous to claim that the
one Christological theologian this century par excellence
has a deficient Christology, and yet the cogency of
Barth´s view rests upon a drastically over-simplified
conception of orthodox Christological relationships. In
short: Barth´s theology too easily severs the connection
between the Revealing Word and the cosmos in which that
Word is revealed.

Barth´s appeal to Christology, to the special-ness of
humankind because of the Incarnation does not preclude a
conception of reverence for all life as advanced by
Schweitzer. Indeed, the reverse is the case. Whatever
the limits of what Barth calls the "mystico-cosmic ethics"
which Schweitzer expounds, they cannot be so easily
opposed to Christian doctrine as Barth thinks. For if the
Logos inheres in his creation, and if the act of uniting
human nature involves the whole of created nature in some
way, then we may reasonably suppose some value to the
created order, quite independent of human utilitarian
calculations. It is understandable, given his
presuppositions, that Barth should faintly recoil at what
he takes to be Schweitzer´s undeveloped theology and
supposedly commonsensical approach. No theologian could
be more disturbed than Karl Barth by the notion that
anything is self-evident in creation. But all this should
not blind us to the real possibility that Schweitzer has
uncovered a practical moral imperative that is deducible
from, if not integral to, Christological doctrine.

Barth is properly fearful of any attempt to build a
theological perspective upon specific creaturely insights
or feelings. But what he overlooks is the possibility
that Schweitzer may have implicitly grasped an essential
implication of Christ-centred theology. The common origin
of all creatures is doctrine that carries with it
implications and consequences which so far only a few in
the Christian tradition have fully appreciated. "Surely
we ought to show kindness and gentleness to animals for

many reasons," writes St. Chrysostom, "and chiefly because they are of the same origin as ourselves" (my emphasis, see Attwater 1960 p59-60). A view similar to that of St. Bonaventure, who says of St. Francis that "when he considered the primordial source of all things, he was filled with even more abundant piety calling creatures no matter how small by the name of brother and sister because he knew that they had the same source as himself (Cousins, 1978). Thomas Traherne likewise speaks of how God "enjoyeth" the whole world so that "all that is therein" are his "peculiar treasures", and that since we are made in his image, "to live in His similitude, as they are His, they must be our treasures (too)" (see Davis, 1980 p83).

In short: doubtless Barth is right that Schweitzer´s concept of reverence cannot constitute "doctrine" as such, but it can be easily defended with the most impeccable Christian doctrines, if not an integral moral imperative of the same. The value of Schweitzer´s thought may lie precisely in this area: that he articulates a frequently-forgotten implication of doctrine which whenever heard - however strange, laughable or incredible - resonates with some sense of the Creator´s will for His creatures.


## (2) RESPONSIBILITY TO ANIMALS

I want now to turn to the question of responsibility to animals. If the notion of reverence has not had a high profile within the Christian tradition, still less the concept of responsibility. Although there are signs of an awakening sense of concern - most notably in Papal pronouncements (for example, Encyclical: Sollicitudo Rei Socialis, 30 Dec 1987) and in the work of some scholars (see, for example, Santmire, 1985) - it is still true, as far as I can determine, that Roman Catholic moral theology denies that humans have direct duties to animals (see Linzey, 1957 p68-98). In order to understand this position we have to examine the thought of St. Thomas Aquinas, whose theology still dominates much Catholic thinking - not least about animals.


## (a) The Scholastic Rejection

I propose to discuss two questions raised and answered by St. Thomas in his Summa Theologica or Theologiae. The first concerns whether it is unlawful to kill any living thing (Aquinas, from CT Campion, 1987 p124). St. Thomas notes three kinds of objections that might be brought against killing. First, on the basis of divine providence, namely that God has "ordained that all living things should be preserved". Second, since depriving an individual of life is murder and since murder is a sin and life is also common to animals and plants, killing animals and plants is also a sin. Third, since in Mosaic Law the killing of another man´s ox or sheep is an offence punishable by death, it follows that killing an animal must be sinful.

Aquinas finds all three objections unconvincing. Following Augustine, he insists:

> "when we hear it said, 'thou shalt not kill,' we do not take it as referring to trees, for they have no sense, nor to irrational animals, because they have no fellowship with us" (Aquinas, from CT Campion, 1987 p124).

If we inquire concerning the philosophical basis of this view, we may not be surprised to find Aristotle cited as its source:

> "There is no sin in using a thing for the purpose for which it is...," answers Aquinas. "Now the order of things is such that the imperfect are for the perfect, even as in the process of generation nature proceeds from imperfection to perfection... Wherefore it is not unlawful if man use plants for the good of animals, and animals for the good of man, as the Philosopher states" (Aquinas, from CT Campion, 1987 p124).

It is this appeal to the natural "order of things" that predominates in Thomist thought. Only subsequently, and almost secondarily, is this interpretation reinforced by an appeal to scripture. Aquinas cites Genesis 1:19 and Genesis 9:3 which concern the giving of food for man to corroborate what he has already accepted, following Aristotle and Augustine, as the providential design of nature.

To our three objections noted earlier, Aquinas replies briefly as follows:

To the first, that God preserves all life in existence, he maintains that "the Divine Ordinance of animals and plants is preserved not for themselves but for man," and hence "as Augustine says... both their life and their death are subject to our use" (Aquinas, from CT Campion, 1987 p125).

To the second objection, namely that life is a common possession of humans and animals, Aquinas answers in a line almost entirely taken over from Aristotle (see Sinclair, 1985) and worth citing in full:

> "Dumb animals and plants are devoid of the life of reason whereby to set themselves in motion; they are moved, as it were by another, by a kind of natural impulse, a sign of which is that they are naturally enslaved and accommodated to the uses of others (Aquinas, from CT Campion, 1987 p125).

To the third objection, that killing another's oxen is contrary to Mosaic law, Aquinas answers that it is only the life of an ox considered as human property that is disputed in the Old Testament. The act of killing another's ox is "not a species of the sin of murder but of the sin of theft or robbery" (Aquinas, from CT Campion, 1987 p125).

In short: three elements distinguish Aquinas' view of the status of animal life. First, animals are irrational, possessing no mind or reason. Second, they exist to serve human ends by virtue of their nature and by divine providence. Third, they therefore have no moral status in themselves save insofar as some human interest is involved, for example, as human property.

In case it is thought that this might be a caricature or misreading of Aquinas' position, it is worth noting that this view is consistently defended throughout his work. Indeed, there are passages where he underlines the absence of moral status by claiming the legitimacy of absolute human prerogatives over animals.

> "(B)y divine providence," he argues in Summa Contra Gentiles, animals "are intended for man's use in the natural order. Hence it is not wrong for man to make use of them, either by killing or in any other way whatever" (see Regan & Singer, 1976).

It is sometimes argued that whilst Aquinas did not accept specific duties to animals, such as refraining from killing, he nevertheless espoused general care and love towards animals (Agius, 1970). Close reading of Aquinas does not support this view, however. Question 65, article 3, in the Summa is precisely concerned with this question whether "irrational creatures also ought to be loved out of charity" (Aquinas, from CT Campion, 1987 p125-127). Here the line taken by Aquinas entirely supports his earlier view that we have no fellowship with animals. "The love of charity extends to none but God and our neighbour," maintains Aquinas. But can animals be regarded as, or at least analogous to, human neighbours? No, claims Aquinas. "[T]he word neighbour cannot be extended to irrational creatures, since they have no fellowship with man in the rational life," and therefore, "charity does not extend to irrational creatures" (Aquinas, from CT Campion, 1987 p126).

Why Aquinas is so insistent upon this point lies in the already defended axiom that animals are irrational. Charity is, according to Aquinas, a kind of friendship, which is "impossible, even metaphorically speaking" to extend to animals. It may be objected that surely God loves all his creatures, to which Aquinas replies "yes", charity towards animals may be appropriate "if we regard them as the good things we desire for others" that is, for "God's honour and man's use" (Aquinas, from CT Campion, 1987 p126). And it is only in this way, Aquinas suggests, that God loves the non-human, insofar as they are good and of use to human beings.

We see then that Aquinas' position is consistent in its

own terms. It has been reproduced by one Catholic textbook after another, for example in 1962 by the Dictionary of Moral Theology (Palazzini) which argues that animal welfare workers "often lose sight of the end for which animals, irrational creatures, were created by God, viz., the service and use of man. In fact, Catholic moral doctrine teaches that animals have no rights on the part of man". We may summarise Aquinas in this way: considered in themselves, animals have no reason and no rights, and humans no responsibility to them.


## (b)  The Challenge of Mercy

Aquinas´ doctrine has become the dominant Western religious position on animals since the thirteenth century. Those in any doubt about this should consult Keith Thomas´ excellent survey entitled Man and the Natural World (Thomas, 1984). Only in the eighteenth and nineteenth centuries do we find Aquinas seriously challenged. I want now to consider the best of these challenges made by a little-known eighteenth-century divine, Humphry Primatt. That so few should have even heard of Primatt may itself be suggestive of oblivion, but in a number of practical ways, his theology, if not his name, lives on.

Primatt´s sole known work is his Dissertation on the Duty of Mercy and the Sin of Cruelty to Brute Animals, published in 1776 (see Linzey & Regan, 1988). Without directly mentioning Aquinas, he challenges key elements within the scholastic Catholic tradition. He appears to agree with Aquinas in rejecting the idea that creation has in some way "fallen" from the original designs of the Creator, but unlike Aquinas (who then goes on to postulate the innocence of parasitical existence and man´s part in it (Primatt, from CT Campion, 1987 p127), Primatt sees in nature "a transcript of the divine goodness". From the starting-point that creation is fundamentally good, the outward result of a Creator who is himself "wise and just and good, and merciful", Primatt deduces the principle that "every creature of God is good in its kind; that is, it is such as it ought to be". It follows, that whatever the "perfections or defects may be, they cannot be owing to any merit or demerit in the creature itself, being not prior, but consequential to its creation" (Primatt, from CT Campion, 1987 p127). In this way Primatt agrees with Aquinas about the essential goodness of creation, but gives this doctrine a new twist in underlining the value of each kind of creature in itself.

Primatt also agrees with Aquinas that there is a natural "order of things", and in particular that humans are superior to other animals.

"At the top of the scale of terrestrial animals we suppose Man," argues Primatt, "and when we contemplate the perfections of body, and the endowments of mind,

31

which, we presume, he possesses above all the other animals, we justly suppose him there constituted by his Maker" (Primatt, from CT Campion, 1987 p127).

So far, then, there is much in common between Primatt and Aquinas. But Primatt makes two further distinctions. Whilst he accepts significant differences between humans and animals, he insists upon the common misery of pain:

"Pain is pain, whether it be inflicted on man or on beast; and the creature that suffers it, whether man or beast, being sensible of the misery of it whilst it lasts, suffers evil; and the sufferance of evil, unmeritedly, unprovokedly, where no offence has been given; no good end can possibly be answered by it, but merely to exhibit power or gratify malice, is Cruelty and Injustice in him that occasions it" (Primatt, from CT Campion, 1987 p128).

The appeal here to justice is significant. For Aquinas – whether he thought animals could feel pain or no – certainly did not include animals, even metaphorically, within the sphere of human justice. Indeed because, strictly speaking, animals could have no friendship with humans, and therefore be subject to charitable constraints, animals could not actually be wronged. The new note in Primatt is the insistence that what happens within the sphere of animal-human relations is not a question of locating some human interest, hidden or otherwise, nor a question of taste or skill, but of plain justice. His argument from consistency is developed in a way that has a familiar ring to modern ears:

"It has pleased God the Father of all men, to cover some men with white skins, and others with black skin; but as there is neither merit nor demerit in complexion, the white man, not withstanding the barbarity of custom and prejudice, can have no right, by virtue of his colour, to enslave and tyrannise over a black man; nor has a fair man any right to despise, abuse and insult a brown man. Nor do I believe that a tall man, by virtue of his stature, has any legal right to trample a dwarf under his foot. For, whether a man is wise or foolish, white or black, fair or brown, tall or short, and I might add rich or poor, for it is no more a man's choice to be poor, than it is to be a fool, or a dwarf, or black, or tawny, – such he is by God's appointment; and, abstractly considered, is neither a subject for pride, nor an object of contempt" (Primatt, from CT Campion, 1987 p129).

And in a crucial step, Primatt – contrary to the Thomist tradition – places animals within this widening circle of sympathy and justice:

"Now, if amongst men, the differences of their powers of the mind, of their complexion, stature, and accidents of fortune, do not give any one man a right

32

to abuse or insult any other man on account of these differences; for the same reason, a man can have no natural right to abuse and torment a beast, merely because a beast has not the <u>mental</u> powers of a man" (Primatt, from CT Campion, 1987 p129).

This further point, that mental superiority does not justify moral abuse, is developed by Primatt throughout his work. In short: unlike Aquinas, who found that man had a right to kill animals precisely because of his rationality, Primatt insists that "superiority of rank or station may give ability to communicate happiness, and seems so intended; but it can give no right to inflict unnecessary or unmerited pain" (Primatt, from CT Campion, 1987 p129). Some may think Primatt is simply anticipating the later secular arguments for equality between animals and humans in the matter of moral treatment. But to understand Primatt properly, we have to appreciate the deeply theological, indeed Christological, character of his endeavours. Living mercifully is, according to Primatt, a matter of revelation (Primatt, from CT Campion, 1987 p288ff). It is because God loves and cares for the creation he has made and because that great creative generosity is shown us in His Son, that we have an absolute moral imperative for our dealings with fellow creatures.

Again, contrary to Aquinas, the usefulness of animals is a sign of the very generosity of God which should inspire in humans a corresponding generosity towards the non-human. For the purpose of animals is not to serve the human species but to glorify God and praise Him. They have a justification for existence which humans themselves have yet to earn, and may earn supremely through the exercise of mercy. Primatt does not pull his punches in this matter so central, as he sees it, to Christian faith:

"We may pretend to what religion we please, but cruelty is atheism. We may make our boast of Christianity; but cruelty is infidelity. We may trust to our orthodoxy, but cruelty is the worst of heresies. The religion of Christ Jesus originated in the mercy of God; and it was the gracious design of it to promote peace to every creature upon earth, and to create a spirit of universal benevolence or goodwill in men" (Primatt, from CT Campion, 1987 p288).

(c)  **Responsibility: Aquinas v Primatt**

How then are we to assess the views of Aquinas, and Primatt's protest against them? From a theological perspective, a major weakness in Aquinas stems from what is most derived from Hellenistic sources. Two axioms – typical or untypical – from Aristotle are taken over almost without question.

The first is that humans alone have a rational capacity. Animals are thought to "have the power of locomotion" and

yet in none but man, "is there intellect" (Aquinas, from
CT Campion, 1987 p126). We find this idea taken over in
its entirety by Aquinas. The second is that animals have
no other purpose save serving human beings. Aristotle
arrives at this conclusion from the rather weak argument
that, since all nature has a purpose, animals must have a
purpose too, and "it must be that nature has made all of
them for the sake of man" (Aquinas, from CT Campion, 1987
p126). Again, this idea of a creation entirely pleasing
and naturally ordered for the sake of human-kind is
assumed throughout the Summa by Aquinas. All that Aquinas
does is to give these essentially Greek ideas a scriptural
and/or theological over-writing.

As regards rationality, for example, this is justified in
terms of the giving of God´s image to man which is
described wholly in terms of an intellectual capacity
which separates humans from beasts (Aquinas, from CT
Campion, 1987 p126). And as regards the utility of
animals, the biblical notion of dominion is used to
confirm human despotism over animals (Aquinas, from CT
Campion, 1987 p124-126).

Unluckily for Aquinas one would have to look very hard
nowadays to find one Old Testament scholar who thought
"dominion" simply meant despotism. If anything, the
concept underlines human responsibility for God´s creation
(see, for example, Westerman, 1974). Worse still, when
Aquinas wants scriptural support for Aristotle´s dictum
that animals were made for human use and that we are
therefore justified in using them indiscriminately for
food, the actual texts he utilises - Genesis 1:29 and
Genesis 9:3 do not unambiguously support his case. In
Genesis 9:3, humankind is only allowed flesh on the
condition that they do not appropriate the nephesh, the
life symbolised by blood. In Genesis 1:29, humans are
actually commanded to be vegetarians. In other words,
influenced by Aristotelian philosophy, Hebrew monarchy
becomes created hierarchy. Genesis is interpreted in
terms of the Aristotelian pattern which sees nature as a
wholly hierarchical system in which it is assumed - as
with human society - that the male is superior to the
female, the female to the slave, and the slave to the
beast and so on. No wonder that Robin Attfield (1983)
argues that "the tradition which holds that in God´s eyes
the non-human creation has no value except in its
instrumental value for mankind has Greek rather than
Hebrew sources" (Attfield, 1983 p26).

What is so problematic about Aquinas is that this great
Christian scholar was not quite Christian or scriptural
enough in allowing for theological argument either drawn
from the humanitarian tradition of the Old Testament,
which acknowledged that humans had at least some
responsibilities to animals, on one hand, or to
theological argument centred on the exercise of costly
merciful loving expressed for us in Jesus Christ, on the
other.

We may be tempted to go further. For the emphasis upon rationality in Aristotle, Augustine and Aquinas has left a bitter legacy in Christian theology. These people, not unfairly described by Alec Whitehouse as "aristocrats of the mind" are "frequently disposed to treat as fully actual, and to envisage as finally actual, only what is incorporated into the activity of rational agents" (see Loades, 1981 p210). Hence Christian theology - from this perspective - comes increasingly to consist in the cure, the development, and the salvation of souls. The effect of all this on the non-rational and therefore mortal souls of animals is not advantageous. God´s providential care, attested by Scripture, becomes telescoped into continuing obsession with individual human soul-cultivation, at the expense of the rest of creation.

One historical footnote is desirable. Although, as regards the treatment of animals, Aquinas remains the dominant historical force throughout Western Christianity, the views of Primatt and others have gained increasing acceptance. We know, for example, that the person who was responsible for the revision of the second edition of Primatt´s work was Arthur Broome, the man responsible for the foundation of the RSPCA, the first nation-wide animal welfare society in the world, in 1824. The Society´s first Prospectus spoke in Primatt-like terms about the extension of Christian compassion towards suffering creatures, and one of its subsequent meetings affirmed its foundation in Christian faith and specifically Christian principles (see Turner, 1980 p43). Little do people appreciate how divided the Christian house is on the question of animals. Whilst the Primatt-like forces were increasing their strength behind the new Society, at the same time in the middle of the nineteenth century, Pope Pius IX forbade the opening of an animal protection office in Rome on the familiar Thomist principle that humans had duties to fellow humans but none to animals (see Regan, 1986 p149).

## (3)  THE RIGHTS OF ANIMALS

I want now to turn to our third question, whether animals have rights. The language of rights is sometimes viewed within contemporary Christian circles as being a secular import into theological ethics. In fact, Christian theological tradition that has been one of the main inspirations for the language of rights; for many centuries and until the present day Christians, both Catholic and Protestant, have placed notions of rights within their theological systems. The question is, however, should the language of rights extend to animals? Again it is worth reminding ourselves that even this question is not as new as it may sound. The first person who used the term "rights" in relation to animals was Thomas Tryon in the sixteenth century. In his lyrical "Complaints of the birds and fowls of heaven to their Creator" published in 1688, Tryon gives voice to the creatures pleading for justice:

"But tell us, O men! We pray you to tell us what injuries have we committed to forfeit? What laws have we broken, or what cause given you, whereby you can pretend a right to invade and violate our part, and natural rights, and to assault and destroy us, as if we were the aggressors, and no better than thieves, robbers and murderers, fit to be extirpated out of creation... From whence did thou (O man) derive thy authority for killing thy inferiors, merely because they are such, or for destroying their natural rights and privileges?" (Tryon, in Magel, 1989).

We may notice here both an appeal to negative, as well as positive, rights - such as is also found in the work of Primatt. Primatt argues, at least on one occasion, for the "undoubted right" of animals "intrusted in our care" to minimal requirements such as "food, rest and tender usage" (Tryon, in Magel, 1989). But he also speaks, more characteristically, of humans having no right to treat animals unmercifully (for discussion, see Clark, 1977).

## (a) Rights and Sentiency

We have seen that the particular basis on which Primatt includes animals within this sphere of human justice is sentiency: it is because animals can feel pain like humans that we should regard their treatment as morally significant. But can sentiency by itself, understood as consciousness and the ability to experience pain, be regarded as the criterion for the possession of moral rights? Such was certainly the view of Justus George Lawler who, in 1965, argued:

"To the question of where one draws the line... it must be replied that one would imagine the line to be drawn at the limits of flesh and blood. One draws the line then at the lowest extremity of creatures who share in spirit, and who are compounded of tissues, nerves and blood... Any creature when it reaches the threshold of experiencing and anticipating pain possesses rights".

Following Lawler, I once thought so too; in my Animal Rights: A Christian Assessment, published in 1976, I tried to give an account of sentient rights within a theological context. In it I queried what had become the classical view that either "personhood" or "rationality" were by themselves sufficient grounds for awarding moral rights. I pointed out that these criteria were "necessarily exclusive" of the claims of animals; their inevitable result was to exclude the non-human from proper moral consideration. The unsatisfactoriness of these criteria should be obvious, I argued, from the marginal cases, such as newly-born children or the mentally handicapped, who also possessed no or diminished moral rights. To be fair, I was not entirely oblivious of the difficulties associated with basing rights on the

36

criterion of sentiency. "I think the question we have to ask," I wrote, "is whether we have erred on the right side. Has the criterion of sentiency met the problem of serious differences of potential and capacity for life and suffering which exist in the non-human world?" (Linzey, 1976 p20). The sentiency criterion, I maintained, was one way in which we could make sense of the value of created beings, the scriptural sense of human responsibility towards animals and the fact that they could be harmed in ways that plants and stones could not.

Not surprisingly, my view, together with that of Peter Singer whose book Animal Liberation (1977) followed closely on my own, aroused much discussion. Philosophers who particularly enjoy detecting inconsistency and unreason in theological argument found my youthful book an easy source of both (see, for example, Paterson & Ryder, 1979; Regan 1979, p189-219). In addition, the book attracted one detailed theological critique from a conservative evangelical standpoint, and it is to this critique that I now turn.

(b) **The Critique of Sentiency**

The Human Use of Animals by Richard Griffiths (1982) makes many criticisms of my work, three of central importance. First, he queries whether there can be any purely natural basis for rights based on sentiency, intelligence or evolutionary kinship. Now, I shall not concern myself at this time with Griffiths' detailed arguments against the sentiency criterion for rights, except to note that he does not rule out all rights completely; he concludes that:

> "the search for an adequate secular basis for animal rights is bound to fail because of the overriding difficulty of establishing any rights at all (even human rights) on a purely two-dimensional plane, without including some notion of God" (Griffiths, 1982 p18).

This interesting criticism is related to his second, that from a theological perspective all nature, not just animals, have worth and value:

> "The value that God places on all nature is a biblical principle which means that the Christian does not have to draw the line anywhere in valuing the world" (Griffiths, 1982 p6).

Third, Griffiths strongly argues that the language of rights is divisive amongst Christians and obscures many of the positive elements which can be found within a biblical view of animals. Griffiths enumerates some of these positive elements: animals have intrinsic value to God; God delights and rejoices in the differentiated creation He has made; they are in His gracious keeping; God feeds them; even the sparrows and the Ninevite cattle are His concern; animals reflect God´s glory and therefore praise Him (Griffiths, 1982 p8). Moreover, Griffiths queries the view that animals "were simply created for man alone",

"In the Creation story God makes the animals before man, and pronounces them good without man (Gen. 1:24-25): they are made by God and for God" (Griffiths, 1982, p8).

It seems to me now that all three of Griffith´s major criticisms can be accepted in part at least[1] and I am grateful to him for his work has helped provide stimulus for a substantial rethinking of the question and a new book, Christianity and the Rights of Animals Linzey, 1987). irony for Griffiths is that, while accepting at least some of his criticisms, it is now possible to make a stronger case for animals having moral rights.


(c) **Rights: Linzey v Griffiths**

For I agree with Griffiths that, if there are rights, it is only God who can properly and absolutely claim them. He is, after all, the Creator, and if Creator then sovereign in His power, however we may understand that sovereignty to be manifest. All creatures are His creatures. All things proceed from His creative hands. I like the line from von Balthasar that "the whole point of creation is for us to know that we are not Creator". If, as Karl Barth (1986) would have it, creation is "grace", the result of the sheer generosity of God, then we do well to pause, as he suggests, in wonder and awe and thanksgiving (Barth, 1966 p54). But if this is true, it is perfectly possible, nay desirable, to talk of God´s own rights in His creation which we should respect by reverencing what is given. Alas, I cannot claim originality even for this idea - for it is expounded and defended with subtlety by Dietrich Bonhoeffer in a much neglected section of his Ethics (see Bethge, 1971):

"To idealistic thinkers it may seem out of place for a Christian ethic to speak first of rights and only later of duties. But our authority is not Kant; it is the Holy Scripture, and it is precisely for that reason that we must speak first of the rights of natural life, of what is given to life, and only later of what is demanded of life. God gives before He demands. And indeed in the rights of natural life it is not to the creature that honour is given, but to the Creator. It is the abundance of His gifts that is acknowledged. There is no right before God, but the natural, purely as what is given, becomes the right in relation to man. The rights of natural life are in the midst of the fallen world, the reflected splendour of the glory of God´s creation. They are not primarily something that man can sue for in his own interest, but they are something which is guaranteed by God Himself" (Barth, 1966 p54).

Second, I agree with Griffiths that from this perspective
all life, indeed all nature, has value, precisely because
it is given by God.  And, third, I also agree with
Griffiths that the biblical picture of animals contains
many elements that are much more favourable to animals
than is commonly supposed.

But our common ground in one sense is precisely the ground
of our difference.  While the biblical material does
suggest that all nature has value to God the Creator, it
also points us to an appreciation that different forms of
life have increased capacities for responding self-
awareness in the presence of God.  It is true that we are
not given in the Bible precise instructions as to the
relative value of beings, but it is also true that the
commonness of the lot of humans and animals is frequently
articulated.  Humans and animals, for example, are made on
the same day, recipients of a common blessing, subject
both to the blessing and curse of the Lord: both are to be
redeemed (Linzey, 1987 p8).  Karl Barth is not wrong when
he suggests that "man and beast thou savest O Lord" is a
common thread running throughout the whole Bible (Psalm
36.6, and Clark 1958, p181).  For what such language is
seeking to express in its own time needs to be re-
interpreted for our own.  To take these elements
seriously, then it seems we do have the wavy outlines of a
theological togetherness between animal and human species
that deserves to be taken seriously.  To hold the biblical
principle that all life and nature has value is not to
hold that all being has the same value or that there are
not morally relevant distinctions between one kind of
being and another.

## (4)  CONCLUSION

I want to propose, therefore, that there is a Christian
basis for what I shall term "the theos-rights" of animals,
that is consistent with those same notions of reverence
and responsibility which the tradition has, at its better
moments, espoused.  At the heart of this proposal is the
conviction that we need a theocentric view of creation.
There are four aspects to this which require some brief
elaboration.

## (a)  The Basis of Theos-Rights

(i)  The first is that creation exists for God.  If the
question be asked "What is creation for?", or "Why do
animals exist?", there is only one satisfactory
theological answer.  Creation exists for its Creator.
Years of anthropocentrism have almost completely obscured
this simple but fundamental point.  What follows from this
is that animals should not be seen simply as means to
human ends.  The key to grasping this theology is the
abandoning of the common but deeply erroneous view that
animals exist in a wholly instrumental relationship to
human beings.  Even if humans are uniquely important in

creation, it does not follow that everything in creation is made for us, to be pleasing for us, or that our pleasure is God´s chief concern. We need to be wary of making absolute claims about God´s chief concerns. The point is made starkly by James Gustafson (1981): "If God is ´for man´, he may not be for man as the chief end of creation. The chief end of God may not be the salvation of man" (Gustafson 1981, p96).

(ii) The second is that God is for His creation. I mean by that that God, as defined by trinitarian belief, cannot be fundamentally indifferent, negative or hostile to the creation he has made. Creation, as Barth suggests, is not only "actualisation" but also "justification" (Barth, in Bromiley & Torrance, 1960 p388). Every creature is a blessed creature or it is no creature at all. The point is grasped by Oliver Wendell Holmes Sr. who argued that "if a created being has no rights which his Creator is bound to respect, there is an end to all moral relations between them" (Holmes volume 1 p274). There is a sense in which this dictum is false and another in which it is true. It is false if it supposes some rights that exist independently of divine graciousness, almost external constraints which must tie the hands of the Almighty so that he is bound to accept them. But the dictum is true if it conveys the sense that God the Creator is tied to what His nature has created in His creation. Since His nature is love, and since God loves His creation, it follows that what is genuinely given and purposed by that love must acquire some right in relation to Him. I do not see how God can be the kind of God as defined by Trinitarian doctrine who is morally indifferent to the creation He has created, sustained, and reconciled, and which He will in the end redeem. To posit that God can be indifferent to His creatures, especially those who are indwelt by His Spirit, is to ultimately posit a God indifferent to His own nature and being.

(iii) The third point is that this - what I shall have to term -"for-ness" of God towards his creation is dynamic, inspirational, and costly. It is dynamic because God´s affirmation of creation is not a once-and-for-all event, but a continual affirmation, otherwise it would simply cease to be. It is inspirational because God´s Spirit moves within His creation - especially within those creatures that have the gift of a developed capacity to be. It is costly because God´s love does not come cheap. "We need to maintain the value, the preciousness of the human," argued Archbishop Robert Runcie in a recent lecture (1988), "by affirming the preciousness of the non-human also".

"For our concept of God forbids the idea of a cheap creation. Of a throw-away universe in which everything is expendable save human existence. The whole universe is a work of love. And nothing which is made in love is cheap. The value, the worth of natural things is not found in Man´s view of himself but in the goodness of God who made all things good

40

and precious in His sight... As Barbara Ward used to say "We have only one earth". Is it not worth our love?" (Runcie, 1988).

(iv)   The fourth point, or rather question, is this:   If creation exists for God, and if God is for creation, how can human beings be other than for creation?   To the criticism that this theological perspective minimises the special gifts of human beings, we should reply that, on the contrary, it may well be the special task of humans within creation to do what other creatures cannot do, at least in a consciously deliberate way, namely honour, respect and rejoice in the creation in which God rejoices. This, incidentally, I take to be one of the salient theological points in the second creation saga in Genesis - not, as so many people suppose, that creation was made for man, rather that man was made for creation, to till the earth and to serve it (Linzey, 1987 p22).

The notion of "theos-rights" then for animals means that God rejoices in the lives of those differentiated beings in creation enlivened by His Spirit.   In short:   If God is for them, we cannot be against them.

## (c)   **Objections to Theos-Rights**

To my proposal, I anticipate a number of objections. First, it may be argued that while it may well be that the case for reverence and responsibility towards animals has been overlooked in the Christian tradition, the language of rights is unnecessary and undesirable.   Why confuse the issue with the concept of rights which adds nothing and is practically divisive?   This is a serious objection if it comes from people who are convinced for one or more reasons that all rights language is misplaced, inappropriate or misleading in a theological context. There are some people so powerfully convinced of the sheer generosity of God in His creation that they would prefer not to speak the language of rights.   This position surely deserves respect.   But it is equally possible, following Bonhoeffer (see Linzey, 1987), to argue the reverse, namely that the sheer given-ness of creation gives rights a secure theological basis.   The position which I think is untenable, however, is the one that holds that human rights have a solid basis but then goes on to "query the appropriateness of rights language when it comes to animals" (Linzey, 1987 p72).   Again, it should not be forgotten that the Christian tradition has historically inspired, if not pioneered, some kinds of rights language, and even now it is hardly possible to read a document from the a collective gathering of churches from the Lambeth Conference, the United States Roman Catholic Synod of Bishops or the World Council of Churches that does not make ample, some might think effusive, reference to human rights (see, for example, Synod of the Church of England, 1976). Theologically speaking, the language of rights is no novelty.

41

Nevertheless, this does not mean that all appeals to rights of whatever kind are acceptable, nor that all understandings of rights are theologically defensible, nor that some claims for rights language have not been exaggerated. My proposal is modest. It does not involve us positing that rights language is the only kind of acceptable moral discourse, nor that rights language is comprehensive, so that nothing else needs to be added from a Christian context.

To those who argue that the appeal to rights makes no difference, I can only say that it is amazing that so much ink should have been spilt on an issue of supposed indifference. In fact, rights language obviously makes a difference, and at least in two directions as I have elsewhere tried to show. In the first place, it concretely reverses years of scholastic neglect, and rejects precisely the Thomist view of animals as morally without status:

> "Language and history are against those who want the better treatment of animals and who also want to deny the legitimacy of the language of rights. For how can we reverse centuries of scholastic tradition if we still accept the corner-stone of that tradition, namely that all but humans are morally rightless?" (Linzey, 1987 p97).

Second, whatever the limitations of rights language and however it may be open to misunderstanding, the quite fundamental point is that "to grant animal rights is to accept that they can be wronged" and in analogous terms to the wrong that may be inflicted upon human beings:

> "According to theos-rights what we do to animals is not simply a matter of taste or convenience or philanthropy. When we speak of animal rights we conceptualise what is owed to animals as a matter of justice by virtue of their Creator's right. Animals can be wronged because their Creator can be wronged in His creation" (Linzey, 1987 p97).

To reiterate: the language of theos-rights is not exclusive, comprehensive or essential, but it is plausible, consistent and desirable. It is for those who reject rights language to show how it is possible to give credence to the theological insights I have outlined "without participating in the moral neglect of the non-human which still characterises continuing elements within the Christian tradition" (Linzey, 1987 p98).

The second objection is as follows: if you believe in God the Creator of all, who loves and cares for His creation, whose creation indeed has certain "theos rights" by virtue of its Creator's right, why is it that this same creation, supposedly the work of a loving and caring Creator, does not uniformly exhibit such divine love and care, and as for animal rights hardly admits of them? Does the lion about to disembowel the gazelle have a right to its food, or indeed does the gazelle have no rights to its life? To posit notions of animal rights in a creation that hardly admits of them is theological fantasy.

At first sight, this appears a pretty cast-iron objection; so deeply does it impress itself even upon the most unfeeling heart that either the notion of a holy, loving God or the notion of animal rights itself seems to go out of the window, never to return.

I cannot claim any special sagacity about this question which has baffled, if not tormented, the great and the holy within the Christian tradition. At the same time, it is not clear to me that the nature of parasitical existence in creation poses any greater problem than the general one of evil itself. In which case the problem of lions eating gazelles is not substantially different from the question why God allows any kind of evil at all in the creation He has made. To this general problem I know of no satisfactory answer other than that provided by the twin biblical insights of fall and redemption. Unlike Aquinas, and to a lesser extent Primatt, I would not want to reject a doctrine of the cosmic fall of creation. While doubtless Primatt is right to suppose that creatures are in some sense right as they are, that is, they are valued for their own sake by God, it does not follow that all creation is as right as it could be or should be or - I would want to add - shall be.

To suppose, with the biblical writers, that the world is in some sense estranged and corrupted as a whole or, as Schweitzer puts it, "a ghastly drama of the will-to-live divided against itself" (Linzey, 1987 p245)., is not of course to answer the problem of why it is so. If evolutionary evidence is to be believed, dinosaurs existed and disappeared before the arrival of humans in the world - and we may safely presume that natural evil existed prior to the existence of man - in which case there is a limited amount of culpability that can be ascribed to the human species in this respect. Nevertheless, I think there is some truth in the biblical sense that humans are morally at the centre of the show of creation and that their violence and their degradation does at least profoundly affect, if not originate, the violence that seems structurally inherent within the creation that God has made. But generally to the problem of natural evil, Christian theism can provide at present no clearly satisfactory answer.

And yet in one sense, it can, and should. If theologians and scholars are divided about how evil came into the world, then we must say that most biblical writers - not to mention the major theologians of the first few centuries of the Christian era - were convinced that such evil could not, and shall not, under God's providential plan, last for ever. It is to my mind not insignificant that the earliest messianic hopes in Isaiah (11.9) and Hosea (2:18) envisage a world free of predatory nature, in which the lion does not eat the gazelle but lies down

peacefully with the kid. It is not too popular at the
present to give much credence to these, and many other,
cosmic redemption passages within Scripture; to do so is
to invite the charge of "naive realism" as one objector
put it to me recently. But it seems to me that this hope
of a world-transforming redemption is actually at the
heart of the Christian kerygma, and essential in order to
make sense of the notion of a holy, just, loving God. God
can just be the kind of God we Christians affirm Him to be
in the light of the incarnation if He allows transient
suffering, but He simply cannot be that kind of God we
suppose Him to be if He eternally refuses to allow
suffering to be transfigured by a greater joy. "For I
consider that the sufferings of the present time are not
worth comparing", writes St. Paul (Romans 8: 28ff), "to
the glory that is to be revealed to us," and not only to
us - as he goes on to postulate - but to the groaning non-
human creation as well.

The third objection holds that the kind of Cosmic
Christology I have espoused, requires a very different
kind of Jesus to the one actually presented in the
Gospels. A vegan, or at least a vegetarian Jesus is
indispensable to the gospel of animal rights, it is
sometimes claimed. The animal movement has not lacked
individuals who supposedly meet this claim by answering in
the affirmative and backing the fantastic long-shot that
Jesus just might have been an Essene prophet committed to
vigorous asceticism (Wynn-Tyson, 1979 p 107ff). To such
Christian asceticism, I like the reply of that pipe-
smoking, wine-imbibing theologian, Karl Barth (see
Bromiley & Torrance, 1961 p111-114), that "(a) powerful
ascetic can be a vessel of much greater wickedness than
even the most indulgent" and in a line that is worthy only
of Barth: "We cannot forget so easily that one may be a
non-smoker, abstainer and vegetarian, and yet be called
Adolf Hitler". No, we may with confidence, some might add
relief, believe the Gospel records that Jesus was not a
thoroughgoing ascetic, and not a vegan to boot. He
certainly ate fish, and although there are no precise
records of him eating meat, we cannot dismiss that
possibility either.

(c)  **Divine Generosity**

But does it then follow that because we have no vegan
Jesus that the Christian case for animal rights fails?  I
think not.  We have to reckon with the fact that the
Gospel records do not supply answers to many of the
contemporary questions we would like to ask of the
historical Jesus.  On this question, as with almost every
other, we have no alternative but to work from the hints
and guesses that are there within the text.  But these are
on the whole undoubtedly more positive than negative.

"We have lived so long with the Gospel stories of
Jesus that we frequently fail to see how His life and
ministry identified with animals... His birth, if

tradition is to be believed, takes place in the home
of sheep and oxen. His ministry begins, according to
St. Mark, in the wilderness "with the wild beasts".
(1:13). His triumphal entry into Jerusalem involves
riding on a "humble" ass (see Matthew 21:1b-5).
According to Jesus it is lawful to "do good" on the
Sabbath, which includes the rescuing of an animal
fallen into a pit (see Matthew 12:10b-12). Even the
sparrows, literally sold for a few pennies in His day
are not "forgotten before God". God's providence
extends to the entire created order, and the glory of
Solomon and all his works cannot be compared to that
of lilies of the field (Luke 12:27). God so cares for
his creation that even "foxes have holes, and the
birds of the air have nests; but the Son of man has
nowhere to lay his head" (Luke 9:58)... Moreover, what
many commentators have failed to realise is that Jesus
literally overturns the already questioned practice of
animal sacrifice. Those who sell pigeons have their
tables overturned, and are put out of the Temple (Mark
11:15-16). It is the scribe who sees the spiritual
bankruptcy of animal sacrifice that Jesus commends as
being "not far from the Kingdom of God" (see Mark 12:
32-4)... Even in the heavily gnostic Gospel of Thomas,
there is the striking saying about the birds of the
air and the fishes of the sea perhaps even preceding
us in the Kingdom" (see Linzey and Regan, 1989).

And yet despite these positive, more or less indirect,
intimations of a positive regard for animals, we do well
to appreciate the very limited kind of argument that can
be drawn from them. Christian discipleship cannot be
translated into more or less historical copying of the
Jesus of first century Palestine. Jesus was a male,
circumcised, Jew. He did not marry. He did not choose
women as His disciples. As far as we know He did not
object to the institution of slavery. Nor indeed to the
morality of foreign occupation. I have sometimes heard it
postulated that if Jesus really cared about animals, He
would surely have said something. But the argument from
silence, if taken to its extreme limit, would have
excluded past concern for the treatment of slaves and, in
our own day, for the status of women, a country's right
to live free of occupation and foreign interference, not
to mention all the range of extraneous subjects - not
covered by Jesus - but which contemporary churches like to
pass judgement about. Christian discipleship should never
mean blind obedience to the past, even our Gospel past,
without a corresponding open-ness to the life-giving,
discerning Spirit of God in our own day.

But even if there are no prepackaged answers to many moral
issues available to us from the life of Jesus, we can, I
think, be relatively certain of some things, the chief of
which is that the lordship of God as expressed in Jesus is
that of service. He is, after all, the one who gives His
life for others, who washes their dirty feet, heals
individuals from physical and spiritual oppression, feeds

the hungry, champions the poor, encourages concern for the least of all, and bids His disciples to do likewise if they are to have any part with Him. And it is in this general, unchallenged, Christological model that we have what should be our pattern for lordship or dominion over the animal creation. For the question we have to ask is this: If the power of God is expressed in humility, self-sacrifice, and costly loving, what right can we have to think that our lordship over God´s good creation will cost us less? How can we claim that the one who has all absolute power and rights may serve us, whilst we can behave as petty tyrants to the rest of creation?

It is this inclusive idea of divine generosity, as well as divine rejoicing, expressed in creation and incarnation which supports a basis for the God-given rights of the animal creation. Again these notions do not obliterate other ideas of reverence and responsibility but give them their sharpest possible point. If utilised carefully, the language of theos-rights helps bring out the fundamental point that what we are dealing with is God´s own Spirit-filled life, which does not belong to us and over which we certainly have no rights as of right. Such language - whatever its limitations or deficiencies - serves to convey to us that the claims of animals are God-based claims of justice. Far from usurping God´s own prerogative in His creation, the perspective of theos-rights champions it, brings it into sharpest contact with our own wants and desires, and determines that we recognise the generosity of God even in what often appears to us to be insignificant.

## (d)  Compromising at the Highest Level

Before I conclude, it may be worthwhile simply outlining the kind of imperative which flows from the position I have outlined. I entirely accept that we are in a difficult, even morally embarrassing, predicament with animals. So deeply entrenched has our exploitation of animals become that it is scarcely surprising that to think, and especially to act, morally has become highly problematical. We hunt, ride, shoot, fish, wear, trap, eat, factory farm, and experiment upon billions of animals every year. As one person put it to me recently: "The only place where one can completely respect the rights of animals is outer space". I do not want to avoid this general point and suppose that is is an easy matter to extricate ourselves from more than a few centuries of hardness of heart, indifference, callousness, and anthropocentrism. None of us, it seems to me, is morally clean when it comes to animals. Self-righteousness, therefore, is not only inappropriate but faintly ludicrous. But having accepted what Schweitzer calls - "our common guilt", what we all need is a programme of personal - and collective - disengagement from injury to animals.

What should encourage us is the fact that the Judaeo-Christian tradition contains within itself the insight that the world is still in the process of being finished, and especially that God is not yet himself finished with us. If we take this deeply biblical picture to heart, then we may yet be able to co-operate with the Spirit in the process of making a new creation. What Christian theology can and should do is to provide a vision of a new world. I accept that we have some difficult decisions to make before we even approximate that vision. I accept the need for compromise, given the constraints of the world as we know it. But I add this caveat: let us all compromise at the highest level.

For those who still regard the issue of animal rights as one of those interesting but largely otiose byways of Christian ethics, always destined to remain, as Barth would call it, "problematical but secondary", let me leave you with these words from Victor Hugo:

> "It was first of all necessary to civilise man in relation to his fellow men. This task is already well advanced and makes progress daily. But it is also necessary to civilise man in relation to nature... Philosophy has concerned itself but little with man beyond man, and has examined only superficially, almost with a smile of disdain, man´s relationship with... animals, which are in his eyes merely things. But are there not depths here for the thinker?... For myself I believe that pity is a law like justice, and that kindness is a duty like uprightness. That which is weak has the right to the kindness and pity of that which is strong".

## Footnote

(1) Though Griffiths is clearly wrong in supposing the Genesis 9 (which concerns the permission given by God to eat flesh under certain conditions) is the "basic" text (Griffiths, 1982 p6). This is simply loading the evidence. The prior text is Genesis 1, where man is commanded to be vegetarian, indicating God´s original will for His creation.

## Bibliography

Agius, A. God´s Animals (London: Catholic Study Circle for Animal Welfare, 1970).

Attwater, D. St John Chrysostom (London: Catholic Book Club, 1960).

Attfield, R. The Ethics of Environmental Concern (Oxford: Basil Blackwell, 1983).

Barth, L. Dogmatics in Outline (London: SCM Press, 1966).

Berthold, GC (Editor) Selected Writings (London: SPCK, 1985).

Bethge, LE (Editor). Ethics (London: SCM Press, 1971).

Bromiley, GW; Torrance, TF (Editors). Church Dogmatics, Volume III, The Doctrine of Creation, Part 1 (Edinburgh: T & T Clark, 1960)

Bromiley, GW; Torrance, TF (Editors). Church Dogmatics, Volume III, The Doctrine of Creation, Part 4 (Edinburgh: T & T Clark, 1961).

Brabazon, J. Albert Schweitzer: A Biography (London: Gollanz 1976)

Clark, SRL. The Moral Status of Animals (Oxford: Clarendon Press, 1977)

Cousins, LE. The Life of St Francis (London: SPCK, 1978).

Davis, D (Editor). Selected Writings (Manchester: Pyfield Books, 1980).

Dominican Fathers: St Thomas Aquinas (Translation). Summa Theologica (New York: Benziger Brothers, 1918).

General Synod of the Church of England. Human Rights: Our Understanding and Our Responsibilities (London: Board for Social Responsibility, CIO Publishing, 1976).

Griffiths, R. The Human Use of Animals (Nottingham: Grove Books, 1982).

Gustafson, J. Theology and Ethics (Oxford: Basil Blackwell, 1981).

Holmes, Oliver Wendell, Sr. Life and Letters of Oliver Wendell Holmes volume 1. p274.

Joy, CR. (Editor). Albert Schweitzer: An Anthology (London: Adam and Charles Black, 1952).

Lawler, JG. (1965) "On the Rights of Animals", in Anglican Theological Review April.

Linzey, A. Animal Rights, A Christian Assessment (London: SCM Press, 1976).

Linzey, A. Christianity and the Rights of Animals (London: SPCK and New York: Crossroad, 1987)

Linzey, A. The Neglected Creature: the Doctrine of the Non-Human Creation and its Relationship with the Human in the thought of Karl Barth (Unpublished PhD Thesis: University of London, 1986).

Linzey, A; Allchin, AM. Brother and Sister Creatures: The Saints and Animals (in press).

Linzey, A; Regan T (Editors). Animals and Christianity: A Book of Readings (London and New York: Crossroad 1989). This contains most of the key Biblical texts.

Linzey, A; Regan T (Editors). The Song of Creation: An Anthology of Poems in Praise of Animals (London: Marshall Pickering 1988).

Linzey, A; Regan T (Editors). Compassion for Animals: Readings and Prayers (London, SPCK and New York: Crossroad).

Loades, A (Editor). The Authority of Grace (Edinburgh, T & T Clark, 1981).

Mascall, E. The Christian Universe (London: Darton, Longman and Todd, 1966).

Palazzini, P. (Editor) Dictionary of Moral Theology (London: Burns Oates, 1962).

Paterson, D: Ryder, RD (Editors). Animals' Rights - A Symposium (London: Centaur Press, 1979).

Peers AE (Editor). The Complete Works (Wheathampstead, Herts: Anthony Clarke, 1974).

Primatt, H. Dissertation on the Duty of Mercy and the Sin of Cruelty (Edinburgh: T Constable, 1776).

Regan, T (Editor). Animal Sacrifices: Religious Perspectives on the Uses of Animals in Science (Philadelphia: Temple University Press, 1986).

Roberts, A: Rambaut, WH (Editors) The Writings of Irenaeus (Edinburgh: T & T Clark, no date).

Runcie, R. "Address at the Global Forum of Spiritual and Parliamentary Leaders on Human Survival". 11 April 1988, pp:103014.

Santmire, HP. The Travail of Nature: The Ambiguous Ecological Promise of Christian Theology (Philadelphia: Fortress Press, 1985).

Schweitzer, A. Civilisation and Ethics (London: Adam and Charles Black, 1987).

Sinclair, TA (Editor) Aristotle, The Politics (Harmondsworth: Penguin Books, 1985)

Singer, P. <u>Animal Liberation</u> (London: Johnathan Cape, 1977).

Singer, P. <u>Practical Ethics</u> (Cambridge: CUP, 1979).

Thomas, K. <u>Man and the Natural World: Changing Attitudes in England, 1500-1800</u> (Harmondsworth: Penguin Books, 1984).

Thomson, RW (Editor). <u>Contra Gentes and De Incarnatione</u> (Oxford: Clarendon Press 1971).

Tillich, P. <u>Morality and Beyond</u> (London: Fontana Library, 1969).

**PART TWO**


**EDUCATION**

Alan Bowd

# THE EDUCATIONAL DILEMMA

## Foreword

When I was asked to speak on the topic of "The educational dilemma", two quotations came to mind. Perhaps because I am an educational psychologist, the first had to do with psychology, the second with education.

In the second chapter of Animal Liberation, Peter Singer (1975) noted:

> "...the researcher's dilemma exists in an especially acute form in psychology: either the animal is not like us, in which case there is no reason for performing the experiment; or else the animal is like us, in which case we ought not to perform an experiment on the animal which would be considered outrageous if performed on one of us".

This dilemma is one all people face in the sense that we are all researchers: learners within a social environment which includes animals, both human and non-human. Our choice is not whether to experiment on animals, but how to treat and make appropriate use of them. For most of us, this involves a judgement, not of whether the animal is like us, but in what ways it is like us.

My second quotation is from Susan Isaacs (1930 p160), whose perceptions of children were often remarkably free of the preconceptions and prejudices of her academic peers. Noting the "extraordinarily confused and conflicting ways in which we adults actually behave toward animals, in the sight of children", she went on to observe:

> "What children make of our injunctions to be "kind", and our horror at any impulse of cruelty on their part, in the face of our own deeds, and the everyday facts of animal death for our uses and pleasures, would be hard to say. There is probably no moral field in which the child sees so many puzzling inconsistencies, as here".

I do not propose to offer a possible resolution to the issues raised nearly six decades ago by Isaacs and more recently by Singer. They are, of course, closely related, and the implications for the educator are profound. Taken together, they articulate the chief paradox, the vexed question facing the humane educator: How to develop in young people an amalgamation of knowledge, values, feelings and the resolution to act ethically toward animals; and how to do this within a cultural context of exploitation on the most massive scale accompanied by the prescription of kindness to individual creatures?

## Education and the status quo

In 1981, Bernard Rollin called for "an educational
blitzkrieg" to develop public awareness of the
exploitation of animals and to arouse feelings of
compassion for them. Rollin envisioned a movement in some
ways analogous to the popularisation of related
philosophical issues which accompanied the American civil
rights movement of the 1960s. He believed that members of
humane organisations along with veterinarians would be in
the vanguard of this revolution. However, he did not see
a comparable role for teachers at any level - elementary,
secondary or tertiary.

This isn't particularly surprising. Educators have a
vested interest in the status quo which extends to the
status quo ante. Quite simply, our schools and
universities are not designed to produce individuals who
will upset the apple-cart. In preparing her young pupils
for "life", the teacher attempts to furnish them with
those skills, facts and values which are most extensively
endorsed by society at large. Provided objectives are
consistent with conventional social norms, however, the
occasional unorthodoxy of method may be tolerated.

It was recently reported, for example, (Canadian
Broadcasting Corporation, July 10, 1988) that a Japanese
elementary school teacher was concerned that her urban
pupils knew nothing of the role of animals as human food.
The packaged fish and chicken on supermarket shelves were
thought to be manufactured products by youngsters who had
never encountered either in other than this environment.
Taking her class to a large city park, the teacher
produced a live chicken which she had bought and
encouraged the class to observe and play with it. The
children were apparently delighted with their new pet;
however, their pleasure was short-lived. They were
informed that it was lunch-time and that chicken was on
the menu. The teacher explained the origin of packaged
chicken from the market and then insisted the class kill,
pluck, eviscerate, cook and eat the bird with which they
had been playing. Although her action was considered
unconventional in Japan, she was nonetheless praised for
her originality and earnestness. One suspects that such a
teacher would be reprimanded, at the least, in Western
Europe or North America. To quote Susan Isaacs again:

> "We have..to let our children face - when it comes
> their way - the fact of animal death, as a fact of
> nature as well as of the necessities of human
> sustenance. There is, of course, no need to go out of
> our way to introduce them to it, or to focus their
> attention on it" (p165).

Like most of us, Isaacs was convinced that consumption of
animal flesh was necessary for human survival, and because
of this, morally justifiable. For her, the educational
dilemma could be resolved by leading children gently to

53

"the world of objective knowledge and common human purpose" (p169). Six decades later, there is little prospect of consensus as to whether objective knowledge and common human purpose actually exist.

An investigation of the educational dilemma must extend beyond schooling which, after all, is only a part of education. Perhaps, as public awareness of the sensibilities of non-human animals develops, presumably along with an increasing disposition towards "right conduct", concomitant change will take place in the classroom. Already there is a significant response to some of the most manifest contradictions in educational practice, for example, the employment of dissection and the use of animals in school science fairs (Roswell, 1980; Russel, 1980). Common sense informs us that invasive teaching methods are counter-productive in realising the goal of biology teaching: "a respect for life". However, well-designed research is needed additional to the small number of studies which tend to confirm this view (e.g. Bowd and Boylan, 1986; Boylan and Bowd, 1985). There has been some progress in the classroom, but for the most part schools are places where children are closeted from the fundamental contradiction of our treatment of animals, a paradox which teachers themselves are unwilling and usually unable to confront.

## Humane education and child development

At the First International Symposium on Humane Education held at the University of Sussex in 1980, David Paterson observed that:

"modern education - and by that I include both formal education within family and in society - ...desensitises us to the needs, demands and rights of others. In being taught to be ´objective´, we become callous" (Paterson, 1981 p4).

Peter Singer (1975) noted that our attitudes toward animals form in infancy, dominated by the fact that we begin to eat meat at an early age, a decision which is never conscious and informed. Singer claimed (p224) that "children have a natural love of animals" although offering no empirical evidence to support this claim. Stephen Kellert (1982) has attempted to demystify this stereotype, arguing that his research indicates very young children are often quite harsh and exploitative in their attitudes toward animals. The socialisation of children´s beliefs about animals and their attitudes concerning kindness and cruelty deserves considerable research.

It is currently becoming fashionable to study the effects that pet animals have on people, including the value of animal companionship for special groups such as institutionalised adults and developmentally exceptional children (e.g. Bowd and Bowd, 1988; Beck and Katcher, 1983; Francis, Turner and Johnson, 1985; Fogle, 1984).

54

This kind of work enjoys broader popular support because it remains essentially anthropocentric; the focus is on practical benefits for people rather than animals. Notably, studies of cruelty to animals (e.g. Felthous, 1980) are similarly oriented, and often justified because such behaviour is usually examined as a precursor to violence against people and property.

Clearly, if we are to change the way people behave towards animals, we must learn about the origins of that behaviour in childhood. From the limited research that is available (e.g. Bowd, 1982, 1984;) it is evident that Singer (1975 p224) was right when he argued there are two conflicting attitudes toward animals, coexisting in each individual, "carefully segregated so that the inherent contradiction between them rarely causes trouble".

The investigation of the development of children's schemata concerning animals within the context of their socialisation is necessary for the effectiveness of humane education programmes, and the academic credibility of humane education itself. Humane educators must address the issues of long-term and broad consequences of both socialisation and instruction concerning animals. To do this, it will be necessary to develop and articulate relevant conceptual and research foundations in affective, cognitive and social development.

## The conceptual basis of humane education

As a field of study, "humane education" lacks academic respectability, even academic credibility. In part, this may stem from its concern with a socially devalued area, the treatment of animals, as well as its origin outside of formal education. Two developments must occur for humane education to receive appropriate recognition: first, the establishment of a relevant conceptual framework (it is doubtful at present that there is even consensus on a definition of the field); second the fostering of research based on this framework. Such a foundation is necessary too for continued growth of effective instructional strategies in the field.

Many years ago, Alfred North Whitehead (1929) warned about the dangers of inert knowledge - knowledge that is used only in a limited set of contexts despite its applicability in a wide variety of domains. He argued that much traditional educational practice has produced knowledge that remains inert (Bransford et al., 1986). This is manifestly evident in respect of most people's beliefs about animals, including many who have received information from humane educators. Research on teaching thinking and problem-solving implies that knowledge is least likely to remain inert when learning activities help students actually experience problems, and then apply and evaluate particular strategies in the resolution of problems (Bransford et al., 1986).

For example, few members of a junior high school class presented with literature and a lecture on the cruelty of battery hen farming will act to change battery hen farming, although they may express a negative attitude toward the practice. Consider, however, a group which visits such a facility, examines alternative egg-producing arrangements, and in this context is required to stop eating battery eggs for a week as part of a project. This behaviour is linked with the students´ and so they can go on to discuss their reactions in this context, and participate in related activities such as calculating how many chickens are saved by their action. Their knowledge is less likely to remain inert, and will be accessed and applied to relevant situations outside the classroom context (such as choosing, perhaps, not to eat egg dishes in restaurants).

As Michael Fox has recently observed (1988 p3):

> "the empathetic educator enables students to change their behaviour in accordance with how they feel once they are informed about the consequences of their behaviour" (my emphasis).

Informing students about the consequences of their behaviour includes providing them with both propositional knowledge (put simply, facts and their relationships), and procedural knowledge (knowing how to act upon the world). Traditional educators have tended to emphasise the former at the expense of the latter. It is important that humane educators avoid following the same path.

## Bibliography and References

Beck, A; Katcher, A. Between pets and people: The importance of animal companionship (New York: Putman, 1983).

Bowd, AC; Bowd, AD. (1988) Companion animals: A positive contribution to social work practice. The Social Worker, 56, 1, 609.

Bowd, AD. (1982) Young children´s beliefs about animals. Journal of Psychology, 110, 263-266.

Bowd, AD. (1984) Fears and understanding of animals in middle childhood. Journal of Genetic Psychology 145, 143-144.

Bowd, AD; Boylan, CR. (1986). High school biology and attitudes toward treatment of animals. Psychological Reports, 58, 890.

Boylan, CR; Bowd, AD. (1985). Enhancing students´ respect for animal life through the teaching of science Australian Science Teachers Journal, 30, 18-23.

Bransford, J; Sherwood, R; Vye, N; Rieser, J (1986)
Teaching thinking and problem solving: Research
foundations. American Psychologist, 41, 10, 1078-
1089.

Felthous, AR. (1980) Aggression against cats, dogs
and people. Child Psychiatry and Human Development,
10, 169-177.

Fogle, B. Pets and their People. (New York: Viking
Press, 1984).

Fox, MW. (1988) Beyond animal rights: Feeling,
caring and the golden rule. Bulletin: Psychologists
for the Ethical Treatment of Animals, 7, 2, 1-4.

Francis, G; Turner, J; Johnson, S (1985) Domestic
animal visitation as therapy with adult home
residents. International Journal of Nursing Studies,
22, 3, 201-206.

Isaacs, S. Intellectual growth in young children.
(London: Routledge and Kegan Paul, 1930).

Kellert, SR. Affective, cognitive and evaluative
perceptions of animals. In: I. Altman and JF.
Wohlwill (Editors.) Human behaviour and the
environment: Current theory and Research. (New York:
Plenum, 1982).

Paterson, D. Welcome to humane education. Chapter 1
in D. Paterson (Editor) Humane Education: A
Symposium. (Humane Education Council, 1981).

Rollin, BE. Animal Rights and Human Morality. (New
York: Promesthus Books, 1981).

Roswell, HC. Experimentation - the Canadian
experience. pp. 85-98 in H. Griffin and N. Brownley
(editors.) Animals in Education: The use of animals
in high school biology classes and science fairs
(Washington, DC.: Institute for the Study of Animal
Problems, 1980).

Russel, GK. Reverence for life: An ethic for high
school biology curricula. pp. 27-34 in H. McGriffin
and N. Brownley (Editors) Animals in education: The
use of animals in high school biology classes and
science fairs. (Washington, D.C.: Institute for the
Study of Animal Problems, 1980).

Singer, P. Animal Liberation (London: Johnathan Cape,
1977).

David Paterson

## ASSESSING CHILDREN´S ATTITUDES TOWARDS ANIMALS

It is not long since makers of natural history films, such
as those which are now so popular on British television,
together with biologists and those concerned with animal
welfare, first realised that there was no recognised
common starting point for their work. No-one really knew
what children, young people or even adults knew or thought
about animals. It was presumed that children and adults
knew this, or thought that, reasoning from personal
knowledge and experience, or from that of friends and
acquaintances; there was no objective basis for these
assumptions.

As a result, much time must have been wasted and a great
deal of unnecessary confusion was certainly caused.
Biology teachers, for instance, all too readily presumed
that their pupils knew and understood what in fact they
did not, or attempted to teach concepts which their pupils
were not yet intellectually prepared to accept, or bored
their classes by going over material with which they were
already familiar. In the same way, film-makers produced
material which a high proportion of their potential
audiences couldn´t understand or, in some cases, couldn´t
stomach because it offended their sensibilities.

Animal welfare organisations in Britain wasted hundreds of
thousands of pounds, and those in America many hundreds of
thousands of dollars, producing ´educational´ material and
programmes which were poorly researched and which often
grossly overestimated the public´s background knowledge of
animals. Even the better educational programmes were
seldom if ever assessed for their educational
effectiveness, except in terms such as factual recall
under examination conditions. Still less was there any
attempt to assess the long-term effectiveness of welfare
programmes ("humane education") in building up knowledge
of animals or in changing attitudes towards them.

All this explains why, only a relatively short time ago,
researchers in several countries set out to determine the
level of children´s knowledge, their depth of
understanding, their attitudes towards animals and any
changes in attitude towards animals which occurred as
children matured.

In 1986, I completed a study which began in 1982, looking
at some 1200 children of all ages, from schools in the
south-east of England. In the meantime,two background
studies undertaken by the Humane Society of the United
States of America were published, followed by a series of
studies undertaken by the United States Department of the
Interior (Fish and Wildlife Service) from 1982 onwards.
Each of these highlighted different attitudes which
maturing children had towards animals, as well as
providing interesting data on children´s relationships
with the natural world.

Building on this work, the BBC Special Projects Department recently completed a nation-wide survey in Britain, using improved statistical methods to ensure better sampling.

Each of these surveys was, in one way or another, rather limited; nor is it always clear how far results from one can be directly compared with results from another, since the methodology used is not always described in sufficient detail.

Despite some preliminary consultation, then, each of these surveys used different methods and covered different material. The Fish and Wildlife survey, for instance, was conducted by distributing questionnaires in Wildlife Magazines, and so its results must be biased towards the opinions of those who read (and who can afford to read) such magazines in the first place. It also concentrated more on 10 year-old to 12 year-old children. I myself used two versions (junior and senior) of a lengthy questionnaire which I administered personally to 1200 children in the South East of England in schools over a four-year period during class-time. This was backed up with random interviews and relied only on the consent of the school and Local Education Authorities. The BBC survey was national, but covered the same age group as mine: it was, though, based on interviews with children in their own homes conducted by different interviewers; it used a novel schedule, and depended upon the consent of individual parents.

There were, of course, reasons for the adoption of such different approaches and, although this made a detailed comparison of results difficult, there did seem to be many areas of similarity, and some interesting divergences which between them give a very useful global picture on which all concerned can build, and from which further research could well begin:

## Likes and Dislikes

These and other surveys all agree that younger children have a predilection for lovable cuddly animals, particularly domestic pets. We can readily compare the three most popular and the three least popular animals found in the three latest surveys (see next page), bearing in mind that the choice of species offered in each case varied somewhat.

The dolphin's position in the BBC survey is rather anomalous, but this is probably due to the popularity of the appealing and anthropomorphic "Flipper" programmes which were showing at the time. The dolphin did not appear in other surveys, though the whale was ranked 14/33 in the American list.

TABLE: **Likes and Dislikes**

| Paterson 1981-1986 | USA Dept Phase V | BBC Survey 1988 | |
|---|---|---|---|
| Dog/horse | Dog | Dolphin | **MOST** |
| Cat | Horse | Dog | **POPULAR** |
| Panda/Chimpanzee | Cat | Cat/Rabbit | |
| | | | |
| Crocodile | Rat | Wolf | |
| Rat | Wasp/Mosquito | Spider | **LEAST** |
| Spider | Rat | Rat | **POPULAR** |

## Variations by sex and age

It is interesting to note that younger children not only favoured larger, cuddly animals, but tended to react more favourably to all animals in both British surveys, seeming to be more sensitive at an earlier age than their American counterparts.

In fact the American Fish and Wildlife Survey found that the younger group of American children (6-10 years) tended to be "exploitative, harsh and unfeeling" in their attitudes. They seemed to lack the emotional identification and empathy with animals which appeared to have evolved in the American 10-14 year age group. Above that age, "ethical concern for the welfare and treatment of animals increased dramatically". The American researchers suggested that these three stages (exploitative - emotional - ethical) should be borne in mind when designing suitable programmes and educational curricula for American school-children (making them in turn affective - factual - ethical/conservationist). British results seem to indicate an earlier emotional involvement and sensitivity - due perhaps to their being more exposed to anthropomorphic programmes and literature.

The dog ranked as a high favourite among boys right through the age-groups in all three surveys, never falling below second choice in my survey, being the most consistent first choice in recent American lists and ranking in the BBC survey next to the dolphin. Ranking third for girls aged from nine to eleven, the dog gave way to the horse for the majority of older girls in my survey.

The rabbit featured highly in both British Surveys, although it would be interesting to know whether children were thinking of the pet rather than the wild variety! In fact, most groups listed at least two recognisably "wild" animals as being highly favoured, younger boys opting for the panda, though girls were torn between this and the chimpanzee. These result are consistent with other surveys, such as one conducted by Desmond Morris in 1960 based on a television series about zoo animals, which showed that "the top ten animal loves all have humanoid features" - in that they are mammals, with large eyes, rounded faces and cuddly bodies!

All surveys found a general trend for younger children to favour larger animals (perhaps regarded as parent substitutes?), whereas older children tended to favour smaller animals (supposedly seen as child substitutes).

The rat was clearly the most disliked mammal, and the spider was generally the most widely disliked animal (the American survey did not mention spiders: their place in the unpopularity stakes was taken by the cockroach).

The animals most disliked in all surveys were either dangerous or were thought to be so, but this seems to have been due more to their having a "bad image" than any sort of objective judgement. Thus, whereas the fox was not unpopular in the BBC Survey, the wolf was very unpopular - stories of the "clever Brer Fox" type still apparently being traditional, whereas the wolf continues to be portrayed as cruel and voracious, as in the tale of "Little Red Riding Hood", or as an evil and hungry character who huffs and puffs at Little Pig´s houses, or eternally chases children through dim dark fairytale forests, so forever influencing their feelings about this much-maligned animal!

For the most part, it was observed that unpopular animals lacked anthropomorphic features, being described during my survey in negative and emotional terms such as "slimy" (snakes) or "hairy and dirty" (spiders). Similarly, the rat is an animal consistently associated with danger, dirt and disease but, although the most unpopular mammal, it still evoked strong feelings of sympathy when thought of as being a subject for school dissections, which must prove something!

## Pets and Anthropomorphism

In another American Survey Boyle (1976) showed that the majority of American children thought of pets as companions (78%) or as family members (91%), those with pets being more animal-orientated and ranking pets higher than other animals as love-objects. Both my survey and the BBC´s found that a very large proportion (over 90%) of British children had kept pets at home: this may well have influenced their general attitude to animals, and is a factor, along with much of the literature for young children, which seems to encourage anthropomorphism. Whose young child, brought up on a diet of anthropomorphic stories, does not sometimes hold "conversations" with the family dog, or chat with the cat?

The BBC survey suggested that both sexes and all age groups are in fact predominantly anthropomorphic in their attitudes. Children prefer pet animals to wild ones, think that wild animals get lonely in the wild, and believe that all animals should be loved. My survey showed an earlier falling off in anthropomorphic concepts, at least from the age of nine. Thus, 50% of nine-year-old children thought that animals could tell each-other stories, so attributing to them a fairly advanced use of language, but few children of this age (16%) thought that animals knew their own birthdays, or that they could tell the time from a clock (4%). Similarly, although some 50% of ten-year-old boys thought that cats and dogs understood most of what they saw on television, this figure fell to under 10% by the age of fourteen.

The BBC Survey also indicated that, by the time that children reached the age of fourteen to fifteen years, they were much less anthropomorphic and "sentimental" in their attitudes than were the under-nines, developing a more rational approach which took in the whole animal kingdom and resulted in positive attitudes to wildlife generally. It was also noticeable that children who live in the country tended to be better disposed to wild animals and less fearful of them than were those who live in cities. Fewer would want to stay near people rather than where wild animals were around if they went camping (51%:62%) and fewer agreed that most wild animals were dangerous to people (37%:53%). Along with these more positive attitudes to wildlife generally, they were also less likely to condone hunting wild animals for sport (9%:12%), but had fewer objections to hunting them for food than have city children (40%:26%).

## Knowledge, Sex and Sensitivity

All three surveys found that although boys tended to be more knowledgeable about animals than girls, girls were generally more sensitive than boys - save in one special case: I found that there was a strong correlation between girl´s views on foxhunting and their social class. Thus, although the majority of boys in both independent and state schools thought foxhunting to be cruel (82%:85%), teenage girls in state schools differed widely from their counterparts in independent schools in thinking foxhunting to be cruel (87%:63%) and unjustifiable. This seemed related to a commitment to horse-riding and related activities such as pony clubs and eventing, in social groups A, B and C1.

As might be expected, the BBC survey showed a clear association between watching wildlife programmes on television and/or reading about wildlife, and children´s positive attitudes towards animals, although this relationship is probably not causal so much as one of mutual reinforcement - children watch television and read animal magazines because they are interested and so they become more interested and watch more animal-based programmes, etc. Likewise, there is a demonstrable and probably similar relationship between scoring high on knowledge of wild animals and watching or reading more about them. Comparable associations were found in America - although there are fewer wildlife programmes on their television.

As might be expected, the most knowledgeable children were the older group (ten to fifteen years), from social grades A, B and C1; such children lived in the country and regularly watched wildlife programmes and/or read magazines about animals.

## Where do we go from here?

These surveys have, between them, established a baseline from which all can work with confidence, whatever their involvement with young people and/or animals. We must now, though, take the next step and determine what factors lie behind the transition which we see in young children´s thinking through the "Flopsy, Mopsy and Cottontail", "Peter Rabbit", "Womble" and "Watership Down" stages, to an active concern for animals in particular, and the environment in general, which we find in fourteen-year-olds and the fifteen-year-olds. We also need to assess the associated development of ethical principles in children, principles which ultimately govern man´s relationships with and attitude towards other living creatures.

## Bibliography and References

Kellert & Westervelt Trends in Animal Use and Perception in 20th Century America Phase Four results: (US Fish & Wildlife Service, 1981).

Kellert & Westervelt Children´s Attitudes, Knowledge and Behaviours Towards Animals Phase Five results: (US Fish & Wildlife Service, 1981).

Paterson, DA. Childrens´ Ideas on Animals Sussex University (MPhil Thesis, 1986).

Paterson, DA. (editor) Humane Education: A Symposium Humane Education Council, 1981).

Paterson, DA; Ryder, RD. Animal Rights - A Symposium (Centaur Press, 1979).

Shaw, I. (1987.1 1988.1 1988.2) Children´s Attitudes towards Animals BBC Research Document.

Patty Finch

## LEARNING FROM THE PAST

This paper will highlight lessons that can be drawn from
U.S. history in regards to humane education, focusing
primarily on the education of five-year-olds to eighteen-
year-olds. It is hoped that these lessons will prove
applicable on a global scale. At the very least, it is
hoped that this presentation will inspire all to re-
examine their own country's history of humane education,
discovering what lessons may be gleaned from the past.

Let me begin, not with a quote from history but rather
with a quote from a recent editorial in the New York
Times:

> "Schools... reflect the dominant influences in our
> country. It is fantasy to expect schools to impose
> values and attitudes on the American society:  they
> can do something, but, broadly speaking, it's bound to
> work the other way around".

A statement like this can seem devastating to many humane
educators. If we're honest, we in humane education see
schools as a vehicle for changing society. That's how
we've always justified humane education. We will fail,
however, if we expect schools to lead the animal
protection movement and be on the cutting edge. Schools,
as agencies of the state, will not stand in direct
opposition to our main societal values, customs and
institutions, some of which of course include
institutionalised abhorrent cruelty to animals.

At the same time, however, there is a long history of
schools being a key element in the process of transforming
the culture and the institution to help ameliorate
negative social conditions. Indeed, the earliest
rationalisations for public schools in America, during the
colonial period, focused on the need for an antidote to
the breakdown in the socialisation process, as the
influence of the family and church weakened and villages
became more heterogeneous. Also, there was a perceived
need for teaching the three "Rs"; but these skills were
taught through the explicitly moral medium of the Bible
and the social catechisms in spellers and readers.

During the mid-seventeen hundred's the schools' rôle as an
agent of social change continued. Schools were called on
to actively form a national character. During the 1830s
and on to Civil War times (1860s), free public education
became a reality, justified by the need to stabilise the
nation in the face of a growing and increasingly diverse
population. Thus public education was established, not
for the benefit of the individual child, but rather for
the benefit of society.

From this very brief overview of history we can see that
the school's rôle, as one professor of education put it,

is "...to reinforce and consolidate commitments already held and to avoid unthinking negation of basic values".

Thus, as humane educators, we can expect to push society, but we cannot pull it. We can push, and probably successfully, in two major ways:

>1) By consolidating commitments. As we are all well aware, there are many commitments that our societies have made to animals. We need to consolidate these. We can focus on commitments like proper pet care, the elimination of the pet over-population problem, the creation of wildlife refuges that are truly refuges, and the saving of endangered species.

As there are advances in general public awareness of humane issues, we can expect to succeed with comparable advances in humane education. In society we can see issues moving from the special interest realm to the public interest realm. When an issue becomes perceived of as being of public interest, that means that we as a society have agreed upon a particular basic value and how to implement it. For example, interest in the welfare of seals and whales is no longer confined to special interest groups. Their welfare is now perceived of as being of public interest in the United States, making this issue ideal for consolidation in the schools; similarly, the crating of veal calves is increasingly being perceived as a public interest topic in the United States.

It is up to us as humane educators to monitor society's values and be ready with lessons and materials appropriate for consolidating new public interest topics dealing with animal protection.

>2) The second way we can push society, as already suggested, is to see that the schools avoid unthinking negation of basic values that we as a society have agreed upon. Yet, unthinking negation of basic values which our society holds about animals is indeed happening in our classrooms. It happens when there is a classroom pet not properly loved, respected and cared for. It happens when dissection occurs in the classroom, because it does seem that it is a basic value in our society not needlessly to waste lives simply because of convention. As we seek educational reform, we need to remind educators explicitly that the classroom practices which we are seeking to reform are practices which indeed constitute unthinking negation of basic societal values.

Continuing with our educational history, we find that in the late eighteen hundred's a shift in emphasis and approach occurred in moral education. Moral education began to shift from a focus on "taming of the savage beast" to a romantic approach - very child-centred, and seen as building on children's naturally good sentiments.

This coincided with the real beginnings of formal humane
education. In 1875, the Bands of Mercy were started in
Great Britain. Humane education continued to grow
thereafter. In 1893, 76,617 humane essays were written in
the 6500 schools of London. Twelve hundred prizes were
awarded for these essays, and were distributed by the
Duchess of Fife at the Crystal Palace on June 2, 1894.

In 1882, Bands of Mercy were started in the United States.
By 1892, they had grown to number 30,000 (a Band was
considered to be formed when thirty or more members had
joined). Two million children had signed the Bands of
Mercy pledge (out of a school population of about 7
million).

One lesson that can be learned from this period of history
is that humane education was, and probably still is, at
its strongest when it is inculcating a value commitment to
the protection of animals, focusing on the affective
domain, rather than focusing on the cognitive aspect (i.e.
what to do about that value commitment).

This is not to imply that we as humane educators should
not focus on the implications of value commitments.
Effective means for doing this will be discussed later in
this paper. Rather, the point is that throughout history,
teachers have been most receptive to humane education when
it focused on value-commitment.

During this Bands of Mercy period of the late eighteen-
hundred´s, when humane education focused on inculcating
values, support was solicited by reference to the
Transference theory. This theory holds that if children
learn to treat animals with kindness, they will also be
kinder to each other as well. Sarah Eddy, writing in
1897, expressed the typical sentiment of the time:

> "The humane movement is a broad one, reaching from
> humane treatment of animals on the one hand to peace
> with all nations on the other. It implies character
> building: Society first said that needless suffering
> should be prevented: Society now says that children
> must not be permitted to cause pain because of the
> effect on the children themselves" (emphasis added).

During this time, there was some focus on the implications
of the value of humane treatment of animals. For
instance, Sarah Eddy suggested children write compositions
on "The Rights of Animals and the Protection we should
give them", "How does Cruelty to Animals Affect Meat, Milk
and Fish?", and "Transportation of Cattle; or, A Journey
from the Western Plains to the Market". Nonetheless, the
affected commitment, justified through the transference
theory, was the main emphasis of humane education at that
time, with infrequent examination of the implications of
the application of values.

Parenthetically, let me re-emphasise that this paper is
focusing on humane education efforts within the school.

The tactics that are most effective within the educational community are often not those which work best in a community and are often not at all the tactics which work best in attempts to educate society as a whole. Too often we as humane educators confuse tactics between the two arenas.

At the turn of the century, support for humane education continued to grow. Three million copies of Black Beauty had been sold by 1909, helping to raise the consciousness of society in general. Whitlock and Westerlund, in their book Humane Education: An Overview write that PP Clackston, United States Commissioner of Education from 1911 to 1921, stated:

"Humane education is an ´inalienable right´ of all children and ´must be included´ in the educational process if we wish to attain the goals of ´freedom and brotherly love´".

Thus humane education was still justified primarily in terms of the transference theory, and was beginning to become institutionalised in the educational system. Clackston´s support was echoed by superintendents of public instruction, principals, the National Congress of Parents and Teachers, and the National Education Association.

However, the progressive education movement had been steadily growing since the turn of the century, and by the nineteen-thirty´s, overt moral education was very much on the decline. Moral education still existed, but it was part of the "hidden curriculum" (i.e. those objectives which are not stated as educational objectives, but are nonetheless taught, whether purposely or inadvertently). The emphasis continued to move from inculcating morals to social problem solving. Indeed, the great education debate of 1934 centred on a discussion of the merits of indoctrination versus the study of social problems.

The progressive educational movement flourished between the two world wars, yet the instructional emphasis of humane education did not change accordingly, and we lost ground. Certainly, one major lesson of this time in history is that our reforms will succeed to the extent that they are in step with current educational reforms. While today we may still firmly see the need for moral education, and while there are cries from some educational leaders for moral education and some grassroots support, our Secretary of Education in the United States has just proposed a model elementary curriculum which contains a heavy content focus. This is perhaps to be expected now when the United States has the lowest literacy rate of any industrialised nation. The model curriculum proposed by the Secretary of Education contains no overt moral education except as it explicitly relates to specific social problems such as drug use and the spread of AIDS. (In fact, the overt moral education models introduced in the nineteen-sixty's have never become widespread and are certainly not institutionalised).

We in humane education can and should follow this current pattern of relating moral education to specific social problems in order to be in step with current educational reforms. We must relate humane education to current social problems such as child abuse and the crime rate among the young.

There are four distinct points which we must convey to educators in relating humane education to child abuse and the criminal acts of youth.

The first point is that animal abuse in the home often means that there are also abused children. Certainly we would prefer that society take animal abuse seriously in its own right, but often this is not the case. To have people be concerned about animal abuse because of the implications for humane welfare is at least a step forward from not being concerned at all. We can emphasise to educators that animal abuse must be taken seriously for it can help identify a family in need of immediate help.

Secondly, a child who abuses animals needs immediate skilled and concentrated help.

Thirdly, humane education has the potential of being one of the most effective ways of teaching empathy toward animals and people. In making such a statement, humane education must dedicate itself to deliberately teaching transference. Recent studies by Vanessa Malcarne indicate that transference of values of kindness from animals to people does not occur automatically: it must be directly taught. This is a task we have hardly even begun.

The fourth point we must convey to educators is that one reason for children turning to crime is their perceived lack of purpose, their feeling of powerlessness. Humane education can put purpose back into children's lives. A well-known educator in the United States, Joseph Featherstone, has stated, "I am amazed that we live in a society in which children are starved to give". Children do not need to be starved to give. That is why in the United States the National Association for the Advancement of Humane Education (NAAHE) is instituting children's campaigns. We want children to feel that they matter and that they are powerful enough to change the world.

One successful children's campaign has been our "Playing Tag For Real" campaign in which children urge the licensing of pets in their communities. In one community, the children tripled the number of pets licensed. That is a powerful lesson for children to learn. In emphasising direct action, we are returning to the strategies of the

late 1890s when there were 200,000 Jack London clubs. To
join a Jack London club, children signed a statement that
they would leave their seat any time that animals were
being used for entertainment on the stage.

Secretary Bennett's heavy content emphasis suggests
another strategy. It is an especially wise time to link
up with environmental education, since this is seen to
have much more of a content focus than moral education,
and it is certainly much more widespread. We need to
demonstrate to environmental educators that they can "make
a good thing better", by incorporating humane education
lessons into their curriculum. We need top remind
environmental educators, who are often predisposed to the
humane ethic, that without humane education, environmental
education reaches the mountains, but not the trapped
coyote; the oceans, but not the aquarium-bound whale; the
Arctic, but not the clubbed seal; the cities, but not the
stray dog; the open ranges, but not the cinched rodeo
horse; the farm-lands, but not the crated veal calf; the
endangered species, but not the abused animals.

Humane educators should also explore promoting the
teaching of humane education through literature. With
literacy being an extremely important goal for all
schools, it is an obvious place to incorporate the
teaching of humane education. One school district in
Philadelphia fulfils its mandate to teach humane education
by teaching it through literature. Teachers read books
that contain a humane message to the students, and then
discuss the books with them. This approach reaches
children not only at the intellectual level, but at the
subconscious and emotional levels as well. This is
perhaps one of the most practical and yet effective ways
to integrate humane education into the normal school
curriculum at a time of heavy content focus.

This is also a time in history when educators are
reforming the "hidden curriculum". We are attacking
sexism and racism through a process that began in the
nineteen-sixty's by, among other things, adding women and
minorities to our textbooks and revising biased language.
No textbook publisher wants to be biased. It is an
excellent time to point out the hidden curriculum that
subtly reinforces animal abuse. Let us expose, for
example, conservation education as often constituting a
deliberately distorted and inaccurate curriculum, designed
to support pro-hunting arguments. Let us bring out the
statistics that show that males much more often than
females are the abusers of animals. Let us point out the
need for boys to receive empathy training as girls have
received assertiveness training. Let us expose dissection
as containing a hidden curriculum of desensitising
children.

The climate is right for these kinds of reform. Yet even
given that, change will not happen overnight. In the
United States school system, we are dealing with, as
retired Proctor and Gamble chairman, Owen B. Butler puts

it, "a business...with 50 totally autonomous divisions and 16,000 subsidiaries, each with its own board of directors and labour agreements".

There is yet another lesson that history teaches us. Humane education has not experienced great growth in the last 100 years. To experience substantial growth, humane education must achieve scholarly integrity. History shows that while educational reforms are often started by those outside the field of education, these reforms become institutionalised only when the reforms are taken up by the educators themselves.

With humane education, the process of institutionalisation began in the nineteen-ten´s and nineteen-twenty´s in the United States. But with the advent of the progressive era in education, and the Depression, this progress was halted. Worse yet, most of the ground we had gained was lost. Today in the United States, very few educators are even familiar with the term humane education.

NAAHE is now working to help ensure that the task of institutionalising humane education is taken up by educators, for we, as animal protectionists, cannot lead the educational reform movement. It must be led by the educators themselves. Thus, NAAHE is in the initial stages of developing a textbook on humane education - not written by those of us in the animal protection movement, although we will undoubtedly contribute a chapter or two - but written by various professors of education, environmental education, research, curriculum models and child development. The goal will be to identify those elements which are basic and essential to humane education.

From the few humane education courses that have been offered in colleges of education at the graduate level for elementary and secondary teachers in the United States, we have discovered that a phenomenal change can occur in educators when exposed to humane education for three hours a day, for four to six weeks. These educators are not only taught humane education techniques, but issues as well. The values of the teachers change at the effective and cognitive levels. They leave their humane education course with statements like "This ought to be required of every teacher", and "This course changed my life". The teachers leave committed to humane education - so committed, that even if the teaching of humane education is never required from them, they will teach it; so committed, that even without a formally established district-wide curriculum, they will teach it; so committed, that even without a solid foundation of educational research yet established, they will teach it. We saw this kind of phenomenon happen in environmental education, and it can happen in humane education as well.

It is wise to focus on the teacher, for their importance in the classroom cannot be underestimated. One teacher, Haim Ginot, put it this way:

"I have come to a frightening conclusion. I am the decisive element in the classroom. It is my personal approach that creates the climate. It is my daily mood that makes the weather. As a teacher I possess tremendous power to make a child´s life miserable or joyous. I can be a tool of torture or an instrument of inspiration. I can humiliate or humour, hurt or heal. In all situations, it is my response that decides whether a crisis will be escalated or de-escalated, and a child humanised or dehumanised".

I would also add that it is the teacher who determines whether or not the child will be made more humane.

As we pass on the task of humane education to the educators in the schools, we must be prepared as animal protection institutions to face the choice some day between building a name for ourselves and building a solid and permanent foundation for humane education. There will come a time when the kinds of materials which we are producing will best be produced by well-respected names in educational publishing with access to a widely distributed market.

Another aspect of obtaining scholarly integrity is to professionalise how we teach the cognitive aspects of the valuing process; that is,the practical application of values to specific situations. As humane educators we lose the respect of educators if we choose issues which are not age-appropriate, issues where the children are not capable of comprehending all the alternatives or the ramifications of those alternatives. For instance, while children are quite capable at a fairly early age of understanding the subtleties surrounding the fur trade industry, children are not as capable of comprehending all the arguments surrounding animal experimentation. Teachers will self-censor such topics out of the classroom, because of their age inappropriateness.

Educators can accept controversy in the classroom, if the content is age appropriate and if free discussion of the options are allowed. Humane education issues can survive critical analysis, and prevail in the free market-place of ideas. This is especially true if we have already established an affective commitment to reverence for life.

NAAHE is also in the process of funding educational research, with an emphasis on research conducted by Professors of Education. One such project involves research on education for pre-schoolers. Preschools in the U.S. are still in the process of formulating curricula. There is a hunger for quality materials which we in humane education can urge professors to fill. Humane education is perceived by pre-school teachers as an especially appropriate topic for the curriculum.

Lastly, history has taught us that direct appeals to

children to join clubs in support of animals has worked well, provided only that little expense is involved. The Bands of Mercy and the Jack London Clubs were highly successful for their times. We at NAAHE have plans in progress to make our KIND Clubs experience phenomenal growth in the United States during the next few years. These clubs are overseen by teachers, with a new club activity arriving every other month. We also plan to launch clubs for secondary students. We have great hope for these clubs, for the ultimate focus of our efforts in humane education, besides the animal, is certainly the student. As Abraham Lincoln said:

"Students are people who are going to carry on what we have started. They are going to sit where we are sitting, and when we are gone, attend to those things that we think are important. We may adopt all the policies we please, but how they will be carried out depends on these students. They will assume control of our cities, states, and nations. they will move in and take over our churches, schools, universities, and corporations. All of our books are going to be praised or condemned by them. The fate of humanity is in their hands".

So it might be well to pay them some attention!

## Bibliography and References

Archives, Massachusetts SPCA.

Business Week, September 9, 1988, page 135.

Eddy S. Songs of Happy Life for Schools, Homes and Bands of Mercy (Providence, Rhode Island: Art and Nature Study Publishing Company, 1897).

Eddy S. Friends and Helpers (Boston: Ginn and Company, 1899).

NAAHE Publication: The Cycle of Abuse.

Shaber JP "Commitment to Values and the Study of Social Problems in Citizenship Education", Social Education March 1985, p196.

Teacher evaluations, Humane Education graduate course, published by the College of Education, Stephen F. Austin University, Nacogdoches, Texas, 1988.

The New York Times, September 8, 1988, editorial page.

Whitlock ES; Westerlund SR (Editors), Humane Education: An Overview, (Tulsa, Oklahoma: NAAHE, 1975).

Cindy Milburn

## INTRODUCING ANIMAL WELFARE INTO THE EDUCATION SYSTEM

It is unwise to isolate education from other systems which affect our perceptions of reality and morality.

I think that morality is a "movable feast" and other speakers will show how perceptions of right and wrong can easily, though perhaps not always consciously, be influenced by self-interest.

It is vital to define animal welfare so that there is a fixed reference point for discussion. Where there is doubt, animals should be give the benefit of that doubt. Science should be called upon not to prove suffering, as at present, but to prove lack of suffering.

In addition to offering a personal definition of welfare, I will draw upon nine years of experience in working with the RSPCA to show how practical steps can be taken to ensure that the status and welfare of animals is given a proper recognition in the education system.

Two hundred years ago, the British philosopher Jeremy Bentham said:

> "The question is not, can they reason, nor can they speak, but can they suffer?".

The question which we must ask today is not "Have they rights?", but "Have we responsibilities?".

Our perception of the status of animals is fundamentally linked with our view of our own status. To many people it is inconceivable that we should measure our civilisation by the way we treat animals. To others it is inconceivable that we should not.


## INTRODUCTION

One of the aims of this conference is to bring together people from different disciplines, including those working in animal welfare and animal-related professions. In order to ensure a balance between theory and practice, most of the sessions have been divided into academic and practical approaches to the different subject areas.

Previous speakers have dealt with research and experience in the area of attitudinal development. I shall concentrate on the practical aspects of introducing animal welfare into the education system. Humane Education is the responsibility not just of animal welfarists but of educationalists in every animal-related profession.

I have to declare an interest in the active promotion of Animal Welfare, and some would question whether being both an educationalist and an animal welfarist are mutually compatible. By admitting a leaning towards welfare one admits to a bias: anathema in conventional educational terms.

The 1987 Education Act requires that controversial material is presented in a balanced way, and who would disagree? But how do we define "controversial"? Is teaching animal welfare "controversial", and if so, why?

Surely any definition of education must refer to whether the end-product is worthwhile, RS Peters argues that education involves the intentional transmission of what is worthwhile: criteria include matter and manner as well as cognitive perspective.

It is my belief that Humane Education is a worthwhile activity. It is not a political doctrine, it is above party politics. Humane Education is an attempt to develop altruism and a sense of compassion in a world where all other pressures are in opposition to it. I´m not under any illusions about the significance of this. In trying to improve the status of animals we necessarily challenge our status as human beings.

In this respect the welfare message is more challenging than, say, that of the conservation movement. The idea of conserving the natural world has an abstract visual and comfortable appeal that the condition of the battery hen or tethered sow does not. The Animal Welfare message challenges people on a very personal level; we cannot distance ourselves in time or place from the choices which we make.

Animal Welfare encompasses husbandry and transcends rights. It is exactly what it says it is - concern for the well-being of animals. It puts animals at the centre of the equation irrespective of their intrinsic rights or their perceived value to human beings. I believe that where doubt exists about an animal´s well-being, the benefit of the doubt should be given to the animal. Scientific onus of proof should be on lack of suffering, not proof of suffering as at present. We have a responsibility to ensure that the animals used by human beings do not suffer.

The scales are weighted against altruism and compassion; how does one present a balance in such a situation? Education does not exist in isolation. What is balance in education when education is seen as one system in the context of many systems hostile to the notion of animal welfare?

Bearing this in mind, I shall begin by putting the education system into the context of some other systems which influence Animal Welfare.

Then I shall consider influences on attitudes and behaviour.

Finally I shall look at Animal Welfare in the context of the education system.

First, then, an overview of Systems: these include:

Welfarists / Consumers / Research Scientists / Investors / Producers / Government / Educationalists / Animals.

Development of attitudes cannot be seen in educational isolation. Education is only one of many influences and systems which affect our beliefs.

## ATTITUDES AND BEHAVIOURS

There are many forces at work which influence an individual´s beliefs and attitudes. In my experience, an individual´s behaviour changes more easily when compassionate choice is made desirable and easy through education, legislation and life-style acceptability.

The recognised stages of learning, knowledge, understanding and synthesis apply not just in animal welfare, but to any new concept or idea.

The difficulty here is an assumption that the mind openly receives new ideas and the only constraints are those of individual learning capacity.

Other speakers have shown the effects of resistance to new ideas when developing attitudes. I believe that resistance springs from fear of the knowable as well as fear of the unknown.

In my opinion it is possible to identify a progression of attitudinal changes; recognition of resistance, analysis and choice.

Researchers are often accused of merely quantifying common sense. However we have much to learn about the development of attitudes - information that can only be gathered by rigorous and committed research. Combine this with valuable insights gained by practitioners world-wide, and Humane Education will become a force to be reckoned with.

In my experience, behavioural changes create and spring from attitudinal change. Developing attitudes and influencing behaviour should not be seen as activities which are in opposition to eachother. They are compatible and interactive processes, but distinct. They must be tackled together because neglect of one undermines the foundations of the other. This does not invalidate concentration on one by an individual or an organisation. What is important is that organisations recognise the significance of both approaches within the overall system. There is a danger in becoming so absorbed by a particular

75

approach that any other seems to be extraneous or, worse
still, a threat. This need to consider attitude and
behaviour as part of a whole applies across the board, not
simply to Animal Welfare organisations.

That of course is one of the aims of this conference: to
provide the opportunity to meet and talk with others in
different, but related, fields of work; to identify
common ground, to establish common interests and to work
towards joint solutions, albeit from differing
perspectives.

This brings me to the third and final part of my paper,
where I would like to talk about practical solutions.

In 1982 I was appointed Head of the RSPCA´s Education
Department. For several years previously I had been
working for them in schools, and knew from my experience
that there were two problems which had to be dealt with as
a matter of some urgency.

The first priority was to deal with the immediate
practical problems: how animals were kept and how they
were used within the education system, focusing on
behaviour rather than attitudes. What was the point of
giving a talk or running a course on responsible pet
ownership if the conditions in which school pets were kept
undermined the message which the children were supposed to
be receiving? If one accepts that caged mammals are kept
as pets, then we have a duty to ensure that only the best
possible conditions prevail, particularly in an
educational environment where standards are seen to be
set. My experience was that standards were appalling, and
that convenience took precedence over welfare. Higher up
the school system, animals were used in dissection without
any systematic attempt to present related ethical issues.
This raised the question of whether this practice
encouraged children to view animals as educational tools
rather than sentient beings.

Our objective was to establish Animal Welfare in
mainstream education by introducing guidelines and codes
of practice.

We focused on two areas - the keeping of animals in
schools, and "A level" dissection. Central to my belief
is the idea that nothing is done in isolation, and every
interested party has a valuable contribution to make,
which is why we enlisted the help of education authorities
in the production of material on Animals In Schools. We
were also greatly assisted by other educationalists,
veterinarians, and biologists. In total, a hundred and
fifty individuals and organisations contributed to the
"Animals in Schools Guidelines".

It was an exercise in co-operation, and the resulting
guidelines were purchased by the thousand by education
authorities. A mention and commendation in both the Lords
and the Commons further underlined my belief that nothing

occurs in isolation. The dissection campaign is ongoing and also involves many organisations. We look to the day when Ethics is included in every "A Level" biology syllabus.

More recently, as a member of the Welfare Promotions Group of the Farm Animal Welfare Council, I was involved in writing to educational establishments concerned with farming. The response was excellent - 100% from Agricultural Colleges. In this case, we weren't asking for help with the production of guidelines, but for their views on the existing welfare codes. We also asked about their own policies on welfare teaching.

Overall, twenty percent taught welfare as a separate subject: sixty percent of Universities do so, forty percent having a member of staff with specific responsibility for welfare teaching. For Agricultural Colleges, this figure is thirty percent, and for schools fifty percent. Eighty percent incorporate the welfare codes into teaching - although this percentage was brought down by schools, where only forty percent of respondents keeping farm animals kept copies of the codes.

This further convinced me that, given the right approach and a willingness to consult and co-operate, a great deal can be achieved. The key to introducing animal welfare into education is through consultation, communication and co-operation.

I would identify eight steps in the process:

    1)    What are the aims and objectives?
    2)    Who should be consulted?
    3)    What channels of communication are available?
    4)    What are the major obstacles?
    5)    If people are resistant, why?
    6)    Whose help should be enlisted?
    7)    What is a realistic timescale?
    8)    And, finally, sustain a vision of success.

In my work I have concentrated on trying to get behaviour right, because this is of more immediate practical benefit to animals. It is unwise to isolate education from other systems which affect our perceptions of reality and morality.


**CONCLUSION**

In my experience, attitudinal changes spring from and create behavioural changes. I think that morality is a movable feast, and other speakers have shown how perceptions of right and wrong can easily, though perhaps not always consciously, be influenced by self-interest.

It is vital to define welfare so that there is a fixed reference point for discussion. Where there is doubt, animals should be given the benefit of the doubt. I believe that science should be called upon, not to prove suffering, as at present, but to prove lack of suffering.

In addition to offering a personal definition of welfare, I have tried to show how practical steps can be taken to ensure that the status and welfare of animals is given a proper recognition in the education system.

Our perception of the status of animals is fundamentally linked with our view of our own status. To many people it is inconceivable that we should measure our civilisation by the way we treat animals. To others it is inconceivable that we should not.

Konrad Lorenz in his recent book, "The Waning of Humaneness", argues that we need a value-based education:

> "Since all the moral responsibilities of humans are determined by their perceptions of values, the epidemic delusion that only measurable reality has validity must be confronted and contradicted. .....The closest possible contact with the living world at the earliest possible age is the most promising way to achieve this (harmony)".

# PART THREE


# FARMING

Donald M Broom

## ETHICAL DILEMMAS IN ANIMAL USAGE

I shall present to you some statements concerning my own
beliefs about ethical matters, mention some problems where
people differ in their opinions, consider some specific
examples of the treatment of animals by man, and give some
definitions. This means that I shall not be dealing with
what is my main area of activity, which is how to assess
poor welfare, and hence find solutions to welfare
problems.

## Man's moral obligations to animals

Man has moral obligations towards the living organisms
with which he interacts. These can be summarised in three
statements:

    a)    Man has an obligation to conserve species and
habitats.

    b)    Man has obligations where, because of human
action, an individual dies.

    c)    Man has obligations to prevent poor welfare in
individual animals.

The first two statements refer to all living things: the
third refers only to animals.

## Human attitudes to animals

Human usage of living things occurs in almost all aspects
of life and some form of usage is considered acceptable by
everyone. Critical questions concern the nature and extent
of the usage.

As we have seen in previous papers, most early
philosophical and religious writings on the usage of
animals were very human-centred. However, there have been
considerable and accelerating changes recently,
particularly with regard to the belief that we are morally
obliged to try to understand more about the living
organisms which we use. One of the substantial changes
which has occurred in recent years is that we do know more
about these organisms. When deciding whether an action is
morally justified or not, we have a better understanding
of the effects on the animal or plant itself. A
consequence of increased knowledge has been, therefore, an
increase in respect for living things.

The Judaeo-Christian approach to species other than man
has long been one of exploitation. Little consideration
has been shown to animals despite various ideas about some

kind of co-existence in heaven and a number of other statements in the Bible and other religious writings.

Over the past two hundred years, there has been a great and increasing change - for example in the meaning given to the term "dominion". In the Bible man as a species is described as having "dominion" over animals. This was interpreted as meaning that animals could be exploited almost totally. But, as the Bishop of Salisbury pointed out in a speech a few years ago, there is also reference in Isaiah to the future Messiah having dominion over man and other animals. He is not seen as bringing exploitation and destruction but respect for all species in their proper place in the world.

Such an interpretation has two implications:

a)     that respect for all living things is necessary.

b)     that we need to know about and take account of the functioning and requirements of the living organism.

We have to know something about the organism in order to decide upon its "proper place", so giving it proper respect and care.

In these comments I have been referring deliberately to "organisms". How far do animals differ from plants?

In fact, in most aspects of fundamental biological functioning they are very similar and when consideration is given to conservation, people do not differentiate very much at all between them. The same often applies when people discuss whether an organism should be killed. When considering live animals and plants, however, most people assume that animals have a different quality of life.

A development in recent years is that we now have a different idea about the cognitive ability of animals and the complexity of their behaviour. When we are talking about welfare we now take into account the fact that animals respond to the world in a way which shows how much they are aware of it. They have an ability to learn; they can establish complex relationships; they have an ability to suffer. This last point will be discussed later.

Studies of the behaviour and physiology of animals in recent times have revealed the great complexity of mammals and birds and, to a lesser extent, other vertebrates and the more complex invertebrates such as the octopus and the squid. When we come to insects and worms, the evidence of their cognitive ability suggests that this is small. Even so, all of these organisms have some such ability, and divisions between species on this basis would be merely a matter of degree.

## Mechanisms for dealing with adversity: the measurement of welfare

All animals have an array of systems which they use to cope with difficulties. These include:

> a)      the brain/adrenal system, which includes the hypophysis in the brain and the adrenal gland. This helps to provide more energy and is brought into play when animals need it.

> b)      the endorphin/enkephalin system, which involves the production of analgesic peptides. These have a pain-killing effect and enable the animal to deal with unpleasant situations, so that it can cope with them by self-narcosis.

> c)      behavioural responses which alter the state of the individual.

We can now provide a definition of welfare which relates to these systems:

> The WELFARE of an individual is its state with regard to its attempts to cope with its environment (Broom, 1986).

Thus the welfare of the animal is not something which we give to it: it is a condition of the animal itself. There are three kinds of consequences of trying to cope with difficulties:

> (a)      The individual may cope easily, in which case there is little or no welfare problem, or

> (b)      It may live in conditions which are difficult for it, developing methods of coping. It survives, grows and reproduces but it has difficulty in doing so and its welfare is therefore poor.

> (c)      The third possibility is that the animal uses its systems to try to cope, but fails to do so.      It either dies or it cannot grow or reproduce. Its welfare is, again, poor: its control systems are overtaxed, and the term "stress" should be used.

What concerns us is where the welfare of the animal is poor, and we can identify this by some measurement. We may measure poor welfare by demonstrating that the animal shows abnormal behaviour patterns, bringing in analgesic peptides in order to cope. The more it does this, the worse its welfare. (see Broom (1988) and Fraser and Broom (1989) for details of welfare assessment).

We can make objective measurements, showing how good or poor welfare is, along a continuum. This measurement is nothing to do with moral considerations. It tells us something about the state of the animal. We are then faced with having to make moral decisions. How poor, for instance, must the welfare be for someone to say that this situation is intolerable?

One other thing that can be measured to a limited extent is pain. Pain is a sensory mechanism which animals use to cope with difficulty. The pain receptor can send a signal to the brain which means "do something about this". The animal will then avoid the situation if it can.

PAIN is a sensation which is itself very aversive. Other things may be aversive, not so much of themselves but because of their associations.

Questions of whether or not to kill are also separate from those of welfare, although the question of whether or not to kill should never be taken lightly. A further question then could be: is the sudden and painless death of an animal any different from the death of a plant? My feeling is that it is not.

If the death of the animal has an effect on other individuals of whatever species, that also needs to be taken into account. Strong emotional bonds can be formed with animals but are seldom formed with plants.

One last point at this stage: assessing the welfare of an animal is totally different to asserting its rights.

## Animal Usage

The important thing is the welfare of the animal during its life: given that, what sorts of use are reasonable?

**a)    Is it reasonable to study an individual in order to benefit that individual itself?**

For example, an animal could be studied to determine its particular needs and disease-state, so as to provide for or cure them. Most people would agree that this 'use' is quite reasonable.

**b)    Is it reasonable to use one individual to help others of the same species?**

For example, studying disease in one dog could lead to a cure for similar disease in other dogs. Most people would agree with this, but would also stipulate the limits of what could be done to the individual dog being studied.

**c)    Is it reasonable to use one individual to help individuals of another species?**

Should we study a disease in dogs to help cats, or study a disease in rabbits to help people, or use guide dogs to help blind people, or keep pets in order to comfort the old or to educate the young? In each of these cases, the answer would generally be that it depends upon the welfare of the individual being used. There has to be a "reasonable" trade-off.

## Factors which affect peoples´ views on welfare

Given this range of situations, what factors affect peoples´ views about, for instance, the level of poor welfare which is "acceptable"? Where, indeed, do the most important welfare problems lie? Three points should be made here.

a)      **Numbers.** The species which is kept in the largest numbers by man, the commonest bird in the world in fact, is the domestic fowl. A corollary of this fact is that if chickens are treated badly, very many individuals are so affected.

After the domestic fowl come other farm animals, then pets and, some way behind, laboratory animals, zoo animals and animals used for entertainment.

If pest-species were to be included here, apart from bacteria, the nematode worms and insects would top the list and pest-mammals would be high on it.

In thinking about any of these animals, think of individuals. Moral issues are about individuals.

b)      **Terminology.** The way in which people view animals is affected by the words which are used to describe them or operations which concern them.

If a word like "harvesting" is used for collecting and killing chickens, we de-humanise our attitude towards the activity. Similarly, some people talk about "cropping" plants and also about "cropping" animals, or describe killing all the hens as "clearing a hen-house" or as "depleting" it. Such impersonal words are easier to use than "killing" or "slaughtering" and do not take account of the fact that the animals may suffer in the process, whereas plants do not.

In a similar way, referring to abnormal behaviour, people say that animals have "vices" such as tail-biting, implying that the individual is largely to blame for these behavioural aberrations. The so-called vice is usually a direct consequence of the conditions imposed on animals, so the term is inappropriate.

My preference is not to use words which de-personalise the organisms referred to.

c)      **How viewed by man.** The way in which we think of an animal affects how we view its welfare. An animal

84

which is a source of revenue, like a pig, is thought of in a different way from an animal which is mainly a companion, like a dog, or one which is principally a pest, like a house-mouse.

In real terms, this differentiation is unreasonable, since questions relating to the welfare of each individual animal must deal with similar issues. All three species can suffer in very similar ways and yet we still tend to assess their welfare by different standards.

It doesn't matter <u>to a rabbit</u> whether it is being thought of as a potential meal, as the subject of an experiment, or as a pet. What counts for the rabbit is the quality of its life. In fact, the ones which fare worst are some of those which are kept as pets and, probably, the best looked after would also be pets.

## Causes of Welfare Problems

These can be summarised as follows:

a)   <u>Abuse</u> and <u>cruelty</u>,

b)   <u>Neglect</u> (either calculated, accidental or due to lack of knowledge),

c)   Maintaining animals in <u>an unsuitable system</u>, which involves some specific deprivation (like a calf not having a teat or living in very boring conditions for a long time, or

d)   Pushing the animal hard because of the <u>method of production</u>.

e)   <u>Disease</u>, which is an important welfare problem in itself.

## Problem areas - a Summary and Review

a)   Ill treatment, use in sport and neglect cause welfare problems for domestic animals in general.

b)   Pets, working animals, farm animals, zoo and circus animals, laboratory animals: welfare problems can arise through the system of housing and management adopted.

c)   Farm animals: problems arise in handling, transport, marketing, and at slaughter (see below).

d)   Laboratory animals: specific procedures used in testing, research and teaching can cause welfare problems.

e)   Wild animals: these may be ill-treated in various ways, and additionally, may be in pain from the method of capture or disablement, e.g., lead shot, hooks, traps etc.

For farm animals in particular, important problem areas include: housing, handling, transport, procedures at slaughter, what happens at markets, various farm operations, type of provision for emergencies (e.g. a fire on the farm), etc. Another factor contributing to poor welfare is the quality of care provided by the people looking after the animals.

Questions to be asked include: Are the animals neglected? What is the quality of stockmanship? Are the animals diseased, given adequate food, being pushed too hard by the system in which they are kept?

Some of these problems are illustrated by looking at particular examples. Contrast, for instance, veal calves in crates, and those in the fields or in groups in straw-yards, and ask what life is like for them as individuals.

Similar issues can be raised by looking at sows in stalls and sows in fields (remembering that there are both advantages and disadvantages here) or sows in a group-housing situation, bedded on straw, with electronic sow feeders. The lives of the animals must be studied in detail and their welfare assessed individually.

If considering transport or farm operations or diseases which are welfare problems, it is necessary to measure the effects on the animals. Legislators take more note of scientific assessment than of emotional responses.

Overall, what needs to be done is gradually to change the attitudes which people have towards animal welfare, providing information and educating children in a balanced way. In order to obtain the information needed to bring about change we need to investigate the welfare of animals, considering every individual in a compassionate way.

**Bibliography and References**:

Broom, DM. (1986) Indicators of Poor Welfare. British Veterinary Journal, 142, 524-526

Broom, DM. (1988) The Scientific Assessment of Animal Welfare. Applied Animal Behaviour Science, 20, 5-19

Fraser, AF: Broom DM. Farm Animal Behaviour and Welfare. (London: Balliere Tindall, 1989)

Richard Guy

ETHICAL PROBLEMS IN FARMING PRACTICE

INTRODUCTION

Working on the assumption that meat consumption by humans
is part of Nature's grand strategy, it is the methods by
which the livestock are obtained where ethics become
involved. The two sides of the relationship between man
and beast are defined by the non-agricultural hunter-
gatherer on one extreme and by fully restrained, high
input intensive livestock keeping on the other (e.g.
crated veal calves, battery hens, stalled sows).

As the hunting-gathering mode can be assumed to be
inappropriate for our modern society, then it is the
extent of intensification and the ethical decisions
involved in designing and running livestock-keeping
systems that is the issue here.

Technological improvements in automation, drugs, genetics
and materials during the last forty years have made it
possible to "factory-farm" certain animals. That this
means improvement in the efficiency of meat production
cannot be questioned, but the removal of any degree of
respect or apparent care for the animals' basic needs and
feelings has gone too far.

In these discussions, I am of course revealing the
personal feelings of myself and of my wife Gillian on the
respect deserved by livestock. These feelings became
manifest as the basis of the codes of the "Real Meat
Company". The Company gives consumers the choice between
Real Meat from un-intensively reared livestock and
"conventional" meat from mainstream farming systems. The
success of the Real Meat Company confirms that many
consumers are dissatisfied with the extent to which
intensively reared livestock is being exploited.


THE MAIN ETHICAL AREAS


1    Livestock Welfare

The decisions involved in welfare are between what is best
for the animal and what is affordable and feasible. A
good example is straw bedding for pigs. Straw is a great
source of entertainment and comfort for a pig. The animal
can lie in it or express its rooting instinct in it.
Straw is a nuisance, however, to the intensive farmer: it
costs money to buy, you have to pay somebody to put it
into the pen and, because it does not allow automatic dung
collection, you have to pay to get the dung and straw back
out again.

If economy is the only criterion, high-welfare makes no
sense.


## 2    Drug/Growth Promoter Usage

The discovery of medicinal drugs to cure sickness and
relieve suffering in humans and animals is an undeniable
credit to modern science.  Sometimes the discoverer of a
scientific advance is horrified by unintended consequences
of their discoveries.  Alfred Nobel hoped explosives would
never be used in warfare.  Einstein tried to prevent the
development of atomic weapons.

It is unlikely that the inventors of the first antibiotics
would have been happy to think that one day antibiotics
might be continuously included in certain livestock
rations in order to allow for intensive livestock rearing.
Good husbandry in chickens will keep coccidiosis to a low
level, although it is still serious when it strikes.  A
cure for coccidiosis (see: footnote) in chickens was a
great breakthrough.  But almost immediately to include
coccidiostat in all table-chicken food in order to prevent
the disease arising is a little bit alarming.  Then to use
this artificially induced resistance to the disease to
reduce the quality of husbandry is, from a moral point of
view, more alarming still.  Apart from anything else the
drugs are being introduced into the food chain for solely
economic reasons.

Sadly, drugs originally intended as curatives, and a new
range of growth promoting drugs, are now generally used to
"prop-up" the performance of livestock kept in conditions
which would otherwise slow growth and cause rampant
disease.

If economy is the only criterion, not using growth
promoters and not giving preventative medication make no
sense.


## 3    Say what you Do/Do What you Say

If we lived in a perfect world, this section would not
have needed to be written.  It will never do in an ethical
sense to call something free-range when it patently is
not, or to claim to use no growth promoters but use them
for a period, however short.

A small-scale example is a chicken farmer near Guildford
who supplies "free-range", additive-free chickens to his
local area.  He offered his produce to the Real Meat
Company.  On inspection we found that not only was there
not a single chicken able to leave the poultry houses, but
the birds inside the houses were living in conditions
worse than the most intensively reared birds.

A large-scale example would be the EEC-approved free-range

laying hen systems. The EEC legislation on free-range laying hens was laid down in rather a hurry and although it did cover available range space per bird, it did not adequately cover house sizes, stocking density inside the houses or availability of access to range. The average free-range egg buying consumer would be alarmed to witness the conditions inside the large fixed free-range houses containing literally thousands of birds on several floors. They would be even more alarmed to discover that the colour of the yolk in the egg is contrived by the use of artificial yolk colourants.

If economy is the only criterion, doing what the consumer expects makes no sense.

## THE REAL MEAT COMPANY - ORIGIN AND METHODS

The Real Meat Company was founded by me and my wife Gillian Metherell in January 1986, to provide an alternative to the cruelty and over-dependence on drugs inherent in intensive livestock farming. The company exists to procure and market farm livestock that has been reared according to a special "code" providing high welfare, no growth promoters and only limited use of therapeutic medication. We produce free-range table birds and straw-yarded pigs; other farms provide the steers and lambs, and additional pigs and chickens.

The codes were drawn up using information gathered from the Ministry of Agriculture (MAFF), Compassion In World Farming (CIWF) and the Royal Society for the Prevention of Cruelty to Animals (RSPCA). The codes and the modus operandi of the Real Meat Company have gained considerable praise from CIWF, the RSPCA and other sympathetic organisations.

## WELFARE

In setting the welfare element of the Real Meat Company Livestock Codes, we have attempted to make sure that the behavioural and welfare requirements of the animal concerned have priority over ease or cheapness of management. I shall deal in summary with each main animal type and try to make clear the basis of the decisions taken in drawing up the codes.

### Table Fowl

(a) No de-beaking or any other form of mutilation is permitted. Cannibalism in table birds is solvable without recourse to de-beaking. Turkeys are famously prone to cannibalism, yet if the young birds are given toys and are let out to range at the earliest possible moment, the hyperactivity that causes the problem can be expressed in other ways.

(b) Natural ventilation and daylight only. The use of forced air ventilation is only necessary when the birds are overcrowded and so is unnecessary under our system. Natural daylight decreases the likelihood of cannibalism.

(c) Space allocation is a minimum of one square foot per adult bird (6-7 lbs) indoors, with a minimum of one square yard per adult bird outdoors.

Birds kept according to these guidelines and with a high level of husbandry will not commit cannibalism, nor will they suffer significantly from coccidiosis.


## Pigs

(a) No castration or tail-cutting. Both operations are normally performed without anaesthetic and although the level of suffering may not be significant, they are performed for solely management or economic reasons and as such are unacceptable. Tooth clipping is permitted in the case of large litters because the consequences of "side biting" cause more suffering than the clipping itself.

(b) Sows must not be kept in stalls or tethers. Loose straw yards are permissible as is outdoor keeping on suitable land.

(c) Weaning. The codes insist on a minimum of four-week weaning and actually prefer weaning to take six weeks or more. Weaning at three weeks or less causes high levels of stress which will cause drastic scouring unless treated.

(d) Straw bedding must be provided at all stages. The code does not insist that pigs are kept at range because the actual benefit to young pigs under outdoor conditions is questionable. Satisfaction of the rooting instinct as well as physical comfort can be provided by giving adequate bedding.

(e) Farrowing. Difficult decisions must be faced here as the level of comfort for piglets and the sow must both be considered. Although the general public would seem to prefer outdoor sows in arcs in all cases, that system assumes a higher level of piglet mortality. In drawing up this part of the code, we have had to rely on a great deal of our own research.

Surprisingly, the code allows the limited use of farrowing crates. Although "visually" rather unacceptable despite compulsory straw bedding, piglet health and welfare has been found to be far higher with the use of crates than any other system. Farrowing boxes or "nests", solaris and free-access kennels look better, but are harder on the piglets. Outdoor arcs are of course allowable, but only with four-week weaning.

(f) Weaners, porkers and baconers need not be kept outdoors but have straw bedding, no total gridded floors, a generous minimum space allowance and enjoy natural ventilation and lighting.

Pigs are the most intelligent farmed animal. It is particularly tragic that they should also be the most subjected to "factory-farming" techniques. Tail-cutting of piglets is not a particularly painful operation, but it is performed to allow for overcrowded rearing conditions. Out-door sow keeping which is visible to the non-farming public does the image of the pig farmer a lot of good because the public do not realise that the system is actually a cheap way in to intensively rearing early weaned, highly drug dependent porkers.

## Cattle

(a) Natural suckling of calves only. Bucket-reared calves are more prone to illness, are likely to have had to travel long distances including through livestock markets at a tender age, and may well be subjected to in-feed medication to combat stress. We avoid all these things by insisting on suckled calves only.

(b) De-horning and castration are permissible only where pain is not caused. We consider these processes allowable for the well-being of the animal. Goring and bull aggression would cause unnecessary injury even in extensively reared cattle. The company does buy entire bulls from those who rear them properly.

(c) Adequate space, light and bedding must be provided for winter accommodation. Once we have located a suckler herd, this is the biggest cause of failure to meet our codes. Overwintering fifty beef store cattle in a small muddy field with only a railway carriage for them to shelter in is not the sort of husbandry we look for.

The methods of beef production we seek may seem fairly easy to achieve. In fact herds which qualify under our codes and which are not subjected to the use of growth promoters are now extremely rare.

## Sheep

Clearly the easiest beast to rear extensively, our codes only seek to see that indoor lambing or overwintering accommodation is spacious and well-bedded and that sheep eating roots have an adequate dry lying area. We expect a close level of supervision, especially at lambing time. A surprising number of flocks are rejected because of poor accommodation.

## Eggs

The standard of husbandry laid down in the EEC rules is totally inadequate to fulfil our codes or indeed the expectations of the buying public. The use of very large fixed houses with a high stocking density is not acceptable. The one and only egg producer supplying the Real Meat Company uses small movable houses, where the birds have genuine access to range. The eggs are collected by hand.

The apparent contradiction in our hen code is that we do not totally disallow beak trimming. The cannibalistic tendency of laying hens is well-known, and as yet we have been unable to locate a producer able to keep birds without being able to resort to this method of control.

## Method of Operation

Having set the codes of livestock rearing standards, which prevent the use of growth promoters and high-level medication as well as protecting the welfare of the stock, it is essential to ensure that livestock can be produced profitably under this system. The Real Meat Company pays a premium over the open market to its producers to compensate them for the extra expense involved in following our methods of animal rearing. This premium is highest for table chickens and lowest for lambs, as would be expected.

A network of over thirty-five independent retailers, including the first company-owned shop in Bath, sell Real Meat Company meat and meat products. The area we reach on a wholesale basis is bounded by Leicester, London and Bristol. The rest of the country is provided for by a direct overnight delivery service in chilled boxes to any destination in Great Britain. Therefore anyone who wants to actively avoid "factory-farmed" animals can do so.

## CONCLUSION

The continued pursuit of cheaper food for the nation has in the case of meat been made at considerable cost in terms of welfare for the livestock. Pork and chicken meat are cheaper than beef and lamb simply because they can be reared intensively.

We have tried, in setting up the codes of the Real Meat Company, to restore a standard of respect for farmed livestock, and to bring about a high level of stockmanship. No written code can perform this task entirely, and a great deal of importance is attached to actually visiting the farms involved.

Some methods used in modern livestock production are unacceptable to many people but are concealed from them inside intensive units.

Clever promotion within commercial practice may also conceal certain unpleasant realities. Most people believe that "corn-fed chickens" are free-range birds fed on a diet of maize and wheat. In reality corn-fed chickens are not significantly different to any other intensively reared chicken except for the maize in their diet. Incredibly, an artificial dye may be included to colour the fat yellow. Many free-range egg buyers would be appalled at the EEC approved free-range hen houses in current use.

It is the duty of those in a position to do so - journalists, animal welfare organisations and consumer protection organisations - to make sure that people are aware of what is right and what is wrong in livestock farming. The excuse "I didn't know how bad things were" has an awesome ring.

People do care and many people can afford to choose. Real Meat Company meat and meat products do cost more. It would be grounds for considerable suspicion if they did not. I would borrow the advertising catch-phrase from Stella Artois beer and call our products "reassuringly" more expensive. You cannot give your pigs straw bedding and pay someone to muck them out and charge the same for the pigs.

Ethical decisions in purchasing are becoming more widespread. A cheap digital watch does not seem such a bargain if it is discovered that it was made by forced child labour in a far-eastern sweat shop. A juicy pineapple loses its taste if you find that Filipino peasant families are starving next to the field in which it was grown.

So let us salute scientific and technological advances which can provide us with a better life, without exploiting our fellow-creatures. But beware of the cheap price tag or the technological advance which is founded on creature suffering.


## APPENDIX

The Real Meat Company:

> Founded by - Richard Guy and Gillian Metherell in January 1986.
>
> Contributing Farmers - Approximately 20.
>
> Annual Throughput - Approximately 350 tonnes of meat and meat products.

Availability:

> a) Any household in Great Britain by direct chilled delivery.

b) Through thirty five outlets in the Leicester, London, Bristol Triangle.

c) Through company-owned in shop in Bath.

Product Range:

Beef, Lamb, Pork, Chicken, Duck, Turkeys, Ham, Bacon, Pies, Sausages, Dairy Products. All manufactured products contain no artificial preservatives, colouring or flavouring (except ham and bacon which contain salt and salt-petre, the traditional Wiltshire Cure curing salts).

## FOOTNOTE

Coccidiosis is the commonest disease of domestic fowl. It is a parasite which can be kept at bay by good husbandry but is usually treated by near-continuous treatment with a variety of "coccidiostats".

PART FOUR


EXPERIMENTATION

Andrew Rowan

## ETHICAL DILEMMAS IN EXPERIMENTATION

(NB: Text edited from tape-recording)


I shall divide my talk into three main sections:

> 1)    Some of the features of the debate which make it
> so passionate and vehement a topic.
> 2)    Some of the ethical aspects.
> 3)    Sentience, and some of the characteristics of
> animals which are morally relevant to this subject.

I shall then illustrate these points with two examples.


## 1    The Vehemence of the Debate

Anyone who is involved with the animal welfare movement in
any way will soon come to realise that animal-based
research has something about it which touches many a raw
nerve and raises the level of passions to a high pitch.

I would like to focus on two factors here. Firstly, strong
empathy with the animal, perceived as a "helpless
innocent". There is a parallel here with one´s own
feelings when in hospital, totally under the control of
the medical profession!

Another feature is the Jekyll and Hyde nature of the
animal/research issue. The goals of the biomedical
establishment are - at least ultimately - humanitarian:
the elimination of disease and suffering. And yet these
goals are achieved through the infliction of disease and
suffering on animals. Historical accounts of the 19th
century debate show this very clearly, but it still comes
over clearly today.

There is a great deal of misunderstanding about this.
Undoubtedly, members of the general public, as opposed to
the scientific community, really think that animals are
"tortured" in the laboratory. Scientists are not perceived
as being particularly believable when they defend
themselves in this respect.

On the other hand, scientists (like others who have to
kill animals) have an "unexamined guilt". Whether this
guilt is justified is not the point: the underlying reason
for their strong reactions is that they have not often
taken the time to justify their work to themselves. Some
who have thought it through do justify it, and do so when
presenting their work to their fellows or the public.

Participant observation of groups such as research
technicians has shown that when they start their career
they have violent dreams about their work. Similarly, some
experimenters actually refuse to come into the laboratory

until the animal is fully anaesthetised and prepared for them - the animal having passed from being "a living being" to being "a research object".

## 2    The Ethical Constructs

When adopting an ethical position one has to begin by deciding what the morally relevant characteristics are. Hair colour and skin colour, for instance, are not morally relevant characteristics in animals or in humans. Singer bases his utilitarian argument on sentience: Regan bases his animal-rights stance on the possession of ideas and desires. A Kantian bases his argument on the theory that mistreatment of animals might lead to the mistreatment of human beings - for him nothing in the animal itself is relevant.

All of these arguments are based on one single characteristic, but a moral system should be based on a "tapestry", a network of characteristics which are internally consistent. Such a network would include:

    Possession of life
    Possession of sentience
    Intentionality
    Rationality
    Self-awareness
    Social interaction and kinship
    etc.

I do not claim that other characteristics could not be included: nor do I claim to fully understand what is meant by these terms. I do feel, though, that any coherent theory has to include them if it is to take into account not only the moral status of humans but also that of animals.

Sentience itself is seldom discussed, though Singer defines it as "a capacity to suffer and/or experience pleasure".

Suffering is NOT the same thing as pain: they are two different concepts. You can have pain without suffering. Human suffering has been defined as "a perceived threat to the integrity of the person" (a person is not the same thing as an organism). From this viewpoint, animals will only suffer to the extent that they are "persons".

At an AVMA (American Veterinary Medical Association) conference on "Pain in Animals, its Cause and Alleviation", we put together a definition of animal suffering as "the unpleasant emotional response to more than minimal pain and distress".

Anxiety in animals is another matter. It seems to be mediated by a system in the central nervous system, which reacts in a similar way to anti-anxiety drugs in both humans and animals.

Other drugs have been discovered recently which do not alleviate anxiety, but cause it. Injection of these substances into humans causes a panic attack which can be arrested with benzodiazapine: in primates or cats, injection causes pilo-erection, squealing, screaming, struggling, vocalisation, urination, defaecation, etc. To the common-sense observer this means that these animals are in some distress - i.e. they are "anxious". Despite this sort of evidence, there are still people who will argue that anxiety is a uniquely human phenomenon, and that animals are not subject to it as they are to fear.

The reason for bringing this up is because anxiety is a very important phenomenon for us to consider in relation to animal suffering, and we pay far too little attention to it. The International Association for the Study of Pain (IASP) recognises that pain is an important moral issue in animal studies, and they have developed guidelines which they feel address some of those moral concerns. Neurochemists who study anxiety have no such guidelines, although I would have thought that they would be equally obliged to develop them.

Anxiety studies may involve a conflict model, such as when an animal is deprived of water, and is then given it, but gets an electric shock every third time it drinks. This situation sets up an anxiety reaction, since the animal never knows whether it is going to get a shock or not. Consequently, anti-anxiety drugs can be tested on it: if they work it simply drinks and does not care whether it gets a shock or not.

There are moral problems involved in this type of research, and one would have expected the individuals concerned to develop guidelines for their own work similar to those developed by the IASP.


## 3    Two Specific Examples

Finally, I would like to discuss two specific examples. I have been involved with one of them more directly than the other.

The first is the idea of using chimpanzees as heart-donors. This was proposed just over a year ago at Columbia Presbyterian College of Physicians and Surgeons. One of the surgeons had already carried out kidney transplants from chimpanzees to humans in the 1960s: these had not been particularly successful because drugs to prevent rejection were not efficacious.

Since there are now drugs which are more effective as anti-rejection agents, the surgeons wanted to try chimpanzees as heart-donors. They were honest in saying that this would be an experiment, and the recipients were to be told this. The chimp's heart was to be used as an "assist", not to replace the human heart but to help it in cases of terminal heart disease.

I was called in to advise, with two advisers from the National Institutes of Health. One of these spoke on the heart-transplant scene (especially on the problems of finding replacement hearts) and the other spoke on the chimpanzee supply etc. Both tended to be negative about the use of chimpanzees. I then spoke on the ethics of using chimpanzees, my argument being that in using them one must bear in mind strong evidence that they are self-aware. I discussed proofs from mirror-experiments, in which chimpanzees used mirrors to examine themselves, and experiments on "intentional deceptive behaviour" (If I try to deceive you, I must first think that you think that I think - there must be some kind of self-concept which is more advanced than simple awareness of oneself in space an time, which is possessed by any higher predator). I argued that self-awareness militated against killing an animal merely as a means to an end.

Ultimately the decision was left to the Animal Care Committee, and all save one voted to prohibit the project. What had worried them most, though, was not the ethical argument, but the endangered status of the chimpanzee. If the research had worked, chimpanzees would have commanded very high prices and would, among other things, have been bred in Third World countries to provide hearts for humans.

The second issue is the Pound-animal issue. This is clearly not very controversial here or in Europe, since purpose-bred animals are used in research. Nonetheless, it illustrates the concept of social interaction and kinship. There is still a major debate in America over whether Pound-animals should be used in research, based originally largely on economic factors, but now going beyond economics and beyond rationality. Both the medical and the animal-welfare communities see this issue as "the one to win" and have taken increasingly hardened positions on it.

The medical community makes up "silly arguments" and the argument from the animal side (the release of animals from Pounds undermines animal-control measures, etc.) is not much better. The general public do not care much either way and irresponsible owners obviously couldn't care less.

When you survey the public it is critical to put the question correctly. If you ask whether it is all right for former pets to be used in research, only 35%-40% would say "yes". If you ask whether Pound animals that are going to be killed anyway should be used for research, then 55%-60% say "yes". They are the same animals, only they are referred to differently.

What one is seeing here is the element of social kinship. We owe something to a former pet. The alternative is to use purpose-bred animals: what is seen here is that there is more to an animal with which we have some "family kinship": the purpose bred animal, which has never been a pet, does not call for so much moral attention.

Judith Hampson

## ANIMAL EXPERIMENTATION - PRACTICAL DILEMMAS AND SOLUTIONS

In this paper I want to make the point that animal experimentation is not simply an activity in which humans indulge which involves the exploitation of animals (such as their use in sport or entertainment), rather it is of such fundamental and central importance that it underpins our whole society. Almost every activity in our western society is dependent, directly or indirectly, on animal experimentation (see: <u>footnote 1</u>). I will argue that, in order adequately to deal with the ethical dilemmas it presents, it is necessary not simply to search for better means of controlling it, but to change our society quite fundamentally: our assumptions, our ethical values, our expectations, our behaviour, even, and perhaps most importantly, our understanding of ourselves as spiritual beings and our place in the scheme of Nature. When people ask me how we can solve the ethical dilemmas of animal experimentation I am inclined to say, after some fifteen years of wrestling with the practical and philosophical issues, we cannot get there from here.

The main way that we have tried to get there to date is by legislation. In the words of the 1875 U.K. Royal Commission, responsible for the first animal experimentation legislation in the world, such laws aim "to reconcile the needs of science with the just claims of humanity". They seek to sanction, without serious impediment, all those areas of animal experimentation upon which our society has now come to rely. At the same time they seek to make the practice generally acceptable to the public, some sectors of which raise serious ethical objections. In other words, they try to resolve an ethical dilemma.

Over the last decade we have seen a plethora of new legislation to control animal experimentation. New laws have been passed or are in the process of implementation in the United States, Australia, and almost every country in Western Europe. In addition, we have a European Convention regulating the twenty-one countries of the Council of Europe and an EEC Directive imposing fairly stringent requirements on the twelve Member States of the European Economic Community. All this (and more) legislative activity has largely been in response to growing public disquiet and protest. We cannot ignore the substantial impact of groups taking part in illegal and sometimes violent acts, nor the serious philosophical debate which now underpins arguments about the legitimacy of using animals in research.

The moral issues raised by this debate have hardly begun to be addressed by any of the laws passed to date, though some have made an attempt, and are flexible enough to allow these issues to be addressed in their administration.

There are basically two types of legislation. One exerts control primarily through a central government administration, by means of a licensing system and a National Inspectorate. This system is most well developed in the U.K., which established the model. A number of European countries may develop control along similar lines in order to comply with the provisions of the EEC Directive, though it is unlikely that any country will develop either an Inspectorate or a project licensing system as sophisticated as that of the United Kingdom.

The other major type of control system has minimal central administration and exerts control at the institutional level, primarily through Institutional Animal Care and Use Committees (ACUs) or Ethics Committees. These implement basic rules laid down in national law and are responsible for project scrutiny and inspection of the facilities. The system is overseen by a National Inspectorate and by the funding agencies.

This is the model developed in the United States and a similar mechanism of control is being established in Australia. Canada also employs this kind of system, though its provisions are not yet enshrined in national legislation.

The intricacies of these and other control systems are too complex to deal with here and have been described elsewhere (Hampson, 1989). I want to give a brief overview of what I see as the major potentials and pitfalls of these two main types of control system so as to put in perspective the possibilities presented by legislation as a tool for the solution of ethical dilemmas in animal experimentation.

The fundamental limitation of any legislation passed to date is that all such laws rest on the basic assumption that it is morally acceptable to kill animals and to cause them pain and distress in order to protect human society from illness and environmental hazard, and to gain scientific knowledge.

Legislation seeks, at least on paper, to impose limits on the degree of pain and distress which it is permissible to cause. Some even places limits on the purposes which may be considered legitimate. But none questions its legitimacy. In any cost/benefit analysis the costs are always to the animals while the benefits accrue to humans or to their domestic animals, never to the experimental "models" incurring the costs.

Five main aims of legislation can be identified:

> to define legitimate purposes for which animals may be used
> to impose limits on pain and suffering
> to provide for inspection of facilities and procedures
> to ensure humane standards of husbandry and care
> to ensure public accountability

Legislation can be, and has been, effective to a degree in limiting pain caused to animals and ensuring they are cared for and maintained in conditions which reach certain set standards. Unarguably there is much further to go in reducing laboratory animal suffering and improving husbandry and care, but these are areas which legislation is competent to address. By these means it can tackle one side of the dilemma: it can reduce the ethical costs of animal experiments. But in order to balance cost against benefit, legislation must also examine the purposes for which animals are used, the justification of that use and public accountability.

Laws currently in force address the question of purpose only in a very general way. Those which require prior authorisation of projects ask the applicant to show that the work is important and necessary and that no viable non-sentient "alternative" is available which could provide the same information. These general requirements can serve to raise consciousness in individual researchers, but the possibility remains that they may be quickly dismissed by a few sentences on an application form.

Under the Animals (Scientific Procedures) Act passed in the U.K. in 1986, the Secretary of State is given statutory responsibility for ensuring that the costs to animals incurred in experiments are properly weighed against projected benefits. The machinery provided is a personal licensing system and a project licensing system, requiring detailed justification on the project licence application form; a trained professional Inspectorate to assess applications and advise on conditions which may be imposed on projects; specialist scientific assessors who are available to provide technical advice as necessary and a national committee, with statutory authority, to which especially difficult projects or work of special public interest can be referred.

This system is unique and comes closest to facilitating some ethical weighing of costs against benefits - a provision hard fought for, and won, by the animal welfare movement.

Yet this scrutiny cannot meet the intentions of reformists unless it also addresses the fundamental ethical question of whether a research project should be conducted at all.

The Animal Procedures Committee has not yet decided whether it is within its brief to advise the Secretary of State not to grant project licences for work which might be considered "unnecessary". A major sector of public opinion has already indicated that it considers "unnecessary" animal tests for the development of new decorative cosmetics, tests to develop new smoking materials, research into drug and alcohol abuse, maternal deprivation and isolation experiments, and much fundamental or basic research, particularly in the behavioural sciences, which have been targeted by animal rights groups as a "soft" area, in which the public can readily grasp the issues.

Since "necessity" is the word most often used in defence of animal experimentation and its sanction by legislation, it is worth stopping for a moment to think more deeply what we mean by it. A recent paper by a linguist on this topic (Rowson, 1988) identified only one way in which the word "necessity" could be applied to the subject of animal experimentation, that is, under the heading of "moral necessity".

An action is considered morally necessary only if it would be immoral not to take it. Some researchers do indeed argue that it would be immoral not to perform animal experiments because of the impedance to medical progress that such a restriction would bring. However, they generalise from particular examples to a justification of all animal experiments. As Michael Balls, Chairman of the Fund for Replacement of Animals in Medical Experiments (FRAME) has put it: "I consider that experimentation on animals should only be permitted if a convincing and specific case for doing it can be made" (Balls, 1988).

The specific justification is often weak indeed. Animal experimentation has simply become an institution whose existence is justified in general terms. In my view, it has not been convincingly shown that the vast majority of animal experiments today have an essential bearing on medical progress.

The word "necessary" can be applied to animal experimentation in only three of its meanings:

**indispensable** - something which is essential for something else to be done or to exist

**imperative** - something which has been ordered; something to which high priority is attached

**requisite** - something required by a policy decision

Claiming that animal experimentation is necessary in the sense of indispensable means that it is the only way of achieving some desired objective. If this is the case, and it is often difficult to establish with respect to individual projects, then a legitimate question is, if this is the only way of pursuing the objective, is that objective worth pursuing?

Using "necessary" in the senses of imperative or requisite means that animal research is necessary in order to fulfil a particular policy. Examples of such policies are national and international regulations which require safety testing on animals of an enormous variety of products from floor polishes to medicines. We can legitimately ask whether such policies are justifiable both generally and specifically in terms of the different

103

types of product which they control. Thus the existence of such policies does not mean that the use of animals for these purposes is indispensable.

It might be argued, for example, that animals must be used in the safety testing of a new drug which is an important advance and whose safety can be ensured in no other way. It is equally arguable that such testing is not justified to ensure the safety of a new headache pill or decorative cosmetic. Such animal use cannot be held as indispensable since the products themselves are not deemed indispensable. In utilitarian terms, high ethical costs cannot be justified by trivial benefits.

A debate on the justification of using animals in cosmetics testing has raged for many years. In the U.K. the arguments became so circular and unresolvable that the government gave an undertaking to refer all such applications for project licences to the Animals Procedures Committee. Rather than take strong action limiting this testing, as the West German Parliament is currently attempting to do, it simply passed the problem on to someone else.

The arguments remain the same as they have for decades, and the Animals Procedures Committee has no more information at its disposal now than has already been made available over the years by wide public debate.

If we take seriously the notion that animals matter in moral terms, then the development of a new decorative cosmetic must be too trivial a benefit to justify the suffering or death of a single animal. That such products have to be animal-tested in order to ensure their safety is totally irrelevant in moral terms. There are already more than enough products, and basic ingredients, which have been tested and established as safe.

In the wake of the recent Green Consumer Week and launch of the Green Consumer Guide, the public has demonstrated its desire and willingness to purchase products which are cruelty-free and which do not destroy our environment. The argument for animal testing is commercial, not medical or scientific, but if all companies were restricted by law to the use of already tested ingredients no one would have a competitive edge in the market in terms of innovation.

Our society's inability to solve so uncomplicated an issue (in ethical terms) is an illustration of how little consideration it is prepared to give to the "cost" side of the cost/benefit equation.

This is what I mean by "we cannot get there from here". Despite all our efforts, our extensive debates, our plethora of legislative initiatives, laboratory animals have virtually no moral standing in fact under current legislation. The most trivial of justifications is considered sufficient for legislation to sanction their suffering and death.

It might be expected that an institutional Animal Care and Use Committee, representing a range of interests and expertise, could be more effective in weighing costs against benefits than a central government licensing system. In Australia, many institutions actually give such committees the title of "ethics committees". The comparison with ethics committees in British hospitals or Institutional Review Boards (IRBs) in the States has often been made. This comparison is superficial.

Committees reviewing animal research are operating in a society where animals have little moral standing, where the fundamental question of whether it is morally legitimate to experiment on animals is not even asked. Human ethics committees, by comparison, work in an atmosphere of human protection being paramount. They are regulated primarily not to sanction the research but to protect the participants in meaningful ways (Dresser, 1985).

For example, federal law controlling the operation of IRBs in the USA dictate that the risks conferred upon experimental subjects must be reasonable in relation to any anticipated benefits to those subjects themselves or to the importance of the knowledge that can reasonably be expected to result. These risks are never expected to result in substantial injury or death of the participants and have to be minimised in project design. Most important, the researcher has to disclose detailed information about the research project, its risks and benefits, to the research subject, and obtain informed consent. The committees do not concern themselves with the ethical weighing, since such decisions are taken elsewhere, but are more concerned with whether the research subject has given properly informed consent. Persons incapable of giving informed consent, such as children, or the psychologically disturbed, can be subjected only to minimal risks in projects designed to benefit themselves, not someone else.

Mechanistically, Animal Care and Use, or Ethics committees can operate in a similar way. They can reduce the costs by attending to humane design of the protocol and adequate facilities for animal care. That is basically what they do. They are not ethics committees. They do not ask the fundamental question of whether research in general, or this research in particular, ought to be done at all. The research animals they purport to protect derive no benefit from the research which the committees sanction. They do not prevent those animals from being subjected to suffering and death.

The animal protection legislation under which such committees operate militates against ethical review. Nothing in the revised US Animal Welfare Act, for example, or in the proposed Regulations, authorises an ACUC to determine the scientific merit of a research protocol. Indeed, the National Institutes of Health Guide which most institutions closely follow, stresses that protocol review is intended to relate to animal welfare issues and not to scientific merit. As one British researcher (Bateson, 1986) has pointed out, the factors to be regarded in any cost/benefit analysis are the scientific quality of the research, the likelihood of medical benefit and the extent of animal suffering (see: <u>footnote 2</u>). How can a committee weigh costs against benefits if the scientific merit of the project is not even open to question?

The US research community, resenting bureaucratic interference in its activities, is mounting strong opposition to the proposal that ACUCs should carry out protocol review at all. This is hardly a climate in which protecting the interests of research animals is paramount.

Whatever country we consider, we are looking at a society where animals, unlike children or the mentally defective, have no guardians to protect their interests.

An ethical dilemma is a situation in which we are forced to choose between two evils. I believe that animal experimentation is a genuine dilemma. It is an evil to allow people to suffer and die if that suffering and death can be prevented by drugs, by vaccination, by surgery. It is an evil for us not to exploit our full intellectual potential, not to push back the frontiers of knowledge. But the means by which we have to do so, are also evil. They involve the imprisonment, suffering and death of countless millions of sentient creatures.

My experience of the convoluted realms of ethical philosophy has convinced me that animal experimentation is morally wrong. More important, its existence offends my understanding of myself as a spiritual being. I do not believe for a minute that there is no solution to this ethical dilemma. I do believe, however, that humanity is not yet ready to look for it.

This is true of our society as a whole. We do not want our deeply entrenched assumptions challenged. We do not want the insecurity that goes with learning entirely new ways of solving problems, new ways of being.

The animal rights debate is just one casualty of this blinkered way of looking at the world. As a result, the debate is fast getting itself inextricably bogged down in a thick glue of inertia. A large proportion of would-be defenders of animals are so weighed down with their own feelings of anger and frustration at our failure to make progress that they can only direct that anger outwards in acts of violence and abuse against those whom they see as "the enemy": researchers, legislators and even fellow animal rights protagonists.

Meanwhile, researchers and legislators fail to address the ethical debate and continue to defend the <u>status quo</u>. The focus is not on looking into the merits of the issue or finding better ways of doing things but on justifying why we should keep carrying on the way we always have. This extract from an editorial which appeared last year in Neuro-surgery illustrates the point:

"The public, with a lack of knowledge of the research process and its benefits and with a love of animals, is an easy target for the actions of animal rights activists. The critical facts and issues must be communicated to the public to counteract this threat. The ultimate goal of biomedical research is improved patient care. Thus, not only must research scientists inform the public of the problem, but physicians, with day-to-day contact with the public through patient care, must become involved in this issue, especially at the local and state levels. The future of research and health care in the United States is in grave peril" (Grubb, 1987).

Such gross exaggerations and distortions of the current state of affairs are counterproductive to any initiatives designed to resolve our ethical dilemmas and should not pass without comment, though frequently they do.

First, if the ultimate goal of biomedical research is improved patient care, then many might argue that a substantial proportion of the millions currently spent on animal research which makes little or no impact on patient care, could better be spent on improving medical facilities available to everyone.

Medical gain is the plea usually made in defence of animal experiments. Its defenders warn us about the scourges of infectious disease and would have us believe that every rat and mouse that dies in the laboratory does so in the service of keeping children out of wheelchairs. Let us not delude ourselves (see: footnote 3). In the U.K. each year, some 23% of experiments are done in order to study normal or abnormal structure and function. A large percentage of this is fundamental research which researchers carry out because they are simply interested in finding things out. It may or may not have a medical spin-off. Examples of experiments which seem to have little or no connection with life-saving medical research are legion. Here are just two:

"Pavlovian analysis of interactions between hunger and thirst" (Ramachanran and Pearce, 1987), looks at the effects of Pavlovian conditioning on hunger and thirst in rats.

"Parturition in the guinea pig: vital role of the mammary gland" (Calvert and Peaker, 1986), concluded that the mammary glands are essential in childbirth after finding out that female guinea pigs die around parturition if the mammary glands have first been surgically removed. The work follows similar work done in goats.

Some 8% of the animals used annually die in the safety-testing of industrial, household or other non-medical products, an issue which I have already discussed. Some 17% are used for "other", non-specified purposes. Almost 60% are used to develop and test medical, dental and veterinary products, most of which are pharmaceuticals and vaccines. We can legitimately question how many of these are essential to our health. Indeed many have argued that the over-production and over-prescription of pharmaceuticals is positively detrimental to our health.

The Department of Health and Social Security survey of the 204 drugs licensed in the U.K. between 1971 and 1980 concluded that drug innovation in Britain has been directed towards commercial returns rather than therapeutic need. Moreover, an abundance of analogous drugs is offered, often with exaggerated claims for their efficacy (Laurance, 1987). Before we run away with the idea that pharmaceutical companies are knights in shining armour locked in a crusade against world disease, we should be aware that the pattern of drug development in the west bears little relation to the pattern of disease in the world. While the Third World is crying out for drugs and vaccines against diseases and parasites which kill and debilitate millions of people every year we continue to produce new drugs in already over-subscribed areas which offer little or no medical benefit over existing ones and often these are areas where prevention of disease and holistic patient care are sadly neglected. For example, in the decade of the DHSS survey, 33 cardiovascular agents and 7 new benzodiazepines (drugs of the valium family) were developed while there was only one agent for the treatment of shistosomiasis, the commonest disease in the world.

The reasons for this state of affairs are easy to understand. The cost of developing a single drug today is at least £100 million. Third World countries cannot afford expensive new drugs which would provide a return for the investment of the company developing them.

Despite the pressing need of these countries, one writer in the Lancet has pointed out that "Drug companies today struggle to find new areas of research, for most firms are working in the same areas: cancer, atherosclerosis, hypertension and thrombosis are examples of areas where a lot of repetitive and costly work is yielding only 'me-too' drugs" (Garattini, 1988). This is borne out by looking at last year's "top ten best-sellers" in the world pharmaceutical market.

These facts might lead us to put a question mark over the statement quoted earlier that the ultimate goal of biomedical research is improved patient care, or at least to ask whether our society is going about providing it in the most cost-effective way possible.

What about the second statement, that research and health care is in grave peril? There is no reason at all why research and health care need be jeopardised by the animal rights movement. By definition, any real and lasting solution to the ethical dilemma must come from a new and deeper understanding, not only of the issues but of ourselves. When we come to understand that the pursuit of knowledge is more than intellectual, that the expansion of our moral and spiritual consciousness can provide us with answers to problems we cannot yet conceive of with our rational minds, then our society will be able to solve this and many other ethical dilemmas. Along with a proper understanding of the moral status of animals would come a deeper understanding of our place in the scheme of things, an holistic approach to our relationship with our environment and a new way of healing our bodies and keeping them healthy. In such a society it is conceivable that medicine could progress much more substantially than it can now with our restricted reductionist outlook, and that it could progress without the exploitation of animals.

This requires nothing less than a _gestalt_ shift in the evolution of human consciousness. It requires that we build a new society in which we can live together harmoniously without destroying our environment, without the constant threat of our own destruction, without wars, without famine, without exploitation of those weaker than ourselves. As Doug Moss, publisher of the international animal rights magazine, _Agenda_, has said, "the animal cause is indissolubly tied to other contemporary struggles for justice and sanity in the conduct of human affairs" (Moss, 1988). Albert Schweitzer pointed out that without developing a reverence for all life and for nature it is inconceivable that we will ever enjoy world peace.

Tom Regan, widely hailed as an intellectual leader of the animal rights movement, makes this plea: "It´s time we stopped serving up the same old ideas in the same old ways. The animals for whom we struggle deserve better" (Regan, 1987).

We deserve better too. We owe it to ourselves as well as to the animals to stop trotting out the same old attacks against one another, the same old defences of the status quo, to start searching together for a saner, more fruitful, more holistic way of being. Until we can build such a society, medical progress as we know it is under no threat from the animal rights movement, because nothing is going to stop animal experimentation. What is under threat is much more significant that that, it is no less than our moral and spiritual evolution. It is only through this evolution that we will be able to solve the ethical dilemma of animal experimentation, and many others which currently elude us. We cannot get there from here.

**FOOTNOTES**

1    See "The Western Society we Live in" RSPCA srs/aerd/6.84.

2       See diagram 2 in <u>New Scientist</u>: "When a Research
        Proposal falls into the opaque part of the cube,
        the experimental part of the work should not be
        done" (New Scientist 20:2:86, 30-32).

3       See "Number of Experimental Animals used in 1986
        categorised by Purpose" RSPCA
        (BSC/RAD/RSPCA/7.87).

## References and Bibliography

Hampson, JE. Legislation and the changing consensus.
In G. Langley (editor) <u>Animal Experimentation: the
Consensus changes</u>, (London: Macmillan, 1989).

Rowson, RH. (1988) A note on the "necessity" of using
animals in research. <u>ATLA, 15</u>, 311 - 318.

Balls, M. (1988) The need to limit animal
experimentation. <u>FRAME News, No 19</u>, 8 - 9.

Dresser, R. (1985) Research on animals: values,
politics and regulatory reform. <u>South Californian Law
Review, 58</u>, 1147 - 1201.

Bateson, P. (1986) When to experiment on animals.
<u>New Scientist</u>, 20 February, 30 - 32.

Grubb, RL. Jr., (1987) Animal rights versus medical
research. <u>Neurosurgery, 20-25</u>, 809 - 810.

Ramachanran, R: Pearce, JM. (1987) Pavlovian analysis
of interactions between hunger and thirst. <u>Journal of
Experimental Psychol Psychology: Animal Behaviour
Processes, 13/2</u>, 182-192.

Calvert, DT: Peaker, M. (1986) Parturition in the
guinea pig: vital role of the mammary glands. <u>Journal
of Physiology, 378</u>, 82 P.

Laurance, J. (1987) An abundance of drugs. <u>Self
Health,</u> December, 32.

Garattini, S. (1988) Remedies for tropical diseases.
<u>The Lancet,</u> June 11, 1338.

David, G. (1988) Glaxo sits up with a glow of health.
<u>Sunday Times</u>, 11 August, S 11.

Moss, D. (1988) Animal rights: broadening our
perspective; broadening our base. <u>Between the Species
4/2</u>, 153 -157.

Regan, T. <u>The Struggle for Animal Rights</u>,
International Society for Animal Rights, Clarks
Summit, PA, x (1987).

**Michael Balls and Jacqueline Southee**

## REDUCING ANIMAL EXPERIMENTS BY QUESTIONING THEIR NECESSITY

FRAME supports "the Three Rs" approach to eliminating the suffering endured by laboratory animals. Our main concern is with the scientific development, validation, acceptance and use of replacement techniques, procedures and strategies. Nevertheless, we also recognise that reduction of the numbers of animals used in laboratories, improvements in their housing and care, and refinement of the procedures applied to them, represent the best ways of reducing suffering in the short-term.

One of the most encouraging developments during the last few years has been acceptance of "the Three Rs" definition of alternatives, which is reflected in a number of new national and international laws, such as our own Animals (Scientific Procedures) Act 1986 (anon, 1986a) and the 1986 EC Directive on the Approximation of Laws, Regulations and Administrative Provisions of the Member States Regarding the Protection of Animals Used for Experimental and Other Scientific Purposes (anon, 1986b).

The year 1986 also saw the publication of the US Office of Technology Assessment (OTA) Report on Alternatives to Animal Use in Research, Education and Testing (anon, 1988a). This document is of major political, scientific and animal welfare significance, and is highly recommended reading, along with the 10-author critical appraisal of it, published in ATLA in 1987 (anon, 1987).

Meanwhile, many scientists directly or indirectly involved in the use of laboratory animals have progressively become more concerned about the scientific and ethical issues raised by what they do, and much sound progress is being made, not least in the development of replacement alternative methods, as well as in the housing and care of laboratory animals.

Thus, when we agreed to prepare a paper on reduction for this congress, we expected to be optimistic in anticipating a continuing and accelerating downward trend in animal experimentation. However, that is not how we feel today - the future looks much bleaker than we had expected, and we feel that more determination and new tactics will be essential, if a satisfactory rate of progress toward our goals is to be achieved and maintained.

## DARKENING CLOUDS

The following four trends are among current developments which threaten real progress via "the Three Rs" approach:

# 1    Growing resistance from the scientific establishment

Editorials have appeared in a large number of journals, warning, for example, that unless the threat represented by the animal rights movement is countered, "the future of research and health care..... is in grave peril" (Grubb, 1987).

The US National Institute of Health (NIH) is also fighting back, as was revealed in a memorandum by Dr Frederick Goodwin, Director of Intramural Research, NI Mental Health, which found its way to the offices of many animal welfare societies and was published in full in "Frame News" (anon, 1988b) and ATLA (anon, 1988c).

More recently, a special committee of the US National Research Council has concluded that "appropriate and humane use" of animals in research should continue, including the use of stray pets, and that the "chance that alternatives will completely replace animals in the foreseeable future is nil" (anon, 1988d). This statement will be seized upon by those who want to maintain the status quo.


# 2    Spreading chaos in toxicity testing

The unjustifiable excess of toxicity testing caused by the vast number of regulatory authorities, and by variation among their demands, seems to be getting worse, rather than better. Fear of litigation and the demands of consumer pressure groups for greater safety seem set to increase the numbers of animal toxicity tests carried out. The Japanese appear to be as intractable as ever in their demands, and the Canadian authorities have drafted a new set of regulations which fly in the face of everything we thought we were achieving in relation to the LD50 and Draize eye and skin irritancy tests (anon, 1988e).

Meanwhile, there is much haste within the EC to get testing standards for biomaterials in place by 1992. The West German Federal government is proposing a two-year systemic toxicity study for dental materials, including polymers which will come into contact with human tissues for less than five minutes. Equally disturbing proposals are emanating from other governments.

And why do the British regulators require cytotoxic anti-cancer drugs to be tested for teratogenic effects in animals, when their very nature indicates that they will be teratogens?

The barriers to real change in the use of animals in toxicity testing are now rarely scientific; they are the result of politics, commercial practices and conservative adherence to traditional methods and standards.

# 3    Increasing use of laboratory animals

Although we must expect an apparent increase in animal experimentation in the U.K., since the 1986 Act has brought under control procedures which were not regulated as experiments by the Cruelty to Animals Act 1876, we can hope that the underlying downward trend will continue. However, we cannot assume that this will always be the case.

Meanwhile, animal use in the USA increased significantly between 1986 and 1987 (anon, 1988f), and there was also a slight increase in the total number of animals used in The Netherlands in 1986 compared with 1984 and 1985 (anon, 1988g).  In addition, although the total number of animals used in Japan fell from 10,823,860 in 1981 to 8,235,250 in 1986-87, unfortunately this fall was almost totally accounted for by a reduction in the number of mice used. Significantly more non-human primates, dogs, rats, guinea-pigs and hamsters were used in 1986-87 (anon, 1988h).

# 4    Undemanding acceptance of fundamental research

Although in the case of two of the main purposes for which animals are used, education and testing, the way ahead is relatively clear if "the Three Rs" approach is stoically adhered to, it is the third main purpose (fundamental research) which gives the greatest cause for concern.  It is far too easy to justify fundamental research, perhaps because it is very difficult for those responsible for imposing controls to make judgements on what is put before them, given the infinite variety of purposes and procedures involved.

Thus, if we are not careful, those of us who favoured the new legislation will, in a few years, find ourselves having to admit that the changes which have followed have merely been cosmetic.  This must not be allowed to happen, so what should we do?

## Real change must be earned

First, we must realise that the new laws only provide opportunities for change, but do not guarantee that they will actually happen.  Real changes will have to be sought and won, and, rather than being pessimistic about the problems ahead of us, we must be more than ever determined to overcome them.

## Our demand for change must be repeatedly restated

Secondly, we must take every opportunity to campaign for a reduction in animal experimentation on various grounds, including the following:

a)   **ethical and moral** - regardless of our views on the difficult subject of "rights", we can all agree that human beings have a    responsibility to behave more properly, not only toward each    other, but also toward other animals;

b)   **compassionate** - the causation of suffering as a result of    pain, distress, deprivation and confinement should be avoided, wherever possible;

c)   **conservationist** - members of threatened or endangered species should not be taken from the wild for laboratory use;

d)   **scientific** - animal experiments can be misleading, because species differences limit the usefulness of the information they provide, when it is applied to man;

e)   **economic** - animal experiments are very expensive, and the resources consumed could be better used elsewhere, e.g. in developing and using alternative methods;

f)   **political** - more and more people, including scientists, want to see animal experimentation reduced, replaced, and eventually eliminated altogether;

g)   **requisite** - national and international laws require that there is a move away from the dependence of biomedical research on traditional animal procedures.


## The "necessity" of animal experiments must be questioned

Thirdly, we must face up to the common general defence of animal experimentation - that, while regrettable, it is "necessary". For example, in commenting on why 4.5 million experiments were carried out in the U.K. in 1984, Sir William Paton (1984) writes, "The answer can only be that that is the number that has been found necessary".

This line of argument must be challenged head-on. It does not involve logical or mathematical necessity, conceptual or analytic necessity, or causal necessity, but conditional necessity (Balls, 1988). That is, whether or not the claim of necessity is acceptable depends on other matters, and it conceals a value judgement.

Assessment of such a claim of necessity involves two stages. First, can the researcher show that the course of action proposed is the only means to the end? That is, is there no alternative way involving fewer animals, less sentient animals, less painful procedures, or non-animal methods?

Secondly, if the objective can only be met using the proposed "necessary" means, can its pursuance be justified and on what grounds? The common grounds put forward (Rowson, 1988) are that it is:

1. **indispensable** for something else to be achieved, e.g. for contributing to basic knowledge or to the training of young scientists and doctors.

2. **imperative,** because of something of a higher priority, e.g. overcoming the suffering caused by cancer, heart disease, or multiple sclerosis;

3. **requisite,** because of laws or policy decisions, e.g. that new drugs and many other kinds of products must be tested in animals before human beings are exposed to them.

Our grounds for using the challenge of necessity approach are well founded in the law; for example, the British Government's White Paper of May 1985 (anon, 1985) said:

"animal experiments that are unnecessary, use unnecessarily large numbers of animals, or are unnecessarily painful are indefensible".

## Challenges must be specifically aimed and based on sound science

Fourthly, we must recognise that changes achieved on a scientific basis will require scientific strategies and scientific expertise. The 1986 Act requires the Home Secretary to "weigh the likely adverse effects on the animals concerned against the benefits likely to accrue", before granting a licence permitting the work of a particular project to go ahead. Quite properly, much effort is currently being put into assessing adverse effects in animals, but the other side of the equation must not be neglected.

## GENERAL GUIDING PRINCIPLES

It is easy to adopt and hold to an extreme position (e.g. all laboratory animal scientists are sadists, industry is only interested in making profits, drugs damage human health instead of curing disease), but it is difficult to have a positive influence on events from such a position. So, the decision about what to attack and on what grounds, requires judgement and discrimination. Some general guiding principles are unavoidable, if only as a basis for dealing with specific problems; for example:

1. Human beings matter more than animals; nevertheless, animals matter; also some human interests matter more than

others (e.g. understanding multiple sclerosis is more important than testing a new lipstick), and some animals matter more than others (e.g. while goldfish matter, chimpanzees matter more).

2. Scientific experiments matter, but some matter more than others, and others should be prohibited.

3. Generalisation from the particular is not useful or acceptable; insulin may have been discovered by animal experimentation, but that does not justify all other animal procedures; similarly, many were appalled at what emerged about the head injury experiments carried out on baboons at the University of Pennsylvania, but that does not make all scientists equally culpable.

4. Conflict between human welfare and animal welfare should not be seen as inevitable, but should be avoided wherever possible.

Similarly, we must try to understand why scientists want to do research. Bessis (1985) gives five reasons, to which we have added a sixth:

a) **insecurity:**   to receive recognition
b) **vanity:**        to become a star
c) **power:**         to direct the course of science
d) **curiosity:**     to obtain intellectual pleasure
e) **altruism:**      to do good for mankind
f) **money:**         to receive monetary rewards

These reasons apply no less to those who work in the animal welfare movement; but it is the balance between them which is vital. To accuse scientists of being motivated only by insecurity and vanity would be as absurd as would be their counter-claim that altruism was their only driving force. Similarly, to accuse industry of a sole and single-minded determination to make profits without regard to any other consideration is as absurd as would be an industry's counter-claim to be only interested in serving its customers, while at the same time protecting the environment.


**STRATEGIES FOR REDUCING ANIMAL EXPERIMENTATION**

We need to target our efforts if significant progress is to be made, and this will involve recognising that animal experimentation in education, testing and fundamental research must be dealt with separately.


## 1.   Reducing animal use in education

This should be the easiest part of animal experimentation to deal with, since it is difficult to argue for it on the grounds of educational or scientific necessity.

Happily, school students in the U.K. and Europe are not permitted to experiment on animals, but so-called research projects in the USA result in appalling injury, pain, discomfort and death. This was the focus of a campaign by Barbara Orlans when she was at SCAW (1985), but was weakly dealt with in the OTA Report (anon, 1988a; Balls, 1987).

Similarly, the use of animal experimentation in First Degree courses can be considered unnecessary. First Degrees in science are now widely used as a background to careers outside science, e.g. in general and financial administration and management. A recent article in Nature (Taylor, 1988) has shown that only a minority of graduates in pharmacy and pharmacology, agriculture and veterinary sciences, and the biological sciences, actually take up careers which might involve animal experimentation. The new British law appears to be leading to a dramatic reduction in animal use in undergraduate teaching, much to the regret of animal physiologists. We would be happy to see practical vertebrate physiology become a post-graduate subject.

These matters, along with animal use in training medical and veterinary science students, were fully discussed in David Morton´s excellent review of the education sections of the OTA Report (1987), as well as elsewhere during this conference. We would further suggest that ethical and societal aspects of animal welfare should be mandatory in all courses in Secondary and Tertiary education.

## 2.   Reducing animal use in testing

Significant reductions in animal use have already taken place in the use of animals in new drug discovery, where the empirical screening of chemicals for biological activity has been overtaken by modern drug design technology, involving computer graphics and in-vitro preparations of target cells and tissues.

We have already referred to the current adverse trends in relation to animal use in toxicity testing and it must be admitted that most of the recommendations of the FRAME Toxicity Committee (Balls, et al, 1983), while increasingly recognised as valid and important, (Anon, 1988a; Balls, 1987) have not yet led to the dramatic reduction in animal use which could be achieved without compromising human health.

The FRAME Toxicity Committee has begun to meet again, with many new members. Our goals include seeking greater harmonisation of regulatory guidelines, especially within Europe, where the day must come when national regulatory bodies will be superseded by a small group of European authorities (Griffin, 1988).

However, it must be remembered that companies operating in world-wide markets must test to meet the guidelines of the most demanding authority, so the day will also come when the requirements of certain non-European regulatory authorities must be faced up to and dealt with. Even then, given a unified set of guidelines, albeit on a world scale, it is the operation of the regulatory process which must be harmonised and made more equitable. At present, the same procedures can be used to delay the marketing of the products of an overseas company, while facilitating the marketing of the similar product of a national company. Like many other aspects of toxicity testing, this has nothing to do with necessity, or with consumer or environmental protection. As one of the world's leading toxicologists, Gerhard Zbinden, recently pointed out (1988), the simple statement that a test is necessary because it is required by a regulatory guideline will not be considered sufficient justification in the future.

## 3. Reducing animal use in fundamental pure and applied research

Much is made by the scientific establishment of the necessity for scientists to be free to exercise their curiosity, to follow up "hunches" and to go down pathways which interest them, whether or not they can see any likely application of what they might discover, i.e. to engage in "pure" research. This line of argument is an attempt to weaken attempts to apply rigorous scrutiny to the benefit side of the cost-benefit analysis of animal suffering versus justification of purpose.

In earlier centuries, or even up to 1979 in the U.K., when monetarist economics became fashionable, this argument might have had some appeal, but it is now much harder for scientists to work in isolation. Even if they succeed for a while, others will adopt their discoveries and apply them for less pure reasons. Also, science in many parts of the world is in a state of crisis because of lack of funding. Much essential applied research is not being done because it cannot be funded. Thus, if high quality of hypothesis and of innovatory approach are required in order to obtain funding, then scientists wishing to use animal experimentation should be expected to spell out the benefits likely to accrue from the work they wish to do.

We have two ways of questioning the necessity of animal experimentation in particular areas of work. First, there is the question of suffering likely to be caused to the animals to be used. Under our 1986 Act, suffering is notionally considered to be of mild, moderate, or substantial severity. Both individual procedures within the project and the project as a whole are given a classification. Initially, this is the responsibility of the applicant. That might explain why some scientists are able to claim that experimental work on visual pathways in cats and monkeys has never involved more than a <u>mild</u> degree of suffering, while others who keep monkeys with electrodes in their brains in chairs with head restraint for six hours a day, five days a week, for up to two years, are able to claim that the animals are "happy" and that only _moderate_ suffering is involved.

The proper assessment of potential suffering is vital, and an acceptable basis for using "mild", "moderate" or "substantial" severity must be developed and agreed. However, being too ready to class procedures as of "substantial" severity will do as great a disservice as would the over-use of "mild".

The second basis for questioning, then, is necessity of purpose, and this will require some more complex assessment system. What is clear is that it is at present too easy for a scientist to heavily load this side of the balance. Facing up to this situation is our biggest challenge, since, like the authorities responsible for administering controls on animal experimentation, we are few in number and the assessment of each area of work needs specialised knowledge and very detailed scrutiny. Only extreme cases will be obvious.

We must insist that the animal concern "credentials" of applicants are considered to be no less important than their expertise as research scientists. The quality of the animal care facilities must be considered to be as vital as the availability of equipment for use in scientific procedures. However, one crucial additional point must also be made. If, in taking part in evaluating necessity, we expect scientists to agree with us that the suffering involved in a proposed programme of work is too great, given the likely benefits to human and animal health or scientific knowledge, we must also be willing to accept that, given proper safeguards and controls, animal experimentation _should_ sometimes be permitted, if only until total replacement by non-animal procedures has become feasible.


**CONCLUSIONS**

As in all complex situations, we can see grounds for optimism and for pessimism, when we consider the current status of laboratory animals.

On the _positive_ side, new and stronger laws are being introduced and implemented in many countries. Scientists are becoming more aware of their responsibilities toward their "models", as well as toward their fields of endeavour. Greater influence and power are being given to those who provide day-to-day care for laboratory animals, and to independent veterinarians who can now, by statutory right, advise and comment on the well-being and treatment of laboratory animals. The "Three Rs" concept is now widely accepted and there are genuine efforts toward finding replacement alternative methods. Of particular importance is the requirement that the likely suffering of the animals to be used in a programme of work must be considered, along with the potential benefits likely to accrue to human beings, other animals, and to science in general. We should all welcome and encourage these developments.

On the negative side, there is evidence of growing conservatism and resistance to change in parts of the scientific community, and the numbers of laboratory animals used in some countries are increasing. Meanwhile, the genetic engineering of animals raises new ethical problems, and the production of biological materials from genetically-engineered organisms raises new problems of safety and toxicity testing. There is also a demand for more toxicity testing in general, and the harmonisation of national and international testing guidelines remains a dream. Insufficient funding is being provided for the development and validation of alternatives, so it is too easy for scientists to say that the use of animals in their particular research is unavoidable. Moreover, scientists have little trouble in justifying the necessity of their fundamental research, and it is not easy to see how more stringency can be applied to the assessment to the benefit side of the cost-benefit equation. Finally, procedures applied to animals are too readily judged to be mild or moderate, and the present operation of the severity banding system must be considered unsatisfactory.

One thing is clear. Those of us who belong to what has become known as the moderate animal welfare movement, who gave our support to help the Government get a consensus Bill through Parliament in 1985 and 1986, now expect results - in the form of significant reduction, refinement and replacement of animal experimentation, which must be obvious to all. As Lord Houghton of Sowerby said in the House of Lords on 15 June 1988 (anon, 1988j):

> "I do not want to utter any warnings, (but) those concerned should bear in mind that there could be a public reaction to failure to achieve what we set out to do in 1986. The whole animal welfare movement is waiting to see what happens. Nobody must be misled into thinking that this is a period of indifference".

## Bibliography and References

Anon. (1985) Scientific Procedures on Living Animals. Cmnd 9521, 255 pp. (London: HMSO).

Anon. (1986a) Animals (Scientific Procedures) Act 1986. 24pp. London: HMSO.

Anon. (1986b) Council Directive of 24 November 1986 on the Approximation of Law, Regulations and Administrative Provisions of the Member States Regarding the Protection of Animals Used for Experimental and Other Purposes. (Official Journal of the European Countries 29 (L358), 1-29.

Anon. (1987) The US Congress Office of Technology
Assessment report on Alternatives to Animal Use in
Research, Testing and Education. ATLA 14, 289-374.

Anon. (1988a) Alternatives to Animal Use in Research,
Testing and Education. 441pp. New York: Marcel
Dekker.

Anon. (1988b) Animal welfare versus medical research.
FRAME NEWS 18, 1-2.

Anon. (1988c) Animal welfare versus medical research.
ATLA 15, 273-275.

Anon. (1988d) Use of Animals in Biomedical and
Behavioural Research. Washington DC: National
Academy Press.

Anon. (1988e) Draft Preclinical Toxicologic
Guidelines. (Ottawa: Bureau of Human Prescription
Drugs, Health Protection Branch, Health and Welfare
Canada).

Anon. (1988f) Laboratory animal use increases.
Animal Welfare Institute Quarterly 37, 16.

Anon. (1988g) Animal experimentation in The
Netherlands. ATLA 15, 113-114.

Anon. (1988h) Animal use in Japan. ATLA 15, 278.

Anon. (1988i) House of Lords Official Report. Medical
research priorities. Hansard 498 (143), cols. 327-
330.

Balls, M. (1987) The OTA Report: a critical
appraisal. ATLA 14, 289-306.

Balls, M. (1988) Animal Experimentation - A Necessary
Evil? FRAME NEWS 20, 5

Balls, M: Riddell, RJ; Worden, AN., editors. (1983)
Animals and Alternatives in Toxicity Testing. 550pp.
(London and New York: Academic Press).

Bessis, M. (1985) Some reflections on scientific
research. Annals of the New York Academy of Sciences
459, 387-390.

Griffin, JP. (1988) A European CSM? British Medical
Journal 297, 312

Grubb, RL. (1987) Animal welfare versus medical
research. Neurosurgery 20, 809-810.

Morton, DB. (1987) Animal use in education and the
alternatives. ATLA 14, 334-343.

Orlans, FB. (1985) Science fairs - a sampling of misguided experiments. Animal Welfare Institute Quarterly 34, 108-111.

Paton, W. Man and Mouse: Animals in Medical Research. (Oxford: Oxford University Press, 1984).

Rowson, RH. (1988) A note on the "necessity" of using animals in research. ATLA 15, 311-312.

Taylor, J. (1988). Degrees of salary and satisfaction. Nature, London 334, 393-394.

Zbinden, G. (1988) A look behind drug regulatory guidelines. In: National and International Drug Safety Guidelines (S. Adler & G. Zbinden), pp. 7-14. (Zollikon: M.T.C. Verlag).

Margaret Rose

## REGULATION OF ANIMAL RESEARCH - THE AUSTRALIAN EXPERIENCE

The 1980s have seen major international developments in the regulation of the use of animals in research and teaching. Most notably, in the United Kingdom there has been the introduction of new legislation to replace the Act which pioneered this area - the 1876 Cruelty to Animals Act. Other examples include in the U.S. amendments both to the Animal Welfare Act and to the Public Health Services Policy, and in Europe ratification of the European Convention to Protect Animals Used for Scientific Purposes.

In Australia, we have also experienced these changes. In two States, Victoria (anon, 1986) and South Australia in 1975, (anon, 1985a) there were major revisions of their respective Prevention of Cruelty to Animals legislation, and specific sections were included relating to the use of animals for scientific purposes. In New South Wales, separate, and specific, legislation was proclaimed at the end of 1985 as The Animal Research Act (anon, 1985b). In principle, these legislative changes in Australia have a lot in common, and embody a common set of principles. Moreover, their ambit encompasses the use of animals in research, in product testing and development, and in teaching - including primary, secondary and tertiary institutions.

I should point out that in Australia the regulation of animal welfare is a State responsibility. We presently have no Commonwealth legislation, although since 1969 there has been a Code of Practice for the Care and Use of Animals for Experimental Purposes which has been sponsored by major Commonwealth organisations. This code was initially sponsored in 1969 by the National Health and Medical Research Council (NH & MRC) and in subsequent revisions by it jointly with CSIRO, and since 1985 by both these bodies with the Australian Agricultural Council (anon, 1985c). This Code has been adopted under regulation in the Victorian legislation and is the instrument of licensing in South Australia. Further, it has formed the basis for the Code of Practice to be incorporated into regulation in New South Wales.

So that this does not appear to be too confusing, I should hasten to add that the Code is currently being revised and the new version is presently being circulated for public comment. It is most likely that that document will be adopted under regulation, not only in Victoria, South Australia, and New South Wales, but also under proposed amendments to regulations in other States. Thus the principles in our legislation will be the same in all States - but the instrument of regulation may differ depending on the needs and interests of individual States. This somewhat tortuous and complex system has evolved because of the nature of our Federal Constitution, in which the interests of the individual States and their rights to autonomy are paramount.

These legislative changes in Australia have occurred against a background of increasing public debate on the issue of animal welfare in general, and animal research in particular. Public interest is such that in 1983 the Senate of our Federal Parliament established a Senate Select Committee on Animal Welfare (anon, 1983). The terms of reference of this committee are very broadly based, but include "animal experimentation" as one of the five major categories for consideration. As an indication of the public interest, this inquiry has generated more submissions than any other held previously by the Senate. The committee has, so far, issued reports on the live sheep export trade (anon 1985d), the keeping of cetacea in captivity (anon, 1985e) and the management of our kangaroo population (anon, 1988). The report on animal experimentation is due early in 1989, and will provide a very comprehensive and authoritative overview of the use of animals for research purposes within Australia. It will also identify our weaknesses and strengths.

One may well ask, why all this activity in so many countries? It seems to me that there have been two major forces at work. First, there is the changing attitude in our community towards the relationship and duties of human beings to other animals. Second, there is increasing demand for accountability and public participation in decisions that relate to the conduct of science, and the implementation of technology. That these factors had influenced the drafting of the Animal Research Act in N.S.W. was acknowledged by the Minister when he introduced that legislation into Parliament (1985f). He indicated that the Government´s primary concern was for the welfare of animals. He went on to say that it was conscious of the varying, and often emotive, attitudes in our community towards the use of animals for research purposes, and whilst acknowledging the significant contribution of animal-based research to both human and animal well-being, and wishing to avoid legislation which was unnecessarily restrictive, nevertheless, the Government believed that scientists should be publicly accountable for the use of, and care for, animals used in research, and that such accountability should be a legislative requirement. He indicated that the legislative proposals acknowledged that there were diverse, and sometimes opposing, views on the use of animals in research, and upheld the rights of groups or individuals to hold and express their differing views.

I believe that there is now a widely based societal expectation that the conduct of research and its use of animals goes beyond considerations of cruelty. Not only must we broaden our consideration of the interests of animals, but we must address the ethical issues involved. Such issues have been addressed at this conference by other speakers.

It seems to me that the problem we face is that we have no consensus in our community as to what is the moral standing of animals. Without that consensus, we have great difficulties in incorporating a set of principles into legislation. Moreover, if to resolve this conflict we opt for the lowest common denominator - which may be the easiest option - will we really achieve anything for animals, or for society? As noted by Tannenbaum and Rowan in an article in the Hastings Centre Report of October 1985, our ability to develop public policy which ultimately could be reflected in legislative principles, is very much limited by lack of a clear understanding of the ethical issues involved. To this end I, for one, await the reports of the Working Parties of the Institute of Medical Ethics in the U.K., and the Hastings Centre in New York, both of which are addressing this very important issue.

Despite these difficulties, I believe we must set mechanisms whereby these issues can be addressed within a legislative framework. The simple legislative approach of prescribing certain practices and procedures is not good enough in this instance. First, it may not ensure that the use of animals in research follows on from consideration of the ethical issues involved. David Britt (1984) has well argued how prescriptive legislation acts against consideration of ethical issues - the expedient justification becomes "it is all right to do this if the law says I can". The second major problem is the limits of prescriptive legislation in effectively regulating the conduct of science. An excellent example of this has been toxicology testing involving the LD50 and Draize tests - both of which would have been phased out sooner on scientific grounds if they were not being performed under the umbrella of "legislative requirements".

To avoid consideration of the complexity and difficulties of the moral issues involved would, I believe, be morally irresponsible. I believe it is better for us as a society to rigorously question the use of animals in research on a case-by-case basis, than to avoid the difficult decisions because we do not have moral consensus. Moreover, the basis of the decision to use animals will be that much better if it follows consideration of the various societal views. The difficulty is how to incorporate this process, with its need for flexibility, and the uncertainty in outcome of decisions, into a legislative framework. We are used to the law being an absolute authority - a statement of moral principle which embodies accepted values in society. And yet, if our judgement to use animals is to encompass consideration of ethical concerns, as I believe it must, we have no agreed principles on which to make a consensus judgement. Can we reconcile this probability of uncertainty with a legislative framework?

I believe we can - not by prescribing practices and procedures, but rather by enshrining the notions of responsibility and accountability in a legislative framework. You may ask whether that is not what all laws do? Yes, it is: but in these circumstances it is the mechanisms to ensure this responsibility and accountability which are so important.

Animal research is an activity of science, and any consideration relating especially to its regulation should take into account the nature and conduct of the scientific process.

I want to make a few quick points about the conduct of science which I see as being particularly relevant to this issue.

First, as noted by Sir William Paton in his book "Man and Mouse" (1984):

"Science is essentially a social activity: it´s purpose is not merely the acquiring of scientific knowledge, but also its communications".

Second, knowledge acquired as a result of the activity of science has an important value in society.

Third, the tradition of scientific freedom in the pursuit of knowledge is a widely held value in any democratic society. This tradition is so important to society as a whole that there must be very important values at stake before it is overridden (Warnock, 1986; Holborow, 1988).

Finally, it is widely believed that a central value of science is its objectivity. The problems of this assertion, particularly when there is conflict of scientific opinion, have been well developed in a monograph by Randell Albury entitled "The Politics of Objectivity" (1983), where he concludes that, in most such cases where scientific consensus is achieved, it is by social pressures and constraints, rather than by the rigour of scientific testing.

Questions relating to the use of animals in research involve two important issues of current debate in relation to the conduct of science. First, there is strong belief in our society in the "neutrality" of science - the notion that science is "value-free". I feel that Bronowski (1956) said it well when he said "....those who think science is ethically neutral confuse the findings of science with the activity of science".

The second important consideration is to establish what are the proper limits of scientific autonomy, particularly if there are competing moral claims as there are with the decision to use animals. Ultimately, the political process will determine the limits of public and scientific authority in research, including the decision not to proceed with a particular line of inquiry. Once again, we come back to the issue of the development of public policy, and the problems in the development of this policy as discussed by Tannenbaum and Rowan.

Clearly, we now recognise that the issue of the use of animals in research is complex. The decision to use animals involves consideration not only of the interests of animals, but the claims of the value of science and potential societal benefits. Thus, the values that we as a community will bring to the final judgement will be influenced by a range of views, not only about the moral standing of animals, but also about the value and impact of particular types of research. This issue is complex and value-laden, and emergence of these characteristics must determine not only the style of regulation but also community expectations of what such legislation will achieve.

We have sought different legislative solutions to these problems in various countries. These differences reflect cultural and regional needs. In Australia, we looked to develop a legislative mechanism to ensure responsibility and accountability for the decision to use animals, and how they are used, but one which will not unnecessarily stifle scientific enquiry. Public participation in the decision-making process is the basic tenet of our approach.

Central to this legislative approach is the operation of Animal Ethics Committees within each institution. Such committees are required by law in New South Wales, Victoria, and South Australia: in each instance there is a legal requirement for there to be a person on their committee who is not associated with the institution other than as a member of the committee. Further, there must be at least one representative on the committee with a demonstrated commitment to animal welfare.

Animal Ethics Committees are not new to Australian institutions, since their approval has been a requirement to receive NH & MRC funding since 1979. These committees have a number of functions, but their primary duty is to ensure that the Code of Practice, which I mentioned previously, is complied with insofar as it relates to the acquisition, housing, care and use of animals. To this end, Animal Ethics Committees must examine written proposals for the use of animals in research or teaching within the institution. They have the power to modify, reject, or approve such proposals. They then have a duty to monitor approved proposals to ensure their continued compliance with the Code of Practice. Other duties include development of specific guidelines including those for the use of alternatives, and ensuring that all personnel involved in animal care and use are appropriately instructed and competent.

The Committees must keep records of decisions and actions on all proposals. The revised Code which I mentioned earlier spells out in considerable detail the areas of responsibility, particularly as relating to institutions, to investigators, and to Animal Ethics Committees.

127

Probably the most controversy about these committees relates to the membership. There is particular concern that by insisting on public participation in the decision-making process, scientific progress will be impeded. However, in another area of conflict of values, the development of the in vitro fertilisation programme, the experience in Australia has been that public participation has made a positive contribution, not only to the decision-making process, but also to the ultimate outcome, and to public confidence in the programme (Bartells, 1983).

Community representation on these committees can influence their decisions in three ways:

1.   They serve the political function of reassuring the public that all is "above-board";

2.   through them the public can exercise its democratic right to influence scientific development, and

3.   they can make a positive contribution by widening the scope of the assessment process, so that broadly-based social concerns are considered.

The qualities which community representatives bring to such committees are important. What are the ideal characteristics of such a person? We have a parallel model to Animal Ethics Committees with Human Ethics Committees. These have been going for a sufficiently long period for some of these questions to have been asked of them. In that regard, Joan Porter (1986) surveyed non-scientist members of over 200 Human Ethics Committees in the USA. She tested the hypothesis that non-scientist members of these committees felt intimidated or unequal to the scientific members because of their lack of scientific knowledge. This was not seen by them to be the case. Based on their responses, she concluded that:

"the ideal unaffiliated/non-scientist member is assertive, self-confident, and intelligent, and able to make mature judgement and be sensitive, with a strong sense of ethical values".

She also sent a questionnaire to the chairpersons of committees. Their major concern was that non-scientist members would not have adequate scientific knowledge - this clearly was not the perspective of the non-scientist members themselves. Perhaps the rôle of lay members on Animal Ethics Committees is best summed up by Karl Obrink (1984) when he said:

".... laymen are indispensable in ethical discussions, both as carriers of a healthy scepticism and as a communication link between the laboratory and the community".

In Australia, the trend is now to have an increasing diversity of membership on Animal Ethics Committees. The effective operation of these Committees is obviously vital for the operation of our legislation. Members are drawn from three categories of persons: scientists, animal care staff and lay persons, each bringing particular skills, interests and knowledge to facilitate the Committees' judgements. The Committees do not seek to draw their membership from people with one point of view. Rather, they seek to bring together people of differing views in an attempt to find a practical solution to the issues involved. In addition to the person representing animal welfare interests, it is seen to be important and valuable to have a person who can bring an independent, community perspective to the decisions of the committee. Depending on the size and nature of the institution, often more than one member is external to the institution. However, we do recognise that there is potential for conflict in the operation and judgement of committees between scientists and non-scientists. We are attempting to address these issues. For example, we recently held a workshop with the purpose of exploring the expectations of the community and the involvement of lay/non-scientists members on Animal Ethics Committees (Kuchel, 1987).

Nevertheless, Animal Ethics Committees are not without their detractors. There are those who believe that such committees are little more than "rubber stamps" (Fox, 1981).

However, a more serious problem and limitation has been noted by Caplan (1987) when he discusses the problems of doing ethics by committees:

"Such a method presumes that the truth is most likely to emerge from the clash of such diverse opinions - a method that may be well suited when issues of law or science are at stake, but is not self-evidently appropriate for moral deliberation".

Similar concerns about the limitations of committees in reaching ethical judgement have been expressed in a recent report of the Science Council of Canada (anon, 1982) and in an article by Rebecca Dresser on the Operation of Animal Ethics Committees in a recent issue of Rutgers Law Review (1988).

Accepting these limitations, there are important advantages which effectively operated Animal Ethics Committees can bring to this vexed problem of the use of animals in research and teaching.

First, they provide a mechanism for connecting ethical and scientific considerations. As discussed by Lehmann (1979), critical judgement is considered to be the province of philosophers, but if it is to be sound and relevant to practical issues it needs to be informed through the kinds of information that is provided by scientists. The constructive interaction of these two disciplines is possible, and indeed essential, to the effective operation of Animal Ethics Committees. Second, the diversity of membership on these committees will bring a wider perspective to the decisions that are made - particularly through community input. Third, by the existence of these committees within institutions they can bring a closer and more direct supervision to the day-to-day operation of the conduct of animal research - an important strength of any system of enforced self-regulation (Braithwaite, 1982). And finally, as noted by Dresser (1985):

> "A review committee scrutinising such practices according to the standards proposed would find it difficult to avoid coping with the serious ethical questions that these practices raise".

However, not only must we have effective operational Animal Ethics Committees, but they must be accountable. There must be mechanisms to demonstrate their effectiveness to the satisfaction of the community.

In its submission to the Senate Select Committee on Animal Welfare, the Australian Vice-Chancellors' Committee believed that for any system to be effective in this area there must be external monitoring to ensure accountability. How this monitoring is achieved will vary.

As I mentioned previously, within Australia the regulatory responsibility for animal welfare is invested in the States and Territories. Under legislation in both Victoria and South Australia, the monitoring of the effective operation of Animal Ethics Committees is by government-appointed inspectors. In New South Wales, we also have government-appointed inspectors, but in addition we will have a system of accreditation, modelled on that which has been developed in North America by both the Canadian Council on Animal Care and the America Association for Accreditation of Laboratory Animal Care. In N.S.W., animal welfare representatives from the Animal Research Review Panel will participate in accreditation inspections.

However, such governmental activities can have only a limited impact in terms of ensuring the effective operation of Animal Ethics Committees. The principles by which Animal Ethics Committees operate, as embodied in the Code of Practice, and their raison d´être, is to promote good practice. Consequently, in addition to the regulatory function of government inspection in Australia, we have placed particular emphasis on the development of additional support systems which will promote and develop the concept of good practice within institutions, and at the level of work in the laboratory.

Some time ago the Commonwealth research body - CSIRO -in the absence of any legislative requirement, established a committee to advise its executive on the ethics of animal research. It brought onto this committee nominees of the RSPCA Australia Inc., the Australian and New Zealand Federation of Animal Societies, the National Farmers Federation, the bio-medical research community, and two eminent philosophers, Professors Peter Singer and John McCloskey. In addition, the CSIRO established an animal welfare liaison group to promote dialogue and discussion between its eighteen separate and diverse Animal Ethics Committees. This system of networking has, within this particular organisation, proved very effective - not only in raising awareness of the issues involved within its scientific community, but also in bringing community representation, and it may be said some of the most articulate and effective opponents of animal research, into the decision-making process.

The success of CSIROs activities has influenced the more recent development of the Australian Council on the Care of Animals in Research and Teaching (ACCART). ACCART was an initiative of the Australian Vice-Chancellors´ Committee and they, together with CSIRO and NH & MRC, are funding its operation for the first three years. ACCART has been developed to provide national networking of all interested parties, including government, scientists, animal welfare interests, and the community.

Finally, in any discussion of the development of regulations one must not forget that such development, by its very nature, involved the political process. In this arena, public perception of science and of the activity and integrity of scientists as well as the community´s values and beliefs about animals, will all come into play in the development of public policy.

In his paper, "The Dilemma of Animals: Real and Political", Senator Christopher Puplic (1987; at the workshop on Animal Ethics Committees which I mentioned previously) noted that, as a result of the interplay of these forces, he, as a legislator, was faced with three questions - first, what weight should he give to the expressed opinions of his constituents on these matters? Second, what are the proper limits of political control and regulation of the activity of science per se? And finally, how would he - as a non-scientist - decide between the competing claims of scientists where there are obvious areas of marked disagreement? Further, he noted that there were problems in the development of public policy if self-interest was promoted rather than a more global conceptual approach - if, for example, the issue was seen entirely as within the province of either the scientists or the animal welfarists.

Obviously the rôle of the political process within a democratic society is to ensure that decisions in the development of legislation will be based on informed judgement. Thus, within the political process, active involvement of all interested parties is essential if we are to resolve the conflicts in this debate - and more importantly, if we are to develop regulation which is effective and meets community expectations of realistic protection for animal interests.

I should not leave this discussion without mentioning the limitations of legislation and indicating the risks and limits of the legislative process in meeting societal objectives. First, as has been noted by authors such as Stone (1988) and Meth (1981), there are significant limits to the ability of legislation to deal with issues when there is a lack of moral consensus. Second, there are problems in the regulation of science.

In this regard, I have found the publication of the Science of Council of Canada, "Regulating the Regulators", to be particularly helpful (anon, 1982). There would seem to be two major problems. First, there is the apparent inflexibility of the legal process in responding to new knowledge and, second, there are major differences between the legal and the scientific concepts of fact, knowledge, probability, and proof.

In conclusion - in Australia institutional Animal Ethics Committees are the corner-stone of our approach to these issues. They must bring considered, collective judgement to the decision to use animals in research. To be effective they must be informed of issues, aware of community and scientific sensitivities, and committed to resolution of conflicts. By so doing they will have fulfilled community expectations of their duties, and will be accountable for their judgements.

I believe it would be fair to say that we are still learning how best to make these committees work. We must keep the operation of these committees, and indeed of our whole legal programme in this area, under critical review. However, as noted by Thomas Moss (1984) in a discussion of the development of an appropriate regulatory system in relation to the use of animals in research:

"If the entire enterprise can be shown to be approaching the standards of best animal treatment and care, most of the tensions at this particular science/public interface could be resolved".

Finally, I would like to return to the theme where I began in discussion of the complexity of the issues involved and close with a quotation by Margaret and Jonathan Stone (1986) in a paper entitled "Principles and Animals":

"If the debate continues without recognition of the complexity of the relationship at its centre, ......then it is likely to remain stalemated.

The constructive alternative, we suggest, is to avoid simplification of the problem, to accept that no simple solution is at hand, and to get on with the job of identifying those problems for which a community consensus seems within reach. We must undertake the hard work of debating, proposing and compromising needed to identify, encode, and continually review the moral values shared within our society.... Moral progress grows from consensus, and those who would solve a complex moral problem must face the compromises needed, not as a second-best way forward but as the only way".

## References and Bibliography

Albury, R. The Politics of Objectivity. (Deakin University Press, Victoria, 1983).

Anon (1982) Science Council of Canada Report. Regulating the Regulators, Science, Values and Decisions. (Canadian Government Publishing Centre).

Anon (1983a) Commonwealth of Australia, Senate Daily Hansard. Wednesday, 16th November, 2615-2620.

Anon (1985a) Prevention of Cruelty to Animals Act, 1985. No. 106 of 1985. (South Australia, Government Printer).

Anon (1985b) Animal Research Act 1985 No.123. (New South Wales, Government Printer).

Anon (1985c) Code of Practice for the Care & Use of Animals for Experimental Purposes, 1985. (Canberra, Australian Government Publishing Service).

Anon (1985d) Export of Live Sheep from Australia. Report by the Senate Select Committee on Animal Welfare. (Canberra, Australian Government Publishing Service).

Anon (1985e) Dolphins & Whales in Captivity. Report by the Senate Select Committee on Animal Welfare. Australian Government Publishing Service, Canberra.

Anon (1985f) New South Wales Parliament Daily Hansard. 2nd October, LA35-La39, continued 30th October 1985, LA127-LA147.

Anon (1986) Prevention of Cruelty to Animals Act (1986). Acts 1986 No. 46. (Melbourne, Victorian Government Printing Office).

Anon (1988) Kangaroos. Report by the Senate Select Committee on Animal Welfare (Canberra, Australian Government Publishing Service).

Bartells, D. (1983) in Albury, R. The Politics of Objectivity: 62-79. (Deakin University Press, Victoria).

Braithwaite, J. 1982 Michelin Law Review., 80:1466-1507.

Britt, D. Nature, 311 (1984): 503-505.

Bronowski, J. Science and Human Values. (Harper & Row, New York 1956).

Caplan, AL. (1987) Laboratory Animal Science., Special Issue, 37: 45-49.

Dresser, R. (1985) South California Law Review, 58:1146-1201.

Dresser, R. (1988) Rutgers Law Review., 40723-795.

Fox, MW. (1981) Psychopharm. Bull; 17:80-93.

Holborow, L. in. Rose, MA. (editor). Animal Experimentation: Ethical, Scientific & Legal Perspectives. (University of New South Wales, Sydney: 130-138, 1988).

Kuchel, TR (editor). Animal Ethics Committees - Their Structure, Function and Ethical Dimension. (Australian Society for Laboratory Animal Science, Canberra 1987).

Lehmann, H. (1979) Animal Regulation Studies 2:255-257.

Meth, TS. (1981). The Limits of Legislation in Achieving Social Change. International Journal for the Study of Animal Problems., 2: 121-124.

Moss, TH. (1984). Science. Technology. Human Values, 9:51-54.

Obrink, KJ. (1984). in Bankowski, A: Howard-Jones, N Biomedical Research Involving Animals, CIOMS. Geneva. 156-164.

Paton, W. Man and Mouse. (Oxford University Press, 1984).

Porter, JP. IRB, Hastings Center N.Y.: 8 (1986):1-4.

Puplic, C. (1987) in Kuchel, T.R. (editor). Animal Ethics Committees - Their Structure, Function and Ethical Dimension. Australian Society for Laboratory Animal Science, Canberra. 10-23.

Stone, M.   (1988) in. Rose, M.A. (editor) <u>Animal
Experimentation:   Ethical,  Scientific and Legal
Perspectives</u>.  University of New South Wales.  145-
149.

Stone, M: Stone, J. <u>Current Affairs Bulletin</u>., 63: 3-
13.  1986.

Tannenbaum, J: Rowan, AN. (1985)  Hastings Center
Report,   15;32-43.

Warnock, M: Conquest. (1986) N<u>o</u>. 175; 1-9.

Gill Langley

## ESTABLISHMENT REACTIONS TO ALTERNATIVES

The systematic development of non-animal research techniques as replacements for animal experiments has a short history, being a concept first expressed fully by Russell and Burch in their seminal work, The Principles of Humane Experimental Technique (Russell and Burch, 1959). Before that time, although there were examples of animal tests being superseded by in vitro methods, such as with the assay of vitamin preparations, this was not part of a deliberate and coherent policy based on humane or ethical considerations.

Motivation is important. Where scientific standards or questions of time and money are the only driving forces for developing humane research technologies, these may well progress in certain restricted fields (such as specific areas of toxicology), but only in a haphazard and unco-ordinated way. Even in these areas the potential of non-animal tests may not be perceived, and animal experiments causing pain or distress may continue unmodified for decades. In the case of original research, as opposed to toxicity testing, alternative methods may be applied where they have been validated and accepted into mainstream science (such as in cell-based cancer research), but they are less likely to be originated in this field. The Medical Research Council (MRC) has often stated that while research that it funds may lead to the evolution of non-animal techniques, the development of new methods "in isolation" from research which they might replace will not be supported. In a recent letter to me, the Secretary of the MRC reiterated this position, and pointed out that in the MRC's view it is not practicable for scientists to be engaged specifically in devising alternatives as their sole or main activity separately from research experiments (Rees, 1988).

Without a broad-based policy founded on an ethical commitment to replacing animal experiments, the process is bound to be fragmented and slower than necessary. The anti-vivisection movement and the humane research organisations have done much to provide the required stimulus, not only by funding novel research in this area but also by focusing the minds of scientists and government authorities on the scientific inadequacies of many animal experiments and the need for a better approach. Theirs were the innovative conferences on alternative research in the early 1970s - such as those of the Universities Federation for Animal Welfare in 1971, the National Anti-Vivisection Society and also the Dr Hadwen Trust for Humane Research in 1973. Company-sponsored or independent symposia on this topic did not occur until 1980 onwards. Considering the general belief that science is a forward-looking, progressive activity, it seems extraordinary that scientists have been content to continue using animal tests which they themselves have

criticised as unreliable or unreproducible. The LD50
test, used since 1927 to assess acute (short-term)
toxicity, and the Draize eye test, used since 1944 to
measure the irritancy of substances to the eye, are
classic examples.

**Table 1**

**British organisations established to promote alternatives**

| Organisation | Founders | Date/Place |
|---|---|---|
| Lawson Tait Memorial Trust | British Anti-Vivisection Societies | 1961, Cheshunt |
| FRAME | Small Group of Anti-Vivisectionists | 1969, Nottingham |
| Dr Hadwen Trust for Humane Research | British Union for the Abolition of Vivisection | 1970, Hitchin |
| Lord Dowding Fund for Humane Research | National Anti-Vivisection Society | 1973, London |
| Humane Research Trust | Lawson-Tait Trustees | 1974, Cheshire |

(Other organisations occasionally fund humane research,
such as UFAW, Potters Bar; and the St Andrew Animal Fund,
Edinburgh. Quest for a Test for Cancer, Harlow, funds
cancer research without animal experiments, although it is
not primarily publicised as a humane research charity).

**Complacency and motivation**

The LD50 test, originally devised as an assay method for
standardising biological medicines such as digitalis, was
adopted on an international basis as a convenient means of
estimating acute toxicity. The LD50 value of a substance
derived by the test gradually assumed the reliability of a
physical constant in some toxicologists' minds, despite
the variability in LD50 values obtained not only in
different species but even in different sexes and genetic
strains of the same animals. In view of the acknowledged
problems with the test, few efforts were made by the
research community to find a more effective technique or a
more humane one.

In 1976 a group of animal welfarists corresponded and had

meetings with the Home Office. One of their demands was that, because of public concern, a review should be undertaken of the LD50 test, and the Home Office concurred. The Report of the Advisory Committee (Home Office, 1979) was disappointing. While acknowledging that severe pain could be inflicted during the test whose results were not always reliable, the Committee made no bold recommendations and launched no initiatives. The anti-vivisection movement, building on this earlier groundwork, targeted the LD50 test in 1980 and drew wider public attention to the suffering it inflicted on animals, as well as to its unreliability.

Since then there has been a flurry of research effort in Europe and America to find cell or organ culture alternatives to the test. Meanwhile, toxicologists found their voices and began to admit publicly that the classic LD50 was not entirely useful; they also discovered that they were able to refine the technique (using fewer animals and lower doses), thus causing less suffering. Between 1982 and 1984, Avon reduced animal use in toxicity testing by about 30 per cent per year. Colgate-Palmolive made a 50 per cent reduction in 1983. In 1987, Du Pont reported a 60 per cent reduction in use of animals. The approximate LD50 test and the Limit test were refinements which could have been adopted at any time in the last twenty years, but this did not happen, presumably due to the complacency of toxicologists and regulatory bodies.

In 1984, the British Toxicology Society (BTS) published a proposed system of assessing acute toxicity which would reduce the number of animals used, and suggested the humane killing of animals which became distressed (British Toxicology Society, 1984). The report referred to an increasing scrutiny of "the ethical and scientific justification for using laboratory animals in toxicological studies", and to the concerns of toxicologists and "those primarily interested in animal welfare". It was followed in 1987 by publication of the results of a feasibility study of the BTS proposals, which were very favourable (British Toxicology Society, 1987). Drug control authorities such as the American Food and Drug Administration and the British Department of Health have announced that they no longer require the classic LD50 test for regulatory purposes - a welcome review of the situation but again, one which should - and could - have come about many years ago.

The case of the Draize eye test is similar. Weil and Scala published a review of Draize test data showing wide discrepancies due to the subjective method of assessing eye damage in rabbits (Weil and Scala, 1971). The variation was extreme between laboratories; the scientific community did little to reduce suffering caused by the technique, although efforts were made to render it more reproducible. The Dr Hadwen Trust for Humane Research funded one of the first efforts to find a replacement, using cell cultures, during 1976 and 1977 - a study which laid the groundwork for later developments. In 1981, coalitions of animal protection societies world-wide singled out cosmetic companies in hard-hitting and professional publicity campaigns against the eye test. As a direct result, a number of companies began to contribute to research programmes and centres to develop humane alternatives to the Draize eye test. There was a surge of research, and several techniques are now at the stage of validation. In 1987, the Home Office belatedly issued guidelines on reducing the risk of suffering during the test, which is finally coming to the end of its 53-year-old history.

## Table 2

### Diary of events regarding the LD50 and Draize eye tests

**Date**     **Event**

1975-6
   Public concern over LD50 test during Animal Welfare Year

1976
   Group of animal welfarists request Home Office review of LD50 test

1976-7
   Dr Hadwen Trust funds one of the first efforts to develop an alternative to the Draize test

1979
   British Home Office Advisory Committee Report on the LD50 test

1980-82
   International coalition of animal welfare/anti-vivisection societies campaign against both tests and demand that user companies fund research into alternatives

1980
   Revlon donates to Rockefeller University, USA, to develop an alternative to the Draize test

1980
   The US Cosmetics, Toiletry and Fragrance Association holds a conference on in vitro and in vivo eye testing

1981
   Cosmetic companies provide start-up funding for the Johns Hopkins Centre for Alternatives to Animal Testing, USA

1981-87
   Numerous research projects to develop alternatives to LD50 and Draize eye test are initiated world-wide

1981-87
  Chemical and cosmetic companies in USA report
  reduction in use of animals in LD50 test

1984
  British Toxicology Society publishes proposed system
  of assessing acute toxicity with reduced animal
  numbers and suffering

1986
  Use of animals in Draize eye Test falls from 31,400 in
  1977 to 11,300

1987
  British Toxicology Society publishes proposals for
  assessing eye irritancy using fewer animals

1988
  Johns Hopkins Centre reports the start of validation
  studies of Draize eye test alternatives


## Failure of imagination

Despite Russell and Burch's enthusiasm for progress in
humane research techniques, nearly 30 years ago,
researchers as a whole have shown little of the flair and
innovation with which the public credits them. The
inactivity of successive governments is perhaps more in
keeping with public perceptions.

The 1959 publication made many far-sighted suggestions of
areas where alternatives to animal experiments could be
explored: toxicity testing and bioassays were singled out
as fields of particular concern, either because of the
suffering caused or the large numbers of animals used.
Despite Russell and Burch's suggestions that human cells
in culture or simple metazoa (primitive organisms) might
be explored as possible alternatives, remarkably little
was done until the early 1980s, when both ideas were
developed further. In part, this lack of progress can be
attributed to the high fidelity fallacy: the assumption
that animals who most consistently resemble humans and are
close to us on the evolutionary scale (ie. are high
fidelity models) are the most suitable for studies of
specific toxicities. The "hi-fi enthusiasts" fail to see
that an organism much lower on the evolutionary tree, or
indeed a cell culture, may be much more sensitive for the
key feature of interest.

An example of a low-fidelity, high discrimination model is
the use of bacteria in the Ames test, to assess the
mutagenic potential of substances to humans. While a
bacterium resembles us very little in general (it is a low
fidelity model), it is similar to us in its sensitivity to
mutagens. The Ames test originated in America in 1971,
and is now used as a pre-screen for carcinogens, thus
reducing the need for long-term rodent carcinogenicity
tests. Rats and mice are considered as fairly high-

fidelity models of humans, and their use in these tests was accepted for many years as reasonably predictive of human responses to carcinogens. After America "declared war on cancer" in the 1970s, animal tests for carcinogens increased in numbers, yet it was not until 1983 that a statistical survey of the results and their applicability to humans was published (Salsburg, 1983). This showed that the tests had a less than 50 per cent success rate in predicting human carcinogens. In 1984, another report surveying data from tests in rats and mice concluded that 46 per cent of chemicals found to be carcinogenic in one species were apparently non-carcinogenic in the other (Di Carlo, 1984).

**Table 3**      (from Brusick, 1983)

**Comparison of rodent and in vitro carcinogenicity tests**

| Test system | Performance time | Cost |
|---|---|---|
| Rodent test | 2 - 3 years | £600,000 – £1,000,000 |
| in vitro (Ames – cell culture) | 3 months | £30,000 – £100,000 |

Thus the high-fidelity animal models have proven to be of low discrimination or sensitivity when it comes to detecting human carcinogens, and the use of more remote models - such as bacteria, yeasts, and human cells in culture - may yet prove more sensitive and relevant in this sphere. The failure of imagination can be seen in this statement made in 1969 by two toxicologists, just two years before Bruce Ames published his technique for detecting mutagens (and hence most carcinogens) with bacteria:

"The investigation of possible carcinogenic or embryoplastic effects, interference with growth and development, or irreversible damage to vital organs, can only be studied in animals" (Frazer and Sharratt, 1969).

Just fourteen years later, having seen many successful developments in these fields, another toxicologist directly contradicted those words by saying:

"Not all types of toxicity tests are amenable to in vitro or sub-mammalian alternative techniques. The three types of toxic phenomena discussed previously, genetic disease, cancer and terata, however, are uniquely adaptable" (Brusick, 1983).

**Inertia and orthodoxy**

In the June 1988 issue of the AV Magazine (the journal of the American Anti-Vivisection Society), Martin Fettman, a veterinarian and adviser to the International Foundation for Ethical Research, expressed the following view regarding the attitudes of scientists to alternatives:

"Pre-existing barriers to this change in gestalt include hurdles we all have encountered in our lives: security with the status quo (if it works, why fix it?), resistance to change (the difficulty of re-training oneself), cynicism (the new technology may only replace old problems with new ones), and fear of failure (the methodology may be inadequate, I may be inadequate, or my colleagues may think me inadequate)".

With many years' experience of specific experimental techniques or establishing an animal "model" of a human disease, it is understandable that researchers may be reluctant to adopt novel approaches; but they often claim they are immune to such fears and worries, and that they embrace new methodologies eagerly once they have been validated. Sometimes a new idea simply may not occur to someone who has used a routine procedure for some time, and knows its wrinkles (cf. Dixon, 1978).

I witnessed a classic example when, in 1980, I attended a conference on in vitro mutagenicity assays. The Ames bacterial mutation test requires the addition to liver enzymes of test chemicals to metabolise as the liver would do in vivo, and the usual source of these was (and is) rat liver, as a mixture called S-9. Robert Sharpe stood up in the audience and asked why the possibility of using human liver enzymes had not been explored, and the assembled toxicologists turned to him with blank expressions and asked why such a thing should be considered. After all, the rat liver system was well understood, and rat livers were in plentiful supply. Robert pointed out that problems of species differences might reduce the validity of the Ames test, since rat livers could metabolise some chemicals differently from human livers. The point was virtually dismissed as irrelevant. Interestingly, the DHSS Guidelines for the Testing of Chemicals for Toxicity, published only two years later, included the following on the subject of mutagenicity testing:

"....in the assessment of risk to man (sic) there are obvious theoretical advantages in the use of S-9 mix prepared from human tissues, which may differ from tissues prepared from rats... in their ability to activate or detoxify chemicals" (Department of Health and Social Security, 1982, p37).

Perhaps this is a rare case of regulatory authorities being more progressive than the scientific community itself, but on the whole such authorities and control bodies, while understandably being cautious, are not as attentive as they should be to animal test alternatives.

The following examples illustrate inertia and resistance to change in the world of science and regulation.

In 1953, the U.K.´s Chief Medical Officer said that the only way to be sure of diagnosing tuberculosis (TB) was to inject tissue samples from suspected patients into guinea pigs to see if they developed the infection. At that time, a cell culture method was being used in conjunction with the guinea pig test, which required 80,752 animals a year. Over a number of years the cell culture technique was improved, and guinea pig tests were conducted less frequently. In 1972, the Tuberculosis Reference Laboratory (TRL) reported that the culture method was more successful and recommended that it replace the animal test (Marks, 1972). This should have spelled the virtual demise of the guinea pig technique. Nevertheless, in 1986 - fourteen years later - it came to light that the Medical Microbiology Department of the London Hospital was still routinely inoculating guinea pigs (as well as using the cell culture method) for the diagnosis of TB, and between 1981 and 1985 it had used 677 animals. Detailed records had been kept, and showed that the two tests produced identical results in 96 per cent of cases, confirming the TRL´s experience of the reliability of the cell test when conducted skilfully. In only one case out of 677 had the guinea pig test provided data of use to clinicians.

A lengthy correspondence ensued between the Home Office and Clive Hollands, who offered the evidence of several leading microbiologists that the guinea pig test is obsolete in all save a very few special cases, and that the culture method is more sensitive, quicker and easier to perform. Just as the Home Office agreed to scrutinise more carefully future licence applications for the guinea pig procedure, the London Hospital announced that it would no longer use the animal technique - ostensibly on the grounds that it had suddenly decided it could not justify the expense.

Another example of lethargy in accepting alternative methods is provided by the history of polio vaccine. Polio vaccine became a medical reality only when it was discovered in 1949 that the virus could be grown in cultured cells. Weller, one of the scientists who received a Nobel Prize for this development, recommended the use of human rather than monkey tissues since there was always a chance that there might be an unknown strain of polio virus which would appear safe in monkey cells but might attack human tissues. Wild-caught monkeys also carried viruses which could be dangerous to humans. His advice was ignored, partly because monkeys were already conveniently present in laboratories, and for many years the vaccine was produced from virus grown in primary (short-lived) monkey kidney cells. This meant, in practice, that enormous numbers of monkeys had to be killed for their tissues. It has been estimated that between 1955 and 1976, 1 to 2 million wild-caught monkeys died in laboratories for the purpose of polio vaccine production and batch testing, discounting the many more which were killed at the time of capture or perished during holding, transport and quarantine. Yet between 30% and 80% of cultures from monkey kidney cells have to be discarded because they contain unwanted and possible dangerous viruses.

An increasing shortage of suitable monkey species in the 1970s called for a different approach, and it was found that in the right conditions the virus would grow in human diploid cells - cells which can survive and propagate in culture for longer periods. The wheel had turned full circle: Weller's recommendations were adopted after thirty years, and the untold suffering of millions of wild monkeys ceased.

Thus, the stable human cell line had been developed in 1961, but was not used until 1971 for polio vaccine production. This delay resulted from suspicions regarding the stability of the cells and from an attitude that it is better to stay with a system whose drawbacks are understood (Hayflick, 1969). The WHO, in its report on the use of cells for the production of biological medicines (World Health Organisation, 1987), touched on the topic:

"it took a decade or more for human diploid cell substrates to be accepted by certain national control authorities, even though all of the available scientific evidence indicated that products derived from them were safe to use".

Dr Frank Perkins, of WHO, also detected the reluctance to adopt new, humane and effective methods, and wrote regarding polio vaccine:

"The arguments, personal positions, misconceptions and preconceived ideas that dominated that situation retarded progress for several years. They were arguments that had no more foundation than those put forward against the use of monkey kidney cells on the grounds that every child given Salk vaccine would have nephritis" (Perkins, 1980).

All vaccines must undergo tests to ensure that the virus has not reverted to a virulent (disease-causing) form, and in the case of the Salk polio vaccine, for 25 years this was done by testing both in live monkeys and by in vitro tests using primary monkey cells. Both are wasteful of life and have relied mainly on wild-caught primates. Dr Perkins questioned the value of the live monkey test by saying:

"Since the early days of the Cutter incident (when many people contracted polio as a result of vaccination), which was never satisfactorily resolved from the laboratory standpoint, I know of no killed poliomyelitis vaccine that has been shown to contain live virus in the monkey test alone.... What value has the monkey test therefore?" (Perkins, 1980).

After a quarter of a century of duplicate testing, the WHO finally recommended in 1982 that the cell culture test should stand alone, and now it seems that a long-lived type of cell may be used so that monkeys will no longer need to be killed for their tissues.

A final example of delayed replacement of animal tests in the polio vaccine saga relates to the use of small animals - rabbits, guinea pigs and adult and suckling mice - to ensure that each batch of polio vaccine is free of contaminating viruses of any sort. These tests have often been conducted both by the vaccine manufacturer and by the national control body, in addition to the normal stringent controls which ensure that no extraneous viruses can infect the vaccine. Dr Perkins again:

"I have not heard of any batch of vaccine that has been shown to be unsatisfactory purely on the grounds of tests in small laboratory animals. In 1962 there were 23 laboratories producing oral poliomyelitis vaccine; today (1980) there are 11 laboratories involved. If we take as an average figure 15 laboratories each year for the last 20 years and if each produced 10 batches of vaccine a year, then 120,000 mice, 60,000 suckling mice, 30,000 guinea pigs and 60,000 rabbits have been used without adding anything to the safety of vaccines. At the very least there should be no necessity to repeat these tests by the control authority" (Perkins, 1980).

Happily, in 1982 the WHO recommended that small animal tests be dropped when human diploid cells are the source of virus for polio vaccine.

Delays of this sort, arising from fixed preconceptions and unnecessary orthodoxy, were documented by Russell and Burch in 1959 for a whole range of procedures involving the refinement and replacement of animal experiments. These included replacing animal assays of vitamins with microbiological tests; the persistent use of a less effective and more inhumane pregnancy test using rabbits when an accurate, more humane and speedy alternative technique existed; delays in the adoption of statistical methods; and failure to tackle areas of experimentation where animal suffering is likely (Russell and Burch, 1959, p157). Bernard Dixon has also noted orthodoxy among scientists when considering novel techniques, in this case those who operate the much-vaunted peer review system of the funding committees. Such a committee, he wrote:

"Is looking to further the progress of science in a way which will also throw credit on the wisdom with which it has distributed the funds at its disposal. But such cabals are invariably packed with currently and previously successful practitioners of the branch of science concerned. They are not, therefore, likely to be receptive to heterodox proposals which offend against their own conventional wisdom" (Dixon, 1976).

A recent report of the US National Academy of Sciences supported this claim, having found that scientists using unconventional systems and models have difficulty in finding funding. The committee took a step in the right direction by recommending that good research should be funded "without taxonomic or phylogenetic bias" (National Academy of Sciences, 1985). The role of the humane research charities since the mid-1960s has been pivotal in countering this funding orthodoxy, by providing "pump-priming" funds to allow the origination of novel methods. As data has accumulated for the new techniques, orthodox funding has tended to follow more easily and, indeed, the humane research organisations rely on later financing from bodies such as the research councils, as they seldom have the funds to see a project through from starting point to final validation.

## Inappropriate expectations

One of the barriers to the acceptance of non-animal methods of research and testing is that scientists, familiar with the old ways, insist that new techniques must provide better data than animal experiments before they can replace them. Obviously we are all keen to improve the relevance of medical research and toxicity testing, but to insist on higher standards than have been accepted for many years in the form of animal tests is to dwell on scientific efficacy to the total exclusion of ethical concern for laboratory animals.

If scientists have happily accepted less than reliable animal-based procedures, they should be prepared to adopt humane alternatives which provide data of equal value. A toxicologist (Brusick, 1983), writing in a special issue of the Annals of the New York Academy of Sciences on alternatives to large-scale animal tests, insisted that two important criteria would have to be met: firstly, that the alternative test will not increase the risk to human health beyond that permitted by animal tests – an eminently reasonable request. His second criterion was that the introduction of the alternative should lead to "greater efficiency" in assessing toxicity than currently available animal models – a quite unreasonable requirement. All tests are scientific compromises, but at least humane technology is not an ethical compromise as well. As Professor Jim Bridges, who has many years' experience with in vitro toxicology, said at a conference in 1983: there is a "natural lethargy" to taking up non-animal methods unless they are better than in vivo ones, even though ethical constraints should dictate otherwise.

This attitude is partly the cause of the irritating habit which the establishment has of claiming that non-animal technology is an "adjunct" but not an "alternative" to animal experiments. The Research Defence Society has actually gone so far in minimising the success of

146

alternatives as to write, in a review of a book funded by
the Dr Hadwen Trust, that the authors review "aspects of
the use of alternatives in experimental work and in
testing in an attempt to ascertain which, if any, offer
real possibilities as alternatives" (Research Defence
Society, 1988). Yet the evidence of replacement, partial
or total, is there for anyone who has eyes to see. The
Ames test has replaced a large proportion of animal
carcinogenicity tests; chemical and physical techniques
have replaced animal assays for numerous hormones and
vitamins; the cell culture diagnostic test for TB has, at
last, replaced the guinea pig method; cell culture methods
have replaced animal tests in the production and testing
of many vaccines, including rabies, polio and yellow
fever; 110 years after mice were first used to measure
levels of tetanus antitoxin in the blood, a non-animal
method replaced them saving about 5,000 mice a year in
Britain alone; pregnancy testing is now done _in vitro_
instead of using rabbits, _Xenopus_ toads and mice; computer
programs have partly replaced the use of animals in
practical classes at university level; the Limulus
amoebocyte lysate test is replacing the rabbit in tests
for pyrogenicity of intravenous fluids.

It seems that new techniques go through several phases of
acceptance. Firstly there is sometimes hostility to the
new idea. More data is demanded, and extra validation is
undertaken. The technique may be accepted as useful in
addition to animal procedures. The goalposts may be
moved, so that better data is required of the new method.
It may run alongside animal procedures for many years
before being accepted in principle as a real alternative.
Usually advantages of cost and time encourage final
acceptance. Pockets of resistance can remain, to be
overcome only when attention is drawn to them, sometimes
by animal welfare groups. Although establishment
acceptance may be withheld for a period, the technique
actually replaces a considerable number of animals in a
gradual way for some time prior to this.

## Progress and problems in the scientific establishment

Having dwelt at some length, and critically, on the
response of the scientific establishment to the need for
the success of alternatives, it is only fair to highlight
some of its more recent and positive reactions.
Admittedly, because of massive public concern generated by
anti-vivisection campaigns, some cosmetic companies in
America and Britain have established and contributed to
specific programmes of research aimed at developing _in
vitro_ alternatives to animal toxicity tests.

Companies such as Unilever in Britain have done a
considerable amount of basic cell culture work, some of it
with the aim of generating replacement tests. During the
1980s, ICI has had a high profile, both for its in-house
research into alternatives (for example the use of
isolated skin fragments for testing the corrosiveness of

chemicals) and its support of selected humane research charities. The American Council on Economic Priorities has presented Proctor and Gamble with a "corporate conscience" award in recognition of its efforts to seek alternatives and persuade federal agencies to consider these techniques. The British Industrial Biological Research Association (BIBRA), funded by industry and by government, announced in its 1985 annual report that £200,000 per annum had been allocated to the development of alternatives. The National Institute for Biological Standards and Control have made remarkable progress in replacing animal-based assays of biological medicines with in vitro and chemical techniques. Beecham Pharmaceuticals have contributed expertise and data to research, funded by the Dr Hadwen Trust for Humane Research, aimed at replacing the Draize eye test, but has been occasionally reluctant to publicise this, to the point that publications have been delayed as a result.

In conversation with researchers in university departments, it has emerged that an element of secrecy prevails in commercial companies in this context, as in others. There has been a general reluctance to release Draize test data for comparison with results using non-animal systems. Unilever has failed to publish in scientific journals up-to-date information about its pre-screen for the Draize eye test, which uses isolated rabbits´ eyes. Despite this very unscientific unwillingness to expose its results to peer review, the Home Office has taken the unusual step of recommending the technique to toxicologists, presumably having access to unpublished information on the merits of the method. There is an industrial in vitro toxicology group, but apparently it has refused membership of non-commercial scientists, possibly on the grounds that the group´s interest is mainly scientific and economic, and it is not primarily concerned about ethical motivations. Such exclusivity breeds the risk of stultification. The feeling is generally that considerable information on in vitro toxicity procedures exists in-house in industry, but pressures to publish are not the same as for the academic scientist. To prevent duplication of effort and hasten progress, it is crucial that these data become more widely available.


## Government inertia and action

Governments are very much a part of the establishment with regard to reactions to alternatives. Successive governments in Britain have been extraordinarily resistant to formally financing and otherwise promoting non-animal technology. A brief historical review of the period when humane research was still young illustrates the general parliamentary approach, which has been negative until events and public pressure forced a different response. The 1965 Report of the Departmental Committee on Experiments on Animals, chaired by Sir Sydney Littlewood, had a pessimistic view based on the questioning of scientific witnesses:

> "The replies have been unanimous in assuring us that such methods are actively sought and when found are readily adopted; and that the discovery of an <u>in vitro</u> test... which will satisfactorily replace a test on the living animal is always a welcome event... Discoveries of adequate substitutes for animal tests have, however, so far been uncommon, and we have not been encouraged to believe that they are likely to be more frequent in the future" (Littlewood, 1965, p26).

The Committee, in its Report, drew attention to one important question which it left unanswered:

> "Who can say whether, if certain biological tests were forbidden, satisfactory chemical of other methods of testing would not be developed?"

Time has shown that, even in the absence of such an edict, many biological tests have indeed been reduced or replaced by alternatives, an indication of what more could be done with additional motivation, skill and funds.

One of the earliest debates on alternatives in the House of Commons was in March 1971, and among the speakers was the then Mr Douglas Houghton, whose persistent and brilliant work on behalf of laboratory animals we are celebrating at this meeting. It was proposed that a special institute be established to develop alternatives and to act as a world-wide information source on the subject. Mrs Thatcher, as Secretary of State for Education and Science, replied that such an institute would be unlikely to be

> "as effective as existing approaches" (virtually non-existent), "mainly because of the difficulties of ensuring that the staff of the institute kept in day-to-day contact with the specific problems for which animal experiments are needed".

Since 1973, the Fund for the Replacement of Animals in Medical Experiments (FRAME) has published abstracts of publications on non-animal research, and similar work was done by the Salem Institute in Munich in the mid-1970s.

It is interesting to reflect on the fact that FRAME received a grant from Mrs Thatcher´s government in 1984 to initiate a computerised database on tissue culture alternatives, some 15 years after her original refusal. And although there is no British institute for alternative research, such centres have been set up in other countries, for example the Johns Hopkins Centre for Alternatives to Animal Testing in Baltimore, established in 1981.

Parliamentary questions have been raised at frequent intervals on the topic of alternatives. In 1970, the Earl of Dalkeith asked Mrs Thatcher what financial assistance she intended to make available through the Medical Research Council to the Lawson Tait Trust. Mrs Thatcher replied in the negative, asserting that it was not government policy to financially assist voluntary bodies as such. Her policy changed in the 1980s with a number of grants to FRAME - presumably in response to increasing public concern about animal experiments and in favour of humane research.

Throughout the early 1970s questions were asked as follows:

1971: Will the Secretary of State appoint a commission to study and publicise alternatives? Answer: No

1975: What action is the Secretary of State taking to promote alternatives to animals in biological testing? Answer: The Medical Research Council welcomes such developments in the course of research and urges their publication.

1975: Does the Secretary of State have plans to divert some funds from animal experiments into non-animal experiments? Answer: The Medical Research Council (MRC) advises that it would not be practicable to allocate funds on the basis of the means rather than the purpose of research.

Yet the government now has offered funds in the region of £60,000 a year to be administered by the Home Office for just such a purpose. In this it has belatedly followed the example of the Swedish government, which in 1979 established the National Board for Laboratory Animals, one of whose tasks was to support the development of humane research by means of special grants.

During the 1970s a number of early day motions were introduced, again with no positive outcome, and there were also several private members' bills. In 1970, a bill introduced by Richard Body proposed an amendment to the Cruelty to Animals Act which would have forbidden an animal experiment "if the purpose of the experiment can be achieved by alternative means not involving an experiment on living animals". The bill failed, as did another with the same intent, introduced by Douglas Houghton in 1972. An identical bill was introduced in 1975, and yet another later the same year which proposed that "no experiment on a living animal shall be performed if the licensee knows or believes that the purpose of the experiment can be achieved by alternative means not involving an experiment on a living animal". These failed too.

The turn of the decade from the 1970s to 1980s was a time of feverish legislative activity in Britain, as two private members' bills vied for the attention of parliamentarians, scientists and anti-vivisectionists. The bill introduced by Peter Fry required the first sponsor for a licence application to certify that the result envisaged "cannot be obtained by an alternative

150

procedure"; but the Fry bill fell early on. The Laboratory Animals Protection Bill carrying Lord Halsbury's name (of the Research Defence Society) progressed surprisingly far through the parliamentary process before falling. The bill required that licensees should consider the possibility of using non-animal research methods before beginning an animal experiment.

Legislation in more than one European country does contain such restrictions on animal experiments, and the long-awaited British replacement for the 1876 Act includes a much watered-down version of what was requested so many times throughout the 1970s:

> "The Secretary of State shall not grant a project licence unless he is satisfied that the applicant has given due consideration to the feasibility of achieving the purpose of the programme to be specified in the licence by means not involving the use of protected animals" (Animals (Scientific Procedures) Act, 1986, section 5 [5]).

## For the Future

There are a number of ways of improving the rate of progress in alternative research. Funds are, of course, essential and the government should establish a coherent programme of development with a funding level far in excess of the miserly £60,000 per annum which they have promised so far. Rather than burdening the already hard-working Animal Procedures Committee with the task of selecting a few successful applicants from the more than a hundred who have applied this year, the government should make use of organisations with expertise in selecting applicants and awarding grants, and as ever, the Medical Research Council remains an obvious choice. A new grants committee with responsibility for funding humane research should be drawn up, comprising research scientists with experience both of animal and non-animal experimental techniques. A national human tissue bank to provide a reliable source of primary cells and cell lines should be a first priority, and a regionally organised human volunteer network is also needed to allow the expansion of volunteer studies using new, non-invasive techniques of analysis and imaging.

However, funds alone are not enough. Attitude is critically important, and while the attitudes which I have described prevail, no amount of funding will overcome the inertia and orthodoxy which have pertained in many areas for so long. Education is important here: scientists must be trained to consider the ethical implications of their work and to have a more catholic approach to methodology. They must be willing to accept humane methods which provide results of (at least) equal value to animal tests. Better inter-disciplinary collaboration is necessary, so that animal toxicologists and research

scientists can more easily apply techniques of cell
culture, microbiology, gene technology, biochemistry,
receptor studies, chemistry and electron microscopy.
Industrial scientists must be allowed to be more open
about their in-house research, to avoid wasteful
duplication of effort. Regulatory authorities should make
a priority of assessing the potential of non-animal
methods as they are validated. The fear of the new must
be conquered: the establishment must be prepared to
forego the illusion of safety which animal experiments
have provided, and really work at bringing non-animal
techniques to the fore.

## References and Bibliography

Animals (Scientific Procedures) Act (1986). (London:
HMSO)

British Toxicology Society (1984). Human Toxicology,
3:85

British Toxicology Society (1987). Human Toxicology,
6:279

Brusick, DJ. (1983) Annals of the New York Academy of
Sciences, 406, 68

Department of Health and Social Security (1982).
Guidelines for the Testing of Chemicals for Toxicity.

Report on Health and Social Subjects 27, (London:
HMSO)

Di Carlo, FJ. (1984) Drug Metabolism Reviews, 15 409

Dixon, B. What is Science for? (London: Penguin
Books, 1976)

Dixon, B. Proceedings of the RSPCA Symposium on the
Reduction and Prevention of Suffering in Animal
Experiments, (Horsham: RSPCA, 1978) p134

Frazer, AC: Sharratt, M On the Use of Animals in
Toxicological Studies, (Potters Bar: UFAW: 1969) p90

Hayflick, L. (1969) Progress in Immunobiological
Standardisation, 3 :86

Home Office (1979). Report on the LD50 Test by the
Advisory Committee, Home Office, London Littlewood, S.
(1965). Report of the Departmental Committee on
Experiments on Animals (London: HMSO).

Marks, J. (1972) Tubercle, 53 :31

National Academy of Sciences Models for Biomedical
Research, (Washington: National Academic Press, 1985)

Perkins, FT. (1980) <u>Developments in biological Standardisation, 46</u> :3

Rees, D. (1988) Personal communication.

Research Defence Society (1988). <u>RDS Newsletter,</u> August

Russell, WMS: Burch, RL. <u>The Principles of Humane Experimental Technique,</u> (London: Methuen, 1959)

Salsburg, D. (1983) <u>Fundamental and Applied Pharmacology, 17</u>: 276

World Health Organisation (1987). <u>The Acceptability of Cell Substrates for Production on Biologicals.</u> Technical Report Series 747, Geneva

# PART FIVE

HUMAN/ANIMAL INTERACTION

Earl O. Strimple

## A PAL AT LORTON

I think we have a very exciting programme at the Central
Facility, D.C., Department of Corrections in Lorton,
Virginia. To put this in perspective, I would like to
give you some basic statistics on prisons: for this
information I give all credit to the Department of
Justice.

1. On June 30, 1987, there were 570,579 inmates in local,
state and federal prisons. This represented 25,579 more
people, or a 5% increase in the first 6 months of the
year.

2. On the same date there were approximately 28,500 women
incarcerated, which was a 6.2% increase over the first 6
months.

3. In Washington, D.C. 7,666 inmates were housed,
representing an 11.8% increase over the previous year.

4. On June 30, 1987, Florida had incarcerated 32,771
individuals, representing a 10.3% increase.

5. In 1984, $10 billion were spent to house 438,000
prisoners - approximately $16,000 per individual.

6. $6 billion were spent on new prison facilities.


I would like to give some information on the recidivist,
the person who has been incarcerated previously. This is
based on a 1979 study. This problem has only become worse
in the last 8 years.

1. 60% of those admitted to prison in 1979 had served a
previous sentence of incarceration.

2. More than 1/2 of the recidivists would still have been
in prison at the commission of the next crime if they had
served the maximum sentence.

3. The recidivism rate was highest in the first 2 years
after release from prison.

    32% were re-arrested after the first year
    47% were re-arrested after the second year

4. Recidivism was higher among men - black, and non high-
school graduates - than women - white, and high school
graduates.

Clearly rehabilitation is not occurring in prisons and
there are a number of reasons why. I'll demonstrate some
of these in this presentation.

Let me take you through a typical day at Lorton:

There is a 06:00 wake-up. Police officers enter the dormitory, turn on the lights, blow a whistle, and yell "show time".

Between 0600 and 0700 is breakfast. You must be back to your dormitory and on your bed for the 0700 count. (Counts occur when there is a change of shifts.)

The count usually clears by 0800. You have between 0800 and 0830 to clean your area, wash, shave, or any other personal activity.

At 0830 everyone is off to their work squad until 1100. This is a great improvement, because when I first arrived in 1982 only about 40% of the population had a job; the others would lie around on their beds.

Let me give you some examples of work. If you work in the laundry, you will receive $176.00 a month for doing institutional contract work. If on the other hand, you were a teaching assistant you would receive only $6.50 per month, not too dissimilar from the pay differential in the larger society as a whole.

Unfortunately, the work in your squad is not the type that leads to productive employment when you leave. For example, if you are on the plumbing squad you may unplug toilets while people try to hide drugs in T-shirts.

Well it´s 1100, and time for lunch until 1200. I won´t go into detail about the quality of the food, but it doesn´t add to the morale. Whereas in college you may occasionally have had "mystery meat", at Lorton it is "mystery food".

There is a 1200 count which usually clears between 1300 and 1330. It is back to work until 1530.

There is another count at 1530 because there is a 1600 shift coming on. Recently this count hasn´t cleared until 1700 or 1730. You now have until 1830 to eat before going to night classes or seeing visitors.

Lights out at 2300.

You may think that the inmates have time to themselves while sleeping. WRONG!! Every hour during the night police officers walk through the dormitory shining a light in your face or grabbing a foot. In between visits by the officers you must sleep with one eye open because other inmates may be marauding, and you may find a "shank" or home-made knife in your abdomen.

If you are hurt and not killed you´d better hope you have enough strength to find a police officer, because nobody in the dormitory will help you. There is a good reason for this. If you report a resident has been "cut" , the police will assume you know who did it and hold you as an accessory. Even if you know you can't tell because you don't want to become a "snitch".

There is no place in prison for a "snitch". Inmates in prison have a code of honour: "Thou shalt not be a snitch". If you do, your days are numbered.

Often the police officers who work closely with inmates are young (21-23) and are seeking some influence or power. Many of these officers show no respect to the residents. They will look for a weaker inmate and hound him until he snaps. They'll say, "hey boy, come here". If he talks back, the officer will give a "shot" or disciplinary report for disrespect to an officer. After so many of these "shots" the inmate will be sent to the "hole" or solitary confinement.

At no time can a resident touch an officer. If an officer proves that you touched him during a dispute, he may get 45 days off with pay, you'll go to the "hole" and 5 years may be added on to your sentence.

This is life in a medium-security prison. Given this daily routine I want to show you how animals play an important part.

It all started this way:

It was early spring, 1982, while reading the Washington Post, that a picture caught my eye. It depicted a man and a bugle with a prison fence and a guard tower in the background. The caption described the life of an older inmate (over 24 years of age) at Lorton Reformatory as eating, sleeping, and playing cards. My thought was, what a waste of time!

At this same prison, I had been co-operating with the Washington Humane Society in caring for some injured cats. Since animals were already present, why not investigate organising an animal-facilitated programme there? Programmes like this had been successful in providing meaningful activities in other institutions.

Meeting with the administrator of the prison was the first big hurdle. Fortunately I had a client who was a probation officer for the D.C. Superior court. I asked her if she know who this person was. She said no, but was willing to find out. She inquired and set up the meeting.

By coincidence I had the Latham Foundation film, Hi Ya Beautiful, describing David Lee's work at a forensic hospital in Lima, Ohio. With this film and a lot of enthusiasm I met with the administrator, Mr Salanda Whitfield, and his programme director, Mr. Melvin Jones. they were pleased with my presentation and asked me to share this film with his staff and some inmates.

Before I had a chance to show the movie several inmates approached Mr. Whitfield about bringing some other animals to the institution. This triggered Mr. Whitfield´s interest and gave additional support to my idea.

A meeting was arranged with about 12 residents to show the movie. Time was made available at the end to discuss its implications. Concern was voiced for the 500 cats that already lived in Lorton and its environs. We decided to meet again in two weeks and discuss how to implement the programme.

When we met, the residents had given some thought to the type of animal they would like. They felt, in addition to cats, they would like to have birds, fish, rabbits and guinea pigs. When piranhas and snakes were suggested Mr. Whitfield made his views known; no piranhas, no snakes and no dogs in the programme.

I was curious about how the cats were cared for. When I asked one inmate how his cats were fed he said: "I eat my breakfast, the cats get my lunch, and we share my dinner". The query about animal ownership produced an interesting response. The cat belongs to you if it comes to your whistle. This was demonstrated when an inmate went to the yard, whistled, and 5 cats went scrambling to his dormitory.

From my discussions with the residents, I knew it was important to improve the cats´ state of nutrition. I asked for help from Dr. Jack Mara of Hill´s Packing Company. When our needs were explained he said Hill´s would be very willing to co-operate.

Vaccines, flea control products, and various medicines were supplied by the Pitman-Moore Drug Company. Bird food, especially pelleted diets, was given by Dr. Ted Lafeber. These donations were essential before any programme could be undertaken.

To authenticate the group, the residents wanted by-laws and a constitution. They insisted that a contract was necessary between the administrator and PAL because, "if it is not in writing it doesn´t exist".

Fortunately, we had 2 women volunteers who made bi-weekly trips to Lorton to help in the organisation of the inmates and to insure the proper care of the animals. A President and a Board of directors were elected by the men, and Committee Chairmen were appointed. We brought in experts who bred birds, studied animal behaviour, or cared for fish. One such person was a curator at the aquarium in the Department of Commerce. This helped the men develop interest in these areas. They requested and received books for a library on animal care.

Soon men developed expertise in bird care or fish husbandry. They shared their knowledge with other inmates. When problems developed, inmates would turn to

the "experts" for help. Mr. Whitfield was amazed at the
communication and co-operation that developed among the
men. The PAL chapter soon enlarged to 40, then to 50 men.
As new members came in, the older ones would tutor them in
the care of animals. Before a neophyte could join, he had
to demonstrate his ability to set up an aquarium or care
for a bird. A strong support group evolved. Men of
different Moslem sects were working together, something
rarely heard of. The animals crossed all types of social
barriers. Animals were bringing these people together in
a way no other organisation could.

Each summer a dinner is held at Lorton sponsored by PAL.
Inmates invite their wives and children so that they can
see what has been accomplished with their animals. It was
clear, in many instances, that the animal is the only
thing the children have in common with their father. The
animals truly bring the children and father together
through a shared experience.

The PAL programme has clearly demonstrated that animals
produce a sustaining interest for the men. Some men
inquired if their interest in animals might help them get
a job. (It must be realised that the bottom line for any
prisoner is to have a job when their sentence is
completed. Without a job, no freedom.) The idea of job-
training produced such questions as "how can we train the
men?", "what are our resources?", and "who can we turn
to?".

I talked to several veterinarians involved in the care of
laboratory animals. It was decided to approach the
Capital Area Chapter of the American Association of
Laboratory Animal Science (AALAS) to see what type of
training programme they could offer.

I made a slide presentation to their membership to show
them what we were doing. This was followed up by meeting
the executive board. I invited some of their members to
help vaccinate and treat some of the animals at Lorton. I
tried to establish a dialogue between this group and
Lorton. Some valid questions were asked, but the majority
felt the <u>Assistant Laboratory Animal Technician</u> course
would be appropriate.

The AALAS educational programme is used to teach entry-
level people the fundamentals of laboratory animal care.
It is designed to be taught for 2 hours a week over a 26-
week period.

One member of the executive committee volunteered to
oversee the teaching of this course. Four or 5 others
said they would help in specific areas. The identical
syllabus is used for any first course. Instead of 26
weeks, it was felt better to take 9 months to cover the
material.

Upon completion of the course, the men will still not meet
all the criteria for AALAS accreditation. However,

recognition will be made and certificates of accomplishment will be given depending on the results of a teacher-evaluation and examination. The men who do exceptional work in the course and are eligible for "work-release" or "work-training´ programmes at Lorton will be helped to find a job in a local laboratory, humane society, or animal hospital.

For men serving a longer sentence, the knowledge gained in the course will help them take better care of all the animals in the institution. It is important that they become more self-sufficient in care of their own animals.

Additionally, the prisoners gain personal knowledge. The course give them a better understanding of how their own body works and the care necessary to keep it healthy. They understand what infection is and how it affects them. They understand the role of nutrition and how it inter-relates with their own well-being. What a way to teach health!

About a year ago, we were asked to help provide support for cats that live at the maximum security branch at Lorton. Food for these animals also came from the dining hall or was smuggled in from the Central facility. No litter was available. Arguments developed over the ownership and care of the animals. The administration found problems in the cell block because cats were going where they weren´t welcome. This gave the inmates reason to complain and maintain unrest.

We were asked to help establish a programme for identification, vaccination, and feeding these cats. About 30 inmates of "Max" have become involved.

An interesting phenomenon has been observed. A number of cats owned by older inmates have become pregnant and had kittens. Some of the newer residents who enter "max" became interested in the kittens. When they saw the cats were being well cared for, they decided they would like to have a kitten. What developed was a relationship where "older" inmates took the "newer" inmates in hand to teach them the proper care for animals. This is a very humanising event - learning to share and to care for something other than themselves.

In closing, I would like to share a poem with you that was written by one of the residents last year for our PAL dinner. I feel that it captures some of the feeling which the men have towards this programme.

> Its like opening a book and finding
> This meaning on every page
> We´re not too much different from
> The animals we have in a cage

Look at the fish we have in our tanks
They're not at liberty to swim the sea
Is that any different from us down here
Not being able to live in society

Take the birds we have in the cages
They're not free to fly all about
Like some of us here in this big cage
May never have the chance to get out

But we still generate enough love
To give these animals T L care
And through this programme
            may we generate our love
For each other
To which, hopefully, nothing can
Compare

James Serpell

## ATTITUDES TO ANIMALS

### INTRODUCTION

Until comparatively recently, people who exploited animals
(or who benefited from their exploitation) were rarely
called to account for their activities. That animals
suffered and died to benefit humans was largely accepted
as an inevitable fact of life, and the few who criticised
this on moral grounds were easily dismissed as cranks or
hopeless idealists. Within the last ten to fifteen years,
however, the growth of the animal welfare/animal rights
movement has produced a relatively dramatic shift in
public opinion. Increasingly, farmers, scientists,
sportsmen and others involved in animal exploitation are
being forced to examine their consciences and defend their
actions as far as they can. The results of this process
of self-examination reveal an array of complex attitudes
and beliefs that deserve careful examination and analysis
by those campaigning for improvements in animal welfare.

The material presented in this paper summarises the
results of a pilot study of attitudes to animals and their
treatment among specific groups who exploit animals for
either professional or sporting reasons. Data were
collected by means of recorded interviews with individual
subjects. Although the sample sizes were necessarily
small they are not, I believe, entirely unrepresentative.

### KILLING FOR SPORT

As in many other cultures past and present (see Serpell,
1986), hunters in Britain display considerable ambivalence
and a variety of peculiar inhibitions about killing
animals. The hunting and shooting fraternity, for
instance, places heavy emphasis on arcane rules of
sportsmanship. Apart from "vermin" (to which different
rules apply), only so-called "game" species can be killed
and only at specific times of the year: it is considered
bad form to shoot "low birds", "sitting ducks" or animals
below a certain age. Wounded animals are assiduously
sought out and dispatched rather than left to die slowly,
and the greatest satisfaction - and, one suspects, the
least guilt - is generally derived from the clean kill in
difficult circumstances, preferably after hours of
tramping about in sub-zero temperatures. Frequent
attention is also drawn to the fact that more animals
escape uninjured than are shot. And many draw the line at
certain types of hunting - for example, deer-stalking - on
the grounds that it is "too easy".

The more enthusiastic hunters deplore the continental
habit of shooting anything that moves, and the majority
despise the city-dweller who only shoots once or twice a
year on a casual basis. Paradoxically, many of them

express considerable admiration and affection for the animals they kill, viewing the quarry not as a victim, but rather as a worthy opponent in a strange game of life and death. Perhaps more surprisingly, none that I spoke to derived any pleasure from the actual business of killing; claiming instead that the social dimension, and the opportunity to express one´s skill as a marksman, were by far the most important attractions of their sport. By way of justification for killing animals, many shelter behind the belief that hunting is a natural instinct we have inherited from our stone-age ancestors, while others are quick to stress their putative role as guardians of the countryside and, somewhat ironically, wildlife.

## PEST CONTROL

Attitudes to pest species or "vermin" are, not surprisingly, very different from those toward game animals. The animals tend to be described in negative and highly anthropomorphic terms as being sly, ruthless, cowardly, blood-thirsty or filthy. Furthermore, they often assume the status of conscious, thinking beings who are aware of the "evil" of their ways. On traditional game-keeper´s gibbets, for instance, the corpses of pest species are conspicuously displayed, ostensibly as a warning to others. The assumption is that these animals recognise the threat and therefore avoid the area. By portraying vermin as individuals who deliberately conspire to cause others harm, they can be thought of in the same light as criminals; enemies of society who can be exterminated with a clear conscience. Unlike sportsmen, pest-controllers can also disclaim some of the responsibility for killing, inasmuch as they are generally employed by someone else.

Some pest-controllers approach their work in a businesslike manner, and the victims are viewed with a degree of detachment. One individual, in particular, admitted that he would be unable to do the job effectively if he allowed his emotions to intrude. It is a highly selective form of detachment, however, that applies only to the animals being controlled. Family pets, such as dogs and cats, will be described in the most affectionate terms, even by individuals who may be employed to exterminate feral cats the following day. And once again, none reported any satisfaction from killing itself; the rewards being derived primarily from accomplishing a variety of difficult practical tasks expediently and, above all, humanely.

## FARMING

The technique of shifting the blame for methods of animal treatment is particularly noticeable in modern livestock farming. Critics of intensive farming methods are often accused of being out of touch with economic realities, and farmers will often claim that the only reason they rear animals intensively is because consumers "demand" cheap produce. By implication, then, they would prefer to farm animals extensively, if it were economically profitable. In other words, the consumer is to blame. Few farmers slaughter their own animals (in fact, it is generally illegal), and they therefore do not feel entirely responsible for their demise. Indeed, some explicitly avoided enquiring too deeply into the fate of their animals once they left the farm. They also place considerable emphasis on the health and productivity of their charges, as if health, growth and fecundity were somehow synonymous with good welfare. Many will also insist that their animals are actually happy, and that they wouldn´t keep them the way they do if they weren´t. Much as sportsmen claim to be guardians of the countryside, farmers are also quick to point out that livestock animals would be extinct if it wasn´t for farming. In this way they convince themselves that their rôle is protective and custodial, rather than purely exploitative. Many also argue that meat-eating and meat production are all part of the "natural process".

Farmers make certain efforts not to get to know their animals too well as individuals. In large production units this is a relatively easy matter, since it is impossible to get to know thousands of superficially similar animals individually. At this level of detachment, the animals, like motor cars or packets of crisps, can be abstracted to the status of mere units of production. The process is often reinforced by the use of euphemisms. In fur farming, for example, mink or silver foxes are typically referred to as a "crop" which will eventually be "harvested", rather than as animals which will be slaughtered and flayed. On more traditional farms and small-holdings, distancing devices of this kind are less easy to maintain and other, more subtle, techniques are employed. The farmer may avoid naming the animals that are destined for slaughter (names, after all, signify personal status), or they may be given special, often comical names, such as "Mint Sauce" or "Rashers", as a constant verbal reminder of their ultimate fate. As Rothschild (1986) points out:

> "Just as we have to depersonalise human opponents in wartime in order to kill them with indifference, so we have to create a void between ourselves and the animals on which we inflict pain and misery for profit".

## RESEARCH

Very similar attitudes and techniques are prevalent among scientists engaged in biomedical and behavioural research involving animals. Like farmers, many will justifiably claim that they are only doing what the consumer demands, and that most of their work will eventually benefit humanity or other animals. Thanks to public pressure and recent legislation, few would now insist that the pursuit of knowledge, in itself, is sufficient justification for animal experiments, although - off the record - some will admit that it is not always possible to predict the potential beneficial outcomes of "pure", as opposed to strictly applied, research. In general, animals that are used for relatively harmless, non-invasive work are often named and treated like pets. This is particularly true of primates, dogs, cats and other large mammals, especially if they are tame and co-operative.

Conversely, scientists tend to make conscious efforts not to become too attached to animals that are destined for more invasive research, and smaller, less easily personified species, such as rodents, are most frequently used. Even in this case, however, it is not unusual for the researcher to keep one or two individual animals aside as named mascots or pets. Thus by nurturing and personifying selected individuals, it appears that the scientist attempts to compensate their more anonymous brethren. One individual I spoke to remembered the days when stray dogs could be used for research, and he admitted that the knowledge that these animals were doomed anyway made his life considerably easier. Scientists engaged in invasive research also tend to stress the importance of anaesthesia and the reduction of pain or suffering in animal experiments. Most of the ones I spoke to strongly disliked the business of killing animals, and a surprising number were vegetarians. Euphemistic jargon is also widely used. Animals, for example, tend to be "sacrificed" rather than killed in research, implying that they have given their lives in a relatively noble cause.

Division of labour within the research community also serves to dilute the burden of individual responsibility. The scientist, for instance, who designs the project and determines the experiments, is often not involved in the day-to-day care of the animals. He or she thus avoids getting to know them too well as individuals. Conversely, the person who looks after the animals is not generally responsible for deciding their fate.

## DISCUSSION

Despite their complexity, these various attitudes and justifications reveal a number of consistent patterns. First and foremost, they indicate that such people, in the main, dislike the actual business of killing or harming animals. Few of them would willingly admit to feeling guilty about it, although it is difficult to think of any other satisfactory explanation for their discomfort on the subject. Guilt is also strongly implied by the various techniques they employ in their dealings with animals.

Perhaps because they are most vulnerable to criticism, the hunters hedge themselves about with elaborate rules of sportsmanship as a means of balancing things, to some extent, in the animal's favour. Those who derive their livelihood from animal exploitation commonly evade total responsibility by passing the blame either onto their employers or the consumer. Both groups also tend to depict the animal in terms that makes its death somehow less culpable: for example, as a criminal, a noble adversary, a sacrificial offering, or a crop to be harvested. Many seek to compensate for their actions in various ways. By ensuring, for instance, that their animals are healthy and "happy", by contributing to wildlife conservation, by giving the animal a "sporting chance", by killing humanely, by becoming vegetarians, or by singling out particular animals for special treatment. And most of them distance themselves to some extent from their victims; either by means of selective detachment and the imposition of arbitrary boundaries, or by avoiding getting to know the animals too well as individuals. As the Red Queen says to Alice in Through the looking Glass, "It isn´t etiquette to cut up anyone you´ve been introduced to". Far easier, therefore, to avoid introductions in the first place.

The central dilemma that seems to confront these individuals - and those campaigning for a change in public attitudes to animals - is that it is difficult for a person to adopt a compassionate view of an animal that he or she intends to kill, injure or devour. The two are, to some extent, incompatible. The natural human response to this conflict is either to distance ourselves from the animal, or to erect a protective screen of attitudes, beliefs and rituals that make our actions towards it seem less blameworthy. Efforts to improve the welfare of animals in society must take careful account of this important element of animal exploitation. The animal rights movement has undoubtedly made considerable progress in persuading people to think seriously about the plight of animals. But, in general, its response to those who exploit animals has been to condemn them outright as insensitive, self-indulgent or cruel. The results of the present study suggest that such labels are neither appropriate nor constructive, and may only serve to increase feelings of hostility and mistrust.

## References and Bibliography

Rothschild, M. Animals and Man (Oxford: Clarendon Press, 1986).

Serpell, JA. In the Company of Animals (Oxford: Basil Blackwell, 1986)

Nicholas Tucker

## ANIMALS IN CHILDREN'S LITERATURE

Animals have a very special place in children's
literature. Just as concern about children's rights from
the eighteenth century onwards often came from the same
type of person who also worried about cruelty to animals,
so in children's literature does a humane attitude towards
children often accompany humane feelings towards animals.
It follows that children's literature embodying harsh
attitudes towards animals has often been criticised by
those sharing similarly gentle feelings towards both
children and animals. In 1967, for example, I corresponded
with Mr Arthur Thompson, then organising secretary of the
Humane Education Society, over his campaign against the
nursery rhyme Ding Dong Bell. He was convinced it caused
some children to imitate the rhyme as best they could in a
society without wells. Inspired by this example, a Leeds
industrialist named Geoffrey Hall actually tried re-
writing various nursery rhymes he did not care for,
including that old shocker Three Blind Mice. His revised
version runs as follows:

> Three Kind mice, three kind mice,
> See how they run, see how they run;
> They all ran after the farmer's wife,
> She cut them some cheese with a carving knife;
> Did ever you see such a thing in your life
> As three kind mice?

I don't think Hall's intention here was to stop children
cutting off the tails of blind mice, as actual attempts to
imitate such cruelty would seem very unlikely. He simply
disliked such an example of cruelty for its own sake, and
re-wrote the rhyme accordingly.

This, then, is one way to approach the appearance of
animals in children's literature: always to be on the
look-out for the setting of bad human examples towards
them. Such critics would not have been pleased by the way
that Richmal Crompton's boy character William casually
kills a couple of cats with his catapult, perhaps
following the example set by the young heroes of Rudyard
Kipling's school story Stalky & Co., where the same thing
happens. Breathing down writers' necks in this way is no
bad thing where such thoughtlessness is concerned, and any
writer today who let a modern child hero get away scot-
free with the cruelty sometimes shown by William would be
soundly scolded, not least by child readers themselves.
But responding to the treatment of animals in children's
literature merely by collecting examples of good and bad
behaviour is obviously not enough. A nursery rhyme like
"I love little pussy", which first appeared in 1830, is
pleasant enough and may well have helped some children
feel kinder towards cats than was always the case at the
time. But it lacks the energy and bounce that goes into
the best nursery rhymes, and anyone urging that some of

these too should occasionally be changed in favour of
always setting better examples is soon going to make more
enemies than friends.  For one thing, no-one has ever
proved any necessary connection between reading about
cruelty and practising it.  For another, attempts to
censor children´s literature always arouse antagonism
from adults who feel that they themselves are under
attack, either as negligent parents  or else as examples
of readers already hopelessly corrupted by such literature
themselves when young.  And trying to limit any sort of
literature to setting inspirational examples and nothing
else is to ruin it both as literature and eventually as
any sort of persuasive medium.  Children and their
literature deserve better than that.

A different critical tack in this area advocates the
desirability of treating animals seriously as animals and
nothing else.  Dressing them up in human clothes,
therefore, and giving them human speech and emotions, is
thought to encourage sentimentality and a deliberate lack
of understanding.  For Mrs. Lyman Cobb, writing in
Philadelphia in 1832, "Dialogue between wolves and sheep
and cats and mice is as destructive of truth and morality
as it is contrary to the principles of nature and
philosophy".  Later on, during the same century, the
author of Black Beauty, one of the finest of animal
stories, was criticised by a cousin for making the horse
Ginger exclaim at one point "Thank Heaven", which for this
cousin at any rate was "A place undreamt of in equine
philosophy".  Another potential fault often found in such
anthropomorphic literature is the way that vegetarian
animals like rabbits or horses tend always to emerge as
lovable, whereas predators such as foxes, or carrion like
vultures, all with their own equally important and logical
part in general ecology, still come off as natural
villains.  More realism and a less human-centred approach
could also spare us, it is argued, from inappropriate
images such as birds singing happily in cages or animals
over-joyed at the experience of performing  pointless and
humiliating tricks at the circus.

Once more, there may be a case for criticism of
anthropomorphism in books that purport to realism (and
still more where various non-fictional, but in fact
highly fanciful studies of animals are concerned).  But
again, trying to impose blanket critical guides as to the
treatment of animals in literature ignores too many other
vital considerations, including the fact that childhood
itself lasts quite a long time, taking in many different
developmental stages as it proceeds.  There is no way a
small child can be expected to see animals other than from
its own typically egocentric viewpoint, and I am talking
here as the father of a son who once declared he was going
to marry the family cat when he grew up.  Even older
children might still be upset by details of animal life
given them too early and too straight, such as the fact of
occasional cannibalism, or the time it can take a lion
quite literally to eat its prey to death.  Early
habituation to this harsher side of animal existence still

seems to be one of those factors that can sometimes trigger off or at least be used as justification by some people for their own cruelties to animals; witness the way that badger-baiters often claim they and their victims are simply part of a natural chain of predators and preyed upon. So a less intimate knowledge of what foxes can do to hens, or badgers to young chicks, may help rather than hinder positive attitudes towards all animal life at an early age when emotions are still so dominant, and more abstract considerations some way off.

But while most animal books for younger children at least are bound to be fairly anthropomorphic, there are still better or worse ways of writing in this vein. In Beatrix Potter's little books, her animals never diverge too much from their natural ways. Peter Rabbit is properly greedy and adventurous and very nearly pays the price. Her foxes do prey on ducks and her pikes swoop on frogs. Such glimpses of reality amidst the usual fantasies of human speech and clothes puts Beatrix Potter far ahead of her rivals. In her books, pigs risk being eaten, with her character Little Pig Robinson very much an intended victim.

Alison Uttley's Sam Pig, by contrast, is life-long friend to both cook and farmer, and while there is room in infants' literature for some drawing of veils this is surely going too far. As it is, modern children often remain unaware quite where their meat comes from, which is hardly surprising considering the fact that in some early animal stories the main characters sometimes themselves tuck into a meat sandwich in a bizarre form of unremarked upon cannibalism. Modern alphabets also tend to pass over the fact that "B" still stands for butcher. My own sister, when young, was put off meat nearly permanently by such an entry under "B" along with a little rhyme, one line which ran "Lovely red rounds of juicy meat". The only reason I can remember this line now, I fear, is because it proved very effective at the time as a way of tormenting the poor girl. But now I rather approve of the old book we found all this in. Literature that dares to tell children at least some of the truth is usually better than stories that persistently lead children away from reality at every stage, and this judgement applies as much to animal stories as it does to any other type of children's fiction.

Animal stories for older children, on the other hand, should be expected to pull fewer punches if the aim is to give some realistic view of animal life. Jack London's epic books <u>Whitefang</u> and <u>The Call of the Wild</u> come to mind here, with the violence running through them - hard work but sadly accurate in its sickening detail. Henry Williamson's <u>Tarka the Otter</u> must also be mentioned, although again rather solemn. In lighter vein, I have a soft spot for Enid Bagnold's <u>National Velvet</u>, despite the fact that its plot revolves around one of the nastiest type of horse-racing still in existence. But I like the way she actually tackles the normally taboo subject of

animal sexuality. This topic is usually dealt with so
lightly that it is hard to know, for example, what sex
Black Beauty is at all, while the rabbits in Watership
Down are on the whole models of fleshly denial. In
National Velvet, however, Jacob the dog is described as
always being after the opposite sex, unlike his friend the
Piebald horse and future Grand National winner, whose
desires - we are told - are gone, but who has still kept
his pride. In one scene Jacob the dog comes slinking
home. "Bitches good?" enquires Mally, sister to Velvet.
"Succulent" says Jacob, making a half-circle round her".
A small point, perhaps, but a significant one when it
comes to transforming animals in children's eyes to
something more rounded than "Children who never grow up
and servants who never complain" - a phrase used by Keith
Thomas in his marvellous book, Man and the Natural World.

As it is, the way that cats and dogs, some of nature's
most promiscuous animals, are regularly transformed in
children's literature into models of husband-and-wife
domesticity both falsifies animal life and also fobs
children off from asking necessary awkward questions about
the whole nature of sexuality of man or beast. I think it
is braver to let children's animal stories be true to
life. Otherwise we have the paradoxical position where
humanised animals in fiction are being used to dehumanise
human beings, standing in as they usually do in their
stories as human symbols living in a settled, sexless and
usually classless society that has little in common with
the real thing as experienced by either animal or man.
Interestingly enough, in Saki's classic adult short story
Tobermory, about a cat who learns human speech, it is the
area of Tobermory's sexuality that provides one of the
funniest scenes in the story, so firmly demarcating it as
grown-up rather than children's humour.

Children's books that manage to suggest that animals are
not always there just to be eaten, or loved, or worked to
death, but may indeed when permitted have some strong
desires that have nothing to do with their human masters
or mistresses, may miss out on the pleasing omnipotent
fantasies that run through so many gymkhana or dog books.
But this growth in understanding may be one further step
forward towards gaining an accurate and less sentimental
view of life which, I believe, should be one of the
criteria for all good fiction, whether it concerns animals
or anything else. Children who learn this from an early
age may also have a better chance of not getting bitten or
scratched while trying to plant an inappropriate kiss on a
domestic or wild animal otherwise engaged in eating or
something else far more important to it at the time than
mere human affection.

Fiction for any age that involves animal characters as
symbols rather than as anything else is of course an
entirely different matter. In such stories, animals can
appear classless, either sexless or else difficult to sex,
of indeterminate age and nationality, and wild rather than
over-civilised and therefore always in close touch with

mother nature. Accordingly both art and literature have
always used them, with satirists, parable or fable-makers
turning to animal characters from Aesop to Orwell, whose
Animal Farm is still sometimes found in the Natural
History section of uninformed bookshops. His great
character Boxer the cart-horse stands memorably for all
oppressed peasantry everywhere in a way that a human
portrait of one particular Russian peasant in his own
right never could. In the same way the animals in
Kipling's Jungle Book each represent particular virtues or
vices, whose presence stands out from the page uncluttered
by any individual, human touches concerning age, class,
nationality or any of the other ways in which we commonly
distance ourselves from our fellow human beings in print
or in our own minds.

This use of animals as symbols is as old as literature or
even sleep itself, given that Freud persistently stressed
the ways in which animals can stand as symbols for the
particularly important adults in our lives during our
dreaming periods. For any new writers thinking of making
use of such very potent symbols, I would simply enter one
plea: do occasionally ring the changes where particular
animals and particular symbolic virtues are concerned. It
may well be that purely visual impressions will always
dictate that robins are seen as gentle and eagles as
aggressive, whereas the opposite is far more likely to be
the case. But elsewhere part of the genius of Kenneth
Grahame was his skill in investing universal
characteristics in fairly unfamiliar animals such as water
rats and moles. Another fine writer, Richard Jefferies,
recreates something like Stalinist Russia in his neglected
masterpiece Wood Magic, simply by using different types of
birds, all made entirely believable by the brilliance of
the writing. Modern writers should also try to be more
adventurous in this way, so avoiding tired, empty
stereotypes from the past such as greedy pigs or silly
sheep. (As a Scottish shepherd once said after being
quizzed as to the intellectual shortcomings of his flock:
"Could you survive in the mountains during winter as well
as they could?") Recently the American writer Richard
O'Brien turned some rats, those symbolic pariahs, into
models of community and child support in his novel Mrs
Frisby and the Rats of Nimh. I personally can now never
see rats in quite the same light again: no bad thing at a
time when arguments about humane attitudes to animals
nearly always miss out where this particular species is
concerned.

Back to realism again. There was a time when
psychologists believed that animals could be conditioned
to do almost anything, given time and appropriate
reinforcements. This is no longer thought to be true: in
their classic article "The Misbehaviour of Organisms"
published in American Psychologist, 1961, Keller and
Marian Breland write amusingly but tellingly about
attempts to make various animals perform silly tricks, and
how gradually what they describe as "instinctive drift"
causes the animals to return to more natural behaviour,

even if this means going short of food and water. In the same way, attempts by humans to become best friends with wild animals have often ended in tears or worse, although usually after rather than before the best-seller about the whole enterprise has been written and successfully marketed. For me, fiction that aims to look at animals straight can help readers to start distinguishing between human perceptions of animals and how the animals concerned in fact like to conduct themselves when left alone. This is not the only way of picturing animals, as I have tried to argue, but it is one I think writers should always have in the back of their mind. Learning to love anthropomorphised animals is one thing when young, but it should surely be followed by discovering more about what animals are really like, and how they have their own vital part to play in our planet as animals rather than as cosy human surrogates or else as slaves to human narcissism whether in fiction or in real life.

# PART SIX

# THE ROLE OF THE VETERINARIAN
# IN ANIMAL WELFARE

Alastair Porter

## THE CLIENT/PATIENT RELATIONSHIP

The title of the paper reflects the fact that a veterinarian has a triangular relationship with an animal under his care and its owner - and one has to acknowledge that the interests of the animal and its owner do not always coincide. The veterinary surgeon may often find himself in the impossible position of realising that one course of action which he might pursue would be best for the animal, while the owner wishes to insist on an alternative course - and has all the rights in law which are implicit in the word "owner". The veterinary surgeon has no statutory right to substitute the decision most favourable to the animal for the one on which the owner is determined, unless in a particular case the power of the courts can be invoked.

Certain decisions in the courts have shown the problems which can arise if the legal title of the owner of an animal is not given full weight.

One remedy for the type of dilemma in which a veterinary surgeon may find himself when instructed by an owner to carry out a particular procedure which he would prefer not to undertake (e.g. the docking of a dog´s tail) would be the passage of protective legislation by Parliament. Regrettably, the interest of successive administrations in legislating in favour of the companion animal appears to be very limited. Farm animals fare somewhat better.

The veterinarian cannot be expected to remedy legislative shortcomings of the use of ethical embargoes in the face of owner´s rights at law, neither should he be expected to act as an auxiliary policeman when he finds that a client has abused his position as owner of an animal, since that would diminish the trust of members of the public that they may consult a veterinary surgeon on any matter affecting their animals, without fear of their affairs being made publicly known.

## The Client/Patient relationship

The first thing I must do is to apologise for having been unable to participate in the whole of this conference - but you, I know, will appreciate that September is "conference month", and I have left the British Equine Veterinary Association meeting at Harrogate in order to be with you. This double commitment has meant that I have not had the privilege of listening to the papers presented in the first five sessions - and that I regret, for I apprehend that each paper should be seen as part of a large jig-saw, the picture on which will only be clear when all the pieces are in place. If that ultimate perception is, therefore, denied me I hope that I will at least be able to contribute something to the picture which others will see - and I also hope that I will not simply be repeating what others have already said more tellingly before me.

The title of the paper assigned to me was one which, initially, I found confusing. Was the intention that I should discuss the relationship between the veterinary surgeon and his client, or between the veterinarian and his patient? And then the penny dropped. Unusually for the health care field, there is here in every case a triangular relationship - between the veterinarian, the client, who is the animal owner, and the patient, which is the animal itself. There are some parallels in the human health care field, of course, where doctor, parent and small child form a similar triangle - but such relationship always exists in the veterinary field.

How then could one describe the relationship between the animal owner and the animal, vis-a-vis the veterinary surgeon? In some ways, the owner is the animal's agent, asking for something to be done to or for the animal which it cannot request on its own behalf. A kind of limitless power of attorney, if you like - except that the power is taken unto himself by the owner, and the animal has no choice in the matter. Sometimes, it is true, the animal may be grateful for the action initiated by its owner on its behalf, if, for example, the animal is ill or injured, and the owner seeks and obtains treatment. In other circumstances, however, the animal may be less appreciative. For example, the bitch which is spayed to prevent the arrival of unwanted pups, or the tom cat which is neutered to curb his romantic tendencies, would probably not have gone along with the action of the owner in arranging for such a procedure to be carried out.

Probably the most extreme variation between the wishes of the owner and the desires of the animal will occur when the question of euthanasia arises. If the animal is desperately ill, or suffering pain which cannot be relieved, there might be a meeting of minds on the virtues of a happy sleep - and indeed it can sometimes be one of the advantages which the animal has over the terminally and painfully ill human being. But what of the act of euthanasia carried out because the owner of a companion animal cannot afford the expensive ophthalmic or orthopaedic surgery needed by the animal? Or worse, the destruction of a healthy animal because its owner has died, or moved abroad, or finds it surplus to requirements, and attempts at re-housing have failed?

Such situations do distress even the most experienced veterinary surgeon, and reduce veterinary nurses to tears. Owners may be subjected to pleas to change their mind, to allow efforts at re-housing, or some other solution, to be tried - but in the end, one has to remember that the owner is just that.

The animal is his property, and the veterinary surgeon has

no god-like or statutory authority to over-ride the
owner´s directions. There has, in my time at the Royal
College, been the very occasional example of a veterinary
surgeon, under directions to destroy an animal, who has
disobeyed those directions, kept the animal alive and
sought to re-home it without permission. Normally, this
well-intentioned disobedience has ended in disaster - in
at least one case when the "thought-to-be-dead" animal
left its foster home for its home of origin, finding its
way back whence it came.

But, of course, there can also be exactly the opposite
situation, in which the owner wishes to keep an animal
alive for purely selfish reasons, when the animal is no
longer enjoying life. Animals paralysed in their hind
legs, and making their way along with little trolleys to
support them; animals totally blind, and bumping into the
furniture. Oh there will be exceptions which can be
quoted, but the test should surely be what is kindest for
the animal rather than what is the wish of the owner.
Here the rôles are reversed and it will be the veterinary
surgeon who will be acting as the animal´s advocate in
urging euthanasia.

Again and again, however, we return to the fact that the
owner is the owner, and it is he who has the legal right
to decide what is to be done to, or for the animal. The
owner is the judge of what should be done in the interests
of the welfare of the animal - unless a situation arises
in which intervention by the law is possible or necessary.

The situation is complicated by the fact that animals are
kept for a wide variety of purposes - for companionship,
for the production of food, for work, for use in
laboratories, etc., and society, as well as their owners,
regard them differently according to their category. As
we are told by vegetarians (and others opposed to eating
food derived from animals which have been slaughtered),
the public is strangely selective regarding the animals
about which it is prepared to sentimentalise. Your
average dog or cat owner is quite likely to dissolve into
tears when told that his or her companion has come to the
end of the road and must be put down, but will take in his
or her stride the proposition that if one is to eat meat,
that means animals being raised specifically for slaughter
and consumption. I appreciate the reality of that
situation, being - quite honestly - both the owner of a
companion animal and a carnivore.

But to return to the difficult relationship between the
animal and its owner: the situation sometimes arises where
the owner is not available when the animal is in a state
of crisis for some reason or another. Given that the
animal cannot speak for itself, can the veterinary
surgeon, if one is called in, replace the owner and make
the decision? There is, unfortunately, no provision in
law which gives this power to the veterinarian, and there
is ample precedent for the sort of case which I am about
to describe.

The dog runs into the road, is in collision with a car, and is injured. The driver stops, is appalled by the injury, even though he had no chance of avoiding the accident - and finds that the dog wears no collar, and that there is no other means of identification. He takes it to his veterinary surgeon and says "look after it. Do what has to be done. If the owner cannot be located, I will pay for the treatment". The veterinary surgeon examines the animal, cleans up the wounds, stitches them and decides he will carry out an X-ray next morning. He does so, finds a break in the leg and sets it. The dog is, in the words of ward sisters, "doing as well as can be expected". It is kept at the practice for a couple of days, and since it is legally a stray, the police are informed, and through their good offices an owner appears. There is a tearful reunion at the surgery, expressions of gratitude (perhaps) and the dog is removed home. The car driver is advised that he is relieved of his responsibilities, and is glad to hear it. However, when the account is rendered by the veterinary surgeon to the owner, there is a flat refusal to pay. Not only, says the owner, did I not instruct you, Mr. Veterinarian, to carry out this treatment upon my animal - so that there is no contract between us - but I did not cause the injuries in the first place. The fact that the dog would not have been injured if it had not been permitted to run loose on a public highway, is conveniently ignored, as is the additional factor that if the dog had been wearing a collar bearing his owner´s name and address, consent to treatment could have been sought before it had been started. The veterinary surgeon considers the owner´s response quite unacceptable and sues for his fees - and the court says with reluctance that it is unfortunately correct that as the work was carried out neither at the request, nor with the consent, of the owner, there is no contract with the veterinarian, and he cannot recover his fee.

Just occasionally, however, the courts do find themselves in a position to be helpful. In another case, a dog was running alongside the railway line, and made contact with a train. It was of a sufficiently glancing nature not to kill the dog, but it was very severely injured. Once more the dog had no collar, and no means of identification. It certainly was not accompanied by its owner. A veterinary surgeon was called to the scene. He formed the view that the injuries were so severe that there was no alternative to euthanasia. In spite of there being no owner to hand, and acting, as he believed, in the best interests of the dog, he put it down.

The dog was buried at the side of the track. A little while afterwards, the owner learned what had happened, went to the scene, exhumed the dog´s body, and, having sought further advice, decided that the dog´s life could have been saved. He therefore sued the veterinary surgeon in an action for trespass, for having destroyed the animal without permission. The court, however, would have none of it. The veterinary surgeon had acted, in the Judge's words as "an agent of necessity". He had examined the dog, and exercising his professional judgement, in the best interests of the animal, had decided that there was no alternative to euthanasia. It was not open to the owner, who was not present or discoverable at the time, to complain subsequently that his consent had not been obtained to the destruction of the dog. Indeed, the judge went further and said that if the veterinarian, having decided that the dog could not be saved and had to be destroyed to prevent unnecessary suffering, had nevertheless held back and decided that he could not do so because he did not have the owner's permission, he (the veterinary surgeon) might have been in danger of being prosecuted under the Protection of Animals Act 1911 for causing unnecessary suffering by omitting to destroy the dog when that was the only way in which its suffering could be ended.

The fact that that case came out satisfactorily for the veterinary surgeon in the long run is, of course, of limited comfort to a veterinary surgeon weighing up the interests of the animal as against the rights of the owner in any particular case. Not only is the veterinarian unlikely to have the legal precedents at his finger-tips, but he is no doubt instinctively aware that, as the lawyers would say, each case turns on its own facts.

The practical dilemmas on which I guess Mr. Tandy will touch, such as the request by an owner to have his cat declawed or his dog de-voiced, with the threat that the animal will otherwise have to be put down, are very real, and are excellent examples of the divergence of the interests of the animal and the owner.

One way in which some dilemmas can be resolved is, of course, by legislation - and here I would make a plea that Government (and I am not speaking only of the current administration) should accept responsibility for the drafting and passage of legislation affecting the welfare of all animals, and not just certain categories such as farm animals, zoo animals, experimental animals and so on. The statute book carries too many Acts of Parliament relating, for example, to the boarding and breeding of companion animals which started life as Private Members Bills and suffer as a result from various inadequacies. In addition, successive administrations have failed to legislate to outlaw various procedures which are carried out or may be carried out without any breach of the law at the present time. There is legislation, for example, prohibiting the docking of the tails of cows, banning the docking or nicking of horses' tails, controlling the severing of the tails of piglets and so on, but legislation revised as recently as mid-March of this year (Schedule 3 of the Veterinary Surgeons Act) still permits lay persons to dock the tails of puppies before their eyes are open. This is not only one example of procedures which the veterinary surgeon may be called upon to perform, where, in most cases, he is reluctant to do so.

He may consider it unethical and unjustifiable to dock puppies' tails, but he may also take the view that if it is a choice of the procedure being carried out in a professional way, or leaving it to the lay person, the former course is preferable. And one would like to extend the scope of this proposition by saying that although it is desirable and proper that a veterinary surgeon should observe the highest ethical standards and always have a concern for the welfare of the patient, it is not reasonable to expect ethical rules to be a substitute for legislation - as the principal point I have been striving to make in this paper is that the owner has over-riding rights of decision in so many situations.

In pursuance of this belief, the Royal College of Veterinary Surgeons has been working for many years upon recommendations to Government regarding procedures - somewhat emotively referred to as "mutilations" - which ought to be prohibited by law. The first stage of this campaign led to the making of the Welfare of Livestock (Prohibited Operations) Regulations 1982, updated in 1987. That was in some senses, the simpler part of the exercise, since all those operations relate to farm animals, and the regulations could be made under the Agriculture (Miscellaneous Provisions) Act 1968. There is, however, no primary legislation on which to hang regulations relating to companion animals.

Nevertheless, last year, the College submitted its report and recommendations to the Home Office with a request that Ministers should consider taking action to legislate against a number of procedures outlined in the document. In making that submission, the College had the support of the BVA, the RSPCA and UFAW among others - and consultations carried out by the College on behalf of the of the Home Office, with a wider circle of interested bodies, have also indicated a wide measure of support. So far, however, we have had no indication of the Home Office's reaction.

It is submitted that some such legislation must be enacted to deal with situations in which the animal's interests and the rights of the owner are continually in conflict.

Finally, I want to speak on a subject on which I am aware there are widely conflicting views, but it would be intellectually dishonest to avoid the issue simply because it is contentious. This is the matter of professional confidentiality, and the extent to which it may be breached by a veterinary surgeon.

All of the major professions, I believe, will be found to observe a professional, ethical rule which says, in broad terms, the anything the client tells the professional or anything which emerges in the course of the client/practitioner relationship, should remain as confidential between them. The basis of the rule is self-evident. Clients will be hesitant to seek professional advice, if to do so will involve the risk of their affairs being discussed with third parties. They will be particularly anxious if the professional is likely to report them to the police, the Inland Revenue, the RSPCA, or other appropriate authority. Confidentiality as between professional and client is therefore jealously guarded, and any exceptions must be delineated with care and precision.

Exceptions which commonly exist include the breaching of confidentiality with the client's consent, or when required by law (e.g. in the animal field, the reporting of a statutorily notifiable disease) or when giving evidence in court. Most professions will also provide that confidentiality may be breached when, in exceptional cases, the public interest would otherwise be so damaged as to outweigh a primary obligation to the client.

This final provision, relating to the public interest, is at the same time of great value in dealing with the exceptional case, and a source of difficulty as people try to urge the Royal College to apply that rule to all cases of particular kinds in which they have a special interest. Thus, within the recent past, the College has been requested to allow, (or, indeed, to urge) veterinarians to report clients to the appropriate authorities in relation to:

(a)   injuries sustained in organised dog fights;

(b) injuries sustained by dogs in the digging out of badgers;

(c)   surgical interventions which may be concealed from show authorities;

(d) ownership of  dogs which have strayed onto the road, caused an accident , and then run off;

(e)   ownership of dogs which may have been involved in sheep-worrying;

(f)   animals which it is suspected have received injuries as a result of rough treatment by their owners.

The list is not exhaustive, but if the veterinary profession were to make reports, as a matter of general practice, to the appropriate authorities in all these cases, it must be clear that the confidentiality rule would virtually cease to exist, and veterinarians would come to be regarded as something akin to auxiliary policemen.

To some of our critics the answer to the problem is simple. The interests of the animal are paramount, the veterinary surgeon is required always to bear the welfare of the animal in mind, and therefore anybody who mistreats or abuses an animal in any way should be reported. Where there is a conflict between the interests of the animal and those of the owner, the animal must come first.

But, with respect, it is not as straightforward as that. It is perfectly true that if a veterinary surgeon reports to the police or the RSPCA the owner of an animal which has been neglected or abused in some way, his may be a means of ensuring that that particular animal is not abused further. It may even be the means of ensuring that that particular owner be disqualified by the courts from owning another animal. But against that, one must weigh the wider interests of animals whose owners may not bring them to the surgery for treatment if there is the slightest risk of a report to the authorities, should the veterinarian judge that the injuries or neglect can be laid at the owner's door. Believe me, it is a real risk as so many cases of child battering which have hit the headlines in recent years have shown.

Children have not been taken anywhere near a doctor because the parent who has been ill-treating them is afraid that the injuries or neglect would be reported straight to the police - and so there is no medical help, no counselling, no warning, no one to take the part of the child. And that in a situation where there is a statutory power to take a child into care when that is justified, without necessarily bringing a prosecution - a power which is not paralleled in the animal field.

I suspect that this is the situation in regard to illegal dog-fights. I have no knowledge of the real extent of the dog-fighting ring, but I know that our best endeavours, at the Royal College, to find concrete cases of veterinarians presented with dogs for treatment which have clearly been injured in organised dog fights have produced virtually a nil return. Where there are organised dog fights, there must be injuries. Why then are veterinarians not seeing the cases? I believe the answer must be that badly injured dogs are destroyed, while others are patched up in an amateur fashion - and it is clear that if progress is to be made in stamping out this barbaric pastime it is more likely to be achieved through police work, RSPCA investigations, investigative journalism and so on, rather than through evidence provided by veterinary surgeons.

Neither in this area nor in any of the others which I have attempted to cover briefly in this paper, are there any simple solutions or clear-cut answers, but in a curious way I believe that if there is greater understanding of the complexity of the issues, that may be a contribution to their resolution.

John Tandy

## THE ROLE OF THE VETERINARIAN IN ANIMAL WELFARE
## - PRACTICAL DILEMMAS

On admittance to membership of the Royal College of
Veterinary Surgeons, a veterinarian makes the following
declaration:

> "I promise that I will pursue the work of my
> profession with uprightness of conduct and that my
> constant endeavour will be to ensure the welfare of
> animals committed to my care".

It is my sincere belief that veterinary surgeons do not
take this promise lightly and that the welfare of animals
is at the forefront of their minds during the course of
their work. Not that there is uniform agreement in the
profession on all matters of welfare: it would be strange
if that were the case.

Welfare is defined as happiness or well-being. These are
states of mind which cannot be measured. Research into
physiological changes brought about by stress is beginning
to allow some assessment on a scientifically quantifiable
basis. But interpretation of these results is still open
to some dispute by workers in the field.

In the main, judgements must be made on changed
behavioural patterns and clinical signs, but these are not
constant and can sometimes be frankly misleading. For
example, take pain - probably the major factor causing
interference with an animal´s state of well-being.
Assessment of the presence of pain, particularly the
degree of pain, based on behavioural patterns is not
always easy. I think it is quite safe to say that cries
and screams from a dog with damaged inter-vertebral discs
in its neck are signs of pain, but what of the horse with
horrendous injuries contentedly grazing, or the pig with
several feet of intestine trailing along the ground,
playing in apparently high spirits with its companions, or
the dog with the fractured femur wagging its tail and
seeking affection. One must assume some pain - but what
degree of pain?

And what about quality of life - how can this be judged?
Is the cold, wet chicken, scratching for food in the mud
on a Welsh farm, enjoying life? Or what about a tethered
sow in a warm dry stall with a regular food supply - free
from the attention of bullying companions, but unable to
turn around?

In this difficult field, with numerous factors to be
considered, many of which are conflicting and difficult or
impossible to quantify, problems may not always be solved
in a completely satisfactory manner. Decisions are made
by the veterinary surgeon based on his training and

experience. But judgements are often fine - and can be open to criticism.

Judgements may be questioned by peers who, using the same parameters, can come to different conclusions. Or they may be questioned by those in ignorance of the full facts, or those who have not had the appropriate training or experience to interpret the signs. It is often the case that those who are not well-informed can see easy black and white solutions to complex problems. However, the more facts that are known, and the greater the experience of those assessing complex problems, the more the options become less starkly black or white.

There can be little doubt that veterinarians working mainly with pigs are the stoutest defenders of current pig-keeping systems, seeing available alternatives to be less satisfactory than the system under scrutiny. The suggested alternative might, for instance, call for a higher degree of stockmanship than is readily available. The same may be said about veterinarians working in the poultry field.

Judgements, then, are not easy and are readily open to criticism. If a veterinary surgeon is considered to be wrong in his judgement, various consequences may follow. Depending on the magnitude of the error there may be reprimand from a professional colleague, or civil action on the grounds of negligence, or criminal charges under the 1911 Act. In addition, a case may be brought before the Disciplinary Committee of the RCVS - which could lead to the veterinary surgeon's name being removed from the register.

Thus a mistaken judgement can lead to dire consequences: awareness of these helps focus the mind. No matter how tired or overworked a veterinary surgeon may be, he or she strives for solutions which result in the best outcome for the animal.

It is my intention to examine more closely some of the dilemmas confronting veterinary surgeons in the course of their work against this background of decision-making and consequences of error.

However, before I move on to specifics, I would like to mention one or two other matters which do from time to time give rise to some misunderstandings.

Firstly, decisions based on training and experience rather than emotion and anthropomorphism can unfortunately be interpreted as callous and uncaring.

Secondly, we must mention economics. There is no doubt that some people both inside and outside the profession perceive that economic considerations cause dilemmas in decision-making. For instance there was a debate at Liverpool University attended by over ninety undergraduates and teachers from the Veterinary Faculty.

The motion was that "Veterinary Surgeons are shirking their professional responsibilities by allowing economic considerations to take precedence over the welfare of animals committed to their care". A substantial majority voted for the motion. This sort of argument is difficult to counter, since it is mainly based on emotions rather than facts.

A veterinary surgeon in practice, like most other professional people, makes his living from the fees charged. There is no access to government subsidies or charitable funds. The fees must cover not only normal business expenses but purpose-built premises, drugs, equipment and the instruments necessary for an increasing range and sophistication of diagnostic, medical and surgical techniques. He must pay reasonable salaries to his staff if they are to be of an acceptable standard. He needs to keep knowledge and skills up-to-date, which requires payment for courses, journals, videos and membership of specialist groups. At the end of the day surveys show the profits from veterinary practice to be extremely modest compared with other professions.

Despite this, there are very few veterinarians who do not reduce their fees or waive them altogether for treatment of guide dogs, wild animals, children´s pets and those who make a genuine case for financial hardship. I have worked closely with the profession for many years and can only state that I am sure that veterinary surgeons do not put economic considerations before the welfare of animals in their care. Their charity compares favourably with any other profession or group. Nevertheless, as long as it is necessary to charge fees there will be those who make unfair accusations. Having said that I will now turn to some of the practical dilemmas experienced by veterinary surgeons in the course of their working lives.

**FARM ANIMAL HUSBANDRY SYSTEMS**

It is a veterinary surgeon´s duty to treat any animal or group of animals kept under any system of husbandry. It is clearly his duty to point out if the system itself is predisposed to health problems. But what should be his course of action if the system is not the cause of the health problem but could be affecting the general well-being of the animals?

Perhaps the system itself is in widespread use and may have been introduced long before the veterinary surgeon qualified. Before suggesting a change of system, he must ensure that alternative systems have more to offer from the welfare standpoint. Here I will quote extensively from a recent paper by John Oldham, my predecessor as Chairman of the BVA Animal Welfare Committee.

He started by stating that the Farm Animal Welfare Council had said that all farm animals should:

184

(a) be free from thirst, hunger or malnutrition,

(b) have appropriate comfort and shelter and

(c) have facilities provided for the prevention or rapid diagnosis and treatment of injury, disease or infestation.

(d) They should also be free from fear, and free to display most normal (natural) patterns of behaviour.

John Oldham went on:

"These are admirable statements, which must surely be wholeheartedly supported by all of us involved in animal exploitation. A problem arises however when we look at them in a dispassionate way and realise that in order to achieve the "best" overall welfare, there must be considerable compromise between the individual parameters mentioned. For instance the achievement of maximum freedom to display normal (or natural) patterns of behaviour can (and does) mitigate on occasions against the provision of appropriate cover and shelter - e.g. outdoor pigs in cold or wet weather. Similarly, any indoor system successful in providing year round comfort and shelter will to a greater or lesser extent limit freedom to display normal (or natural) patterns of behaviour. If freedom from fear were taken as the ultimate criterion of pig welfare we would never handle a pig to vaccinate it, or treat disease by injection".

It is wrong to assume that the free-range systems are necessarily the best for the animal. In a recent paper by John Webster, discussing poultry systems he says:

"the idea is to itemise and analyse the specific pros and cons of the battery cage and work towards a better one containing, for example, a nest box, perch and sufficient space. This is more logical than insisting on a free-range system with all its potential abuses in terms of cold, parasites and predation".

Roger Ewbank, Director of UFAW, has made the point:

"There are a lot of people who dislike intensive husbandry systems for scientific reasons, for moral reasons, or for aesthetic reasons, and often these are linked to the size of operation".

Once the veterinary surgeon has assessed a system it is then his duty to advise or persuade the owner to take action - pointing out the welfare advantages of doing so. Unless there were gross welfare problems it would not be to anyone's advantage for the veterinary surgeon to threaten or initiate any punitive action.

At the end of the day, it is just not possible for

individual veterinarians to exert sufficient pressure to bring about widespread changes in established systems. This is the responsibility of the veterinary associations - the BVA in particular - in conjunction when necessary with other organisations. You will no doubt hear a little more of this in the following paper by Neal King. This brings us nicely on to the subject of client confidentiality.

## CONFIDENTIALITY

Members of the veterinary profession are expected to maintain the highest ethical standards when carrying out their work and public duties. An ethical code is spelled out in great detail in the Guide to Professional Conduct produced by the Royal College of Veterinary Surgeons. High regard is given to client confidentiality. Except under clearly spelled-out circumstances the veterinary surgeon must not break the confidence of a client. Animal welfare is not considered to be a sufficient reason to break the code. In fact the Royal College have made this quite clear in recent advice relating to suspected illegal dog fights. Under no circumstances must this suspicion be reported to a third party. The breach of confidence, it is said, could lead to other injured dogs not receiving treatment.

On the other hand in relation to farm animals, a highly placed official in the welfare department at the Ministry of Agriculture has publicly stated that:

".... a practising veterinary surgeon has a major rôle to play in welfare. To retain credibility, the profession must seek to maintain the standards of care and husbandry of the animals under their care. I know that they can find themselves in difficult circumstances but they must not shrink from reporting clients whose welfare standards are low and who are not amenable to advice".

You can understand the dilemma in which a veterinary surgeon finds himself if during the course of a visit to a farm he spots practices in livestock husbandry which are leading to welfare problems. He can advise change, he can then later threaten action, but at the end of the day he must choose between adhering to the profession's ethical code on client confidentiality or pass on information relating to his client to a third party for appropriate action.

## MUTILATIONS

A few minutes ago, Alastair Porter predicted that I would wish to discuss the practical dilemma caused by requests that a client's cat be declawed or their dog devoiced. He was right - as always! These are included by the Royal College of Veterinary Surgeons (and in the main by the

British Veterinary Association) in a long list of procedures described as mutilations. Included in this list of course, is the tail-docking of puppies. In chapter four of the Brambell Report, it is stated that "we are prepared to tolerate mutilation only where the overall advantage to the animal, its fellow, or the safety of man is unmistakable".

Although the major professional bodies endorse these sentiments, in practice the matter is not clear cut. Take the docking of puppy's tails, for instance. Virtually to a man - or woman - the profession feel that this is an unnecessary procedure, carried out only for traditional and cosmetic purposes. Despite weak arguments to the contrary, there is no advantage to the dog. Some veterinary surgeons will not carry out the procedure - but others, including myself, will continue to tail-dock until it becomes illegal for lay persons to do so. During my years in practice I have witnessed the appalling consequences of amateur tail-docking all too frequently, particularly in the short-docked breeds. I have seen dogs caused pain and discomfort due to infections, anal injuries and chronic granulations.

It is my view, but not that of all my colleagues, that it is better to ensure that this operation is carried out painlessly, aseptically and in a correct technical manner than to drive my clients into the hands of those who are incapable of any of these things.

A veterinary practice is very rarely asked to declaw a cat or devoice a dog - in a busy practice less than once a year. After a discussion with the owner, it is sometimes possible to persuade them that it is unnecessary and that there are acceptable alternatives.

However, take the case of the elderly person who moves into a relative's home and takes along a beloved pet cat which sets out to destroy the furniture: an ultimatum is given - "stop the cat wrecking my furniture, or else it must go". Under these circumstances it is my view, again not universally accepted, that it is better for the cat to be declawed than euthanased. I once owned a Siamese cat which had been declawed. It lived to the ripe old age of twenty, and never showed the slightest sign of physical or mental stress due to the absence of its front claws.

Similar circumstances arise occasionally with a barking dog, or dogs: a complaining neighbour, a court order or a move to a new flat. "Stop the barking or the dogs must go". Again I would devoice rather than destroy, if after discussion, I was convinced that there was no acceptable alternative. But the dilemma is clear.

## CONGENITAL ABNORMALITIES

One of the major groups of disease causing welfare problems for companion animals, particularly the dog, are hereditary diseases which produce anatomical or physiological problems which in turn may cause pain or affect the quality of life.

When presented with an animal which has a defect causing pain or disease, the veterinary surgeon is duty-bound to alleviate the problem with surgery or appropriate medical treatment. The dog with a painful ulcerative keratitis due to entropion (inturning eyelid), for example in the Chow, or with a large facial fold, as in the Pekingese, must be given surgical relief. The dog with respiratory problems due to an abnormal soft palate must be given surgical relief. The bitch with an abnormal pelvis, or pups with abnormal heads which will give rise to parturition difficulties, must be given a Caesarean section. Without the protection of a domestic environment such animals would probably die, and their problems would be self-limiting. Veterinary interference allows a pain-free existence and continued breeding potential. Castration or spaying can be strongly advised, but cannot be carried out without the owner's agreement. Until such time that agreements can be reached with the Kennel Club on these matters, the veterinarian's treatment designed to improve quality of life can be a factor in passing on further problems to succeeding generations. The veterinary surgeon is cast in the rôle of saint <u>and</u> sinner.

## EUTHANASIA

Unlike their medical counterparts, veterinary surgeons have the power to carry out euthanasia when the circumstances deem it necessary. For companion animals, euthanasia can be used to terminate life which would otherwise be of unacceptable quality due to pain or chronic debility. For some conditions there can be no doubt when the time is right - but for others choice of the appropriate time can be extremely difficult for both veterinary surgeons and owners.

Take the case of Chronic Degenerative Myelopathy in German Shepherds. This is a problem affecting the spinal cord. It starts as a barely discernible weakness of one hind leg and slowly progresses over many months to complete paralysis of both hind legs accompanied by faecal and urinary incontinence. It is obvious that euthanasia is not indicated when the condition is first diagnosed - there being no pain or reduction in quality of life. It is equally obvious that a completely paralysed and incontinent dog is not a happy dog. The difficulty lies in deciding at which stage euthanasia should be carried out, when the deterioration in any one day is virtually imperceptible from the previous day.

There are other similar dilemmas. For instance, Progressive Retinal Atrophy is a fairly widespread problem in various breeds of dogs: its onset is difficult to detect. Its course is many months or even years - but the outcome is often total blindness. Since the changes are gradual, the dog usually adapts well to the incapacity. It is often the opinion of the owner that the dog's life remains a happy one. But further changes may take place in the eyes, leading to glaucoma, which is extremely painful. If this cannot be controlled medically or surgically one or both eyes must be removed. There are those who would find this repugnant or "cruel". But if this is the case, at what stage in this slow process should euthanasia be carried out? This is a dilemma for both owner and veterinary surgeon.

The dilemma experienced by the veterinarian in large animal practice is not so much <u>when</u> to carry out euthanasia as <u>where</u> to carry it out. I refer now to casualty slaughter. Decisions must be made on whether a diseased or injured animal is fit to be transported to a slaughter-house, or whether slaughter should be carried out on the farm. The situation in many parts of the country has improved during recent years. More slaughter-houses have agreed to accept animals for casualty slaughter provided they are accompanied by a certificate signed by a veterinary surgeon. Even more pleasing is the number of abattoirs which now agree to accept carcasses of animals slaughtered on the farm, and will even provide the personnel to do this, once again if the carcass is accompanied by a veterinary certificate. Thus for many veterinary surgeons the dilemmas of casualty slaughter have diminished. Improvements in this field have been achieved to a large extent by the establishment of Local Welfare Liaison Groups. Meetings of these groups are attended by representatives of slaughter-houses, those involved in transport, representatives from local authorities and veterinary surgeons from the State Veterinary Service and private practice.

## THE USE OF ANIMALS FOR RESEARCH

The use of animals in research is a subject which could fully occupy not just the time allocated for this paper but the time allocated for the full symposium. It is not therefore my intention to become deeply involved in discussing the dilemmas faced by the veterinary surgeon in this area but merely to make one or two general remarks. Firstly, the profession almost to a man sees the tremendous benefits which accrue to man and animals from research and so support its continuation. But the welfare of the animals used in research must be constantly in the minds of all those involved, and the number of animals used must be reviewed on a continuing basis. We firmly believe that the 1986 Act was a major step forward for the protection of the animals used. The main dilemma faced by veterinarians in this field is not one of ethics but one of protecting themselves and their families from the attentions of those who suffer from the contemporary sociological disease in which violence is used as a substitute for intelligent and logical debate.

## OTHER PRACTICAL DILEMMAS

Obviously there are many more examples of practical dilemmas for the veterinary surgeon: time curtails discussion, but brief mention must be made here of two of them.

Firstly, in the livestock market - the veterinary surgeon in his capacity as a Local Veterinary Inspector often finds the time he has been allocated by MAFF to be insufficient to carry out his duties to the standard he would like. The responsibilities of the various enforcement agencies represented at the market are not always clearly defined or sufficiently well organised. It is hoped that the FAWC and MAFF proposals on markets and law enforcement will help overcome some of these problems. Secondly, the duties of the veterinary surgeon in the slaughter-house are not as clearly defined or as extensive as the profession would wish. The veterinary surgeon in this situation cannot be fully satisfied that any decision he or she makes will receive the full support of the enforcement authorities.

These problems constantly produce dilemmas for the veterinarian.

## CONCLUSION

Let me summarise the situation. The field of animal welfare is not an easy one. Welfare is difficult to define and almost impossible to quantify. Society's requirements and expectations are constantly changing, depending on economics, political attitudes and technological change. The veterinary surgeon is in the front line of the fight to ensure the highest possible standards. He or she must use all their training and experience to solve the practical problems which they face.

Some practical dilemmas have been discussed. The profession knows that the spotlight of public opinion and the welfare lobby is constantly upon it and that mistakes in judgement can lead to unfortunate consequences for .the welfare of animals and the veterinarian.

I finish as I began by stating that it is my sincere belief that my colleagues in the veterinary profession, despite practical difficulties, do constantly endeavour to ensure the welfare of the animals committed to their care.

**Neal King**

## THE ROLE OF THE VETERINARIAN IN ANIMAL WELFARE
## - A NEW APPROACH

My given title implies that there is a radical new approach to improve the efficacy of the veterinary profession's contribution to animal welfare. Because the fundamental dilemmas highlighted by the two previous speakers are unlikely to change dramatically, there may in fact be no such radical new approach.

It is arguable that the individual veterinary surgeon's rôle in animal welfare is somewhat akin to the service padre's rôle in human welfare.

Both are there to mitigate damage done to individuals by circumstances which flow from human actions which are beyond our control. As long as society continues to use animals, the veterinarian's main responsibility will be to mitigate the consequences for the animal. This situation is unlikely to change.

Nevertheless members of the veterinary profession are in a pre-eminent position from which to influence animal welfare:-

(a)     as individuals who provide daily care and treatment for animals and who are in contact with those who care for them.

(b)     through their collective bodies.

The exercise of this influence can always be improved - by evolution and not by revolution.

An essential element of the evolutionary approach is education.  A recurrent theme throughout this symposium, throughout the BVA Animal Welfare Foundation's first symposium, "Priorities in Animal Welfare", and the subject of the next paper.  I would like to stress the importance of  continuing professional development - opportunity for the qualified veterinary surgeon to keep up to date with developments in the scientific (and ethical) fields - as an influence for evolutionary change in the field of animal welfare.

Another essential element in the evolutionary approach is the stimulation of riding with the tide of change - moving with the tide while encouraging it along.  There is a tide of change in the profession's attitude to animal welfare: it ebbs and flows a bit, but it is there.  It ebbs because all change is resisted by some, and veterinary surgeons are no different to others in this respect. If challenged on my vested interest, on my practices and procedures long-established, on my conviction that I am doing my job to the best of my ability, and on my belief that my concern for animals is as deep as the next man's, I am likely to defend and protest.

Many veterinary surgeons are revulsed by the scientific illogicallity and criminal actions of the extremist. Many of the encouraging steps forward in the profession's attitude to the welfare movement are set back by the latest extremist outrage. If criticism is to be effective in stimulating and encouraging the tide of change, it must be well-founded and constructive otherwise it will arouse antagonism and defensiveness - the polarisation and tribal warfare mentioned by previous speakers.

But the profession heeds, and indeed invites, criticism from those with a right to criticise. And there are those who do so with effect. Clive Hollands, an Honorary Member of the BVA, but a critic nevertheless, spelled out his concerns at the BVA Congress in Warwick last year in a lecture entitled "What the Animal Welfare Movement Expects of the Veterinarian". These are some of the points which he made:

He quotes Professor Ron Anderson, Department of Animal Husbandry at Liverpool Veterinary School, who said in his Weipers Lecture:

> "Animal welfare issues generate a puzzling lack of interest among the academic members of the veterinary profession. Veterinarians should not shy away from discussion on welfare issues simply because of the extreme opinions often expressed on the subject".

Clive went on to say:

> "the animal welfare movement as a whole does not have a very high regard of the veterinary profession on welfare issues".

He quotes Professor John Webster of Bristol University in a paper at Centaur Services annual meeting who asked the question:

> "Were veterinary practitioners achieving the right balance between animal welfare and a desire for an adequate income?".

He said: "It is important that practitioners question their motivation for practice", quoting from a letter by PG Dunn in the <u>Veterinary Record</u>:

> "Animal welfare is a subject to which too little attention is paid. Many have grown immune to the insidious development of unsatisfactory animal husbandry conditions for our farm animals. By tolerating such practices we support a system of animal agriculture which is immoral. How many veterinarians feel totally unconcerned at the sight of sows in stalls on a cold winter day? How many of us

have a completely clear conscience when we see four
layers in a battery cage?"

The significance of these quotes, apart from the fact that
they are all by distinguished members of the profession,
is that I, in turn, reproduce them verbatim from John
Tandy´s speech to the Society of Practising Veterinary
Surgeons annual congress in May this year in a hard-
hitting talk entitled "Practitioners´ responsibility for
animal welfare".

If rebutting the criticisms referred to above, I would
have to say that I am, by and large, proud of what
individual veterinary surgeons do for animal welfare
already. There is no doubt that the most important
contribution we can and do make - at the services´ padre
level, as it were - is our continued competence at
treating and relieving pain and distress in illness and
injury in the front-line. The most serious threat to
animal welfare remains illness. The most important of the
five freedoms is freedom from disease: the second is
freedom from pain and distress. Please let us not forget
that these remain, in the real everyday world, the main
contribution which veterinarians can and do make to animal
welfare.

But by and large, the tide flows because veterinarians do
want to promote good animal welfare whenever and wherever
they can, and to do so above and beyond their everyday
commitment.

As individuals, veterinarians represent as wide a cross-
section of the religious/political/economic/social types
as any other profession.

Common factors, at least at the point of entry to the
profession, are the ability and opportunity to get very
good A levels in the biology-based sciences, and a
conviction that they want to be trained in the treatment
of animal disease. These common factors are soon modified
by the necessary breadth and intensity of veterinary
education and by each individual´s emerging experience and
commitment to various careers open to veterinarians, let
alone pre-existing beliefs, interests and hobbies.
Although all veterinarians have a commitment to the relief
of suffering, this is modified by other life pressures and
the end result will be a wide diversity of opinions: it is
not possible to speak for individual veterinarians, let
alone to pretend that all have similar opinions. It is
possible to assess and represent politically mainstream
opinion, and this is a function of the political bodies.

Meanwhile, as individuals we can and should:

(a) maximise our competence as veterinary surgeons

(b) minimise our isolation as arbiters of animal
welfare

(c)  examine and then develop our philosophy on animal welfare issues

(d)  enhance our personal authority in matters of animal welfare and

(e)  enhance our influence on the various users of animals with whom we interface.

In turning to the profession´s bodies and Association, it is important to avoid a litany of the involvement of the veterinary profession in each of many topical welfare issues.  However it is worth noting the subject-headings from a recent BVA Animal Welfare Committee, if only to illustrate the breadth of the professions´ concern, and to illustrate what it is already involved in.  Agenda items included a submission to the Farm Animal Welfare Council on the welfare assessment of pig production systems; guidelines for the care of sick and injured farm animals; meetings with other welfare bodies to counter the government´s failure to ban the religious slaughter of livestock; a new welfare code for goats; a pilot scheme in conjunction with ATB for training the drivers of farm transport; the FAWC revue of livestock in transit; livestock in markets; Local Veterinary Inspectors in markets; the Deer Slaughter Bill; emergency slaughter; dog-fighting; tail-docking; the welfare of game birds; poultry production systems; the electro-ejaculation of sheep; experimental animals, with particular reference to training and guidelines relating to the 1986 act; circuses; parrots in small cages; RCVS Mutilation Report; welfare of horses in livery yards; various government bills on welfare legislation; a review of BVA policies on animal welfare; liaison with the RSPCA, NFU, LAMC, FRAME and CRAE on welfare matters.

Alastair Porter has already alluded to some of the areas of Royal College activity.  En passant, it is worth noting that the Veterinary Surgeons Act - implemented by the RCVS - is an extremely important piece of animal welfare legislation in its own right.

The BVA and the Royal College, as democratic bodies albeit of differing constitutions and remits, formulate opinion amongst their members which is in itself an important educative process for members, and which is itself important in promoting standards and reducing isolation. Having formulated opinions, they use their influence to promote animal welfare, by political pressure on government, politicians and the media, through consultation and liaison with other bodies such as the RSPCA and the NFU, and through submissions to FAWC, and through Europe.  Both bodies are also committed to the continuing professional development of their members and the promotion of standards of care within the profession.

There are limitations:

a) because of the breadth of opinion within the

profession, policies are rarely as radical as some would have and would like. We have been accused from both sides of the animal welfare spectrum of being in the pockets of the other:

(b) the professions' views are rarely newsworthy - just because they are moderate:

(c) limited resources lead to a limited impact in the press and parliamentary lobbies.

On the other hand, the mainstream considered views of the RCVS and BVA are:

(a) based on scientific rather than emotive principles, and

(b) are projected through civilised democratic channels of national and European governments.

I have been around long enough to see at first-hand policies formed within the Councils of the profession progress - slowly though it might appear - to become the accepted objective of progress and in turn to become legislation and, more important, to become accepted by animal users. I mention as examples only the Zoo Licensing Legislation, RCVS Mutilations Initiatives, the 1986 Animal Scientific Procedures Act and Calf Movements Through Markets.

Of these, the 1986 Act is probably the best example of progress through the statute book to improve animal welfare. In this case, the profession's views were found acceptable enough by two major welfare groups in the field to form the BVA/CRAE/FRAME alliance so that a common, broad-based, moderate, well-founded position could be embraced by government. Those suspicious of the political approach to animal welfare could well note the sentiments of Lord Houghton expressed in his acceptance speech at the BVA Animal Welfare Foundation's Alice Stanley Jay Award for his outstanding contribution to animal welfare. He denied (and I paraphrase rather than quote) that he was an animal welfare extremist, or bigot, or convert, or fanatic, or even an enthusiast, when he embraced the cause politically. It was indeed that he could not bear to see so much concern and energy and commitment by so many different groups going to waste for lack of political co-ordination and direction. Thereby hangs a lesson for all animal welfare groups. While the road to progress remains the democratic one, pooling of resources and co-ordination of political endeavour is essential. It is my conviction that the profession has enormous potential in rallying moderate and sane animal welfare opinion, providing a scientific rather than an emotional basis for it, and projecting it, in alliance with other bodies, to government.

Veterinarians as individuals influence animal welfare in a number of miscellaneous capacities and groups, of which time precludes discussion. But the veterinary influence within the welfare societies, the Home Office Inspectorate, the animal treatment charities, the pharmaceutical companies in particular and industry in general, can all impinge on animal welfare politics, legislation, and in the front-line.

Some other groups within the profession are worthy of special consideration.

The State Veterinary Service has a statutory responsibility for farm animal welfare behind the farm gate. This responsibility was conferred relatively recently on a cadre of state-employed veterinarians whose original and primary rôles were the protection from catastrophic epidemic disease of an important national asset - the livestock industry. Additionally, they have important public health responsibilities, including the eradication of TB and brucellosis, and meat hygiene. The accomplishment of these tasks within the agricultural community has been superbly executed by a policy of working with the farmer as a friend and advisor, resorting to the statute or rule book only when obstructed.

There are those who claim that this cosy relationship is not so beneficial for animals: that when the vet´s friendly advice is neglected, it is difficult to turn nasty and prosecute. The number of successful prosecutions for infringements of animal welfare legislations is tiny, they say. The counter-arguments are that most infringements of farm animal welfare standards are sins of omission rather than commission: when welfare standards fail, the farmer needs all the help he can get to overcome a crisis, be it of health, competence, finance, poor harvest or downright inadequacy. Prosecution by then is of little help to the animal.

Moreover, the legislative framework for policing farm animal welfare relies heavily on the farm animal welfare codes, infringement of which, like the highway code, is not per se a crime, but which can be used as telling evidence against the farmer if and when (if ever) he is prosecuted. But, one could point out, at least the driver on the highway knows that prosecution frequently occurs and he is expected to show some knowledge of the codes before he is let loose on the roads!

Meanwhile, it is arguable that by far the majority of farm animal welfare abuses take place beyond the farm gate - in transport, whether or not through market, to the slaughterhouse floor. In this area, piecemeal legislation and split responsibilities between MAFF, County and District Government, and the Police leaves much to be desired.

To solve some of these problems, and as an opportunity to enhance the rôle of the State Veterinary Service in Animal Welfare, the establishment of a clearly identifiable farm animal welfare inspectorate within the State Veterinary

Service was proposed by the BVA, and remains BVA policy. It was envisaged that a small cadre of experienced veterinarians, recruited from within and without of the State Veterinary Service, would be distributed at divisional level of the service. These officers, in remuneration and in career structure akin to the Home Office inspectors, would have opted out of their normal state veterinary service rôle, and would expect to remain in their divisional appointment for several years, work in close liaison with the farm animal welfare council, from whom they would take their guidance, and to whom they would feed back their experiences. Their rôle would be as welfare experts

(a) to advise and co-ordinate the standards expected by front-line veterinary advisors, be they veterinary officers or LVIs, either in interpretation of the codes or in standards at markets, for example;

(b) to be called in as the "big stick" on difficult cases;

(c) to co-ordinate prosecutions;

(d) to vet all new livestock enterprises before they are established;

(e) to take over responsibility, by primary legislation if necessary, for those murky areas of animal welfare legislation in transport, markets and slaughter houses.

It is possible that such a structure would significantly improve the implementation of farm animal welfare in a number of ways:

(a) the front line state veterinary officers and practising veterinary surgeons would retain their cosy advisory relationship with the farmer, but with the tacit or big-stick threat of the animal welfare inspector to give point to their advice. For example, each state veterinary visit could require a box to be filled in on the accompanying forms, "Are welfare codes being complied with?" A negative reply would elicit a visit from the welfare inspector;

(b) the private veterinary surgeon would have a recognisable, identifiable local expert to call in for advice and the inspector would carry the authority and knowledge to see that the interpretation of standards were even. This could reduce the isolation factor;

(c) In the event of a prosecution, the inspector would co-ordinate all the interested parties with authority. His position and opinion would carry clout in the courts where so often, after painstakingly amassing a welfare case, the magistrates seem to be unimpressed by the evidence and derisory penalties are often imposed;

(d)    the welfare societies, public and all others
interested in animal welfare would have an
identifiable authority to whom they could confide,
complain or from whom they could seek informal advice;

(e)    The inspectorate would, if required, take on
board a system of licensing livestock keepers (a
knowledge of the welfare codes would be a prerequisite
of the licence and a clean slate a prerequisite of
reissue of the licence) and they could also "vet" new
systems before they are installed;

(f)    The farm animal welfare council could have a
direct feedback from the field as new developments and
techniques emerged and the farm animal welfare
council, through its links with the inspectorate,
would have an enhanced value.

Since the development of the idea in 1982, the State
Veterinary Service has to its credit evolved a long way
towards some of the objectives sought by the establishment
of this inspectorate.

The establishment of local welfare liaison groups, the
appointment of regional veterinary officers with special
responsibility for welfare and much greater in service
training on animal welfare, are steps in the right
direction but still fall short of the original concept in
many respects.  Continued development of the State
Veterinary Service in this direction is an important part
of the new approach.

In terms of the profession's groups, contributions to
animal welfare, the launch and development of the Animal
Welfare Foundation is arguably the most significant
feature.  It was founded on a legacy to establish a
professorial chair in animal welfare with a remit to build
a new veterinary-based national animal welfare charity
with the residue of the bequest.

The idea of a chair in animal welfare at a veterinary
school goes far beyond the work of one man in one post.
The fundamental objective is to establish animal welfare
as the multi-disciplinary science it should be rather than
the emotive cause it so often is.  The choice of the
Cambridge Veterinary School juxtaposed as it is to schools
for other disciplines and departments of, for example,
animal behaviour, architecture, land economy,
neurophysiology and the like, allows the discipline to be
wider-based than veterinary science, and yet remain
essentially veterinary.  Eventually, the Centre of
Excellence which should develop around the Chair will
provide a national, if not international, reference point
for scientific evidence for those needing to make
political and moral judgements about animal welfare
issues.

The development of the Animal Welfare Foundation as a

fund-raising body for the direction of animal welfare research and endeavour, and for the furtherance of education at all levels provides an opportunity to harness the vocational expertise of the profession to the collection and wise distribution of urgently needed funds. The recently produced "Priorities for Research and Development in Animal Welfare" document of the Farm Animal Welfare Council points to the need for urgent funding from all quarters: government, industry and the charities. If the AWF can meet its fund-raising potential, and commit itself to supporting such soundly considered research needs, the profession's contribution to the new approach will be further strengthened.

**To Summarise**: The profession's principal rôle is the mitigation of the consequences of society's use of animals at the front-line, by providing high-quality treatment and by the prevention of disease and suffering. The framework within which this activity is constrained limits radical change: we already do it well, we can continue to improve. All the evolutionary changes in the profession are already in the right direction. Shrill and unfounded criticism is counter-productive to evolutionary change. The contribution of individual veterinarians to animal welfare can be enhanced by education, by communication with his peers on acceptable standards, by strengthening resolve to be outspoken on standards - while still retaining the confidence of those who seek his services.

Our professional bodies have a key position in:

(a)   The formation of political alliances with moderate opinion to further animal welfare in the political arena;

(b)   The strengthening of the State Veterinarian's rôle in animal welfare, particularly from the farm gate to the slaughter house floor;

(c)   The establishment and development of the Chair in animal welfare and the extension of its influence;

(d)   The collection and distribution of funds for animal welfare research, development and education, and

(e)   Continuing professional development of our members.

The tide of change - already discernible - is the main propellant to this "New Approach".

M F Stewart

## TEACHING OF ANIMAL WELFARE TO VETERINARY STUDENTS

The teaching of animal welfare to veterinary students in the western world has in recent years been receiving increased attention, both from within and without the veterinary profession.

Mike Appleby found in his 1986 Churchill Fellowship survey of welfare teaching in European veterinary and agricultural institutions, that the variation in approaches to welfare was a reflection of differences in the agricultural industries, of public opinions, and of government legislation in each country studied.

The U.S. system of teaching depends a lot on elective courses, some being stronger on welfare than others, with four actually requiring course work in veterinary ethics.

In the U.K., animals in general already have more protection than in some other countries, so we start off from a relatively positive welfare baseline. In 1986, a Universities Federation for Animal Welfare (UFAW) sponsored workshop investigated and compared the place of the teaching of welfare in our U.K. veterinary and agricultural schools (anon: 1987)

With one exception, British veterinary schools expect students to attend the full course, with no electives, and they all get specific welfare teaching. Although we found differences in the structuring of welfare courses and in the amount of integration with other subjects, and though the complexities of ethical and economic concerns were approached in different ways, there was agreement about the desired outcome: that the students be familiar with all the factors which contribute to the health and well-being of the animals which may come under their care, that they should learn to assess the effects of various environments and management systems on welfare, and that they should be able to recognise and identify the signs of discomfort, distress, pain and suffering in different species of animals. Where there are "grey areas", students should be encouraged to develop an attitude of mind which will enable them to give the animal the benefit of the doubt.

When asked "how much actual course time is allotted to welfare?" the question is hard to answer. For instance, a veterinarian colleague who holds a post as a "lecturer of welfare" writes that his subject (welfare) was described as including "management, nutrition, environment, behaviour, health, transportation, marketing and slaughter of farm animals. The range of application includes farm animals, companion and laboratory animals" (M Cockrane, personal communication). With this range of subjects all coming under the heading of Welfare, one could say that most of the Animal Husbandry course comes into that category.

These subjects are covered in all veterinary schools, hopefully with welfare in mind but not necessarily all listed as part of the welfare course. In fact, when we consider the remit of the basic welfare codes which mention housing, environment, nutrition, prevention and treatment of parasitism, disease, illness, injury, behavioural needs (including social aspects) and freedom from fear (and all the implications of that statement), then it is apparent that all parts of the veterinary curriculum have direct or indirect links to welfare.
Anatomy, Biochemistry and especially Physiology are building blocks without which there can be no informed understanding of the biological mechanisms involved in stress and pain etc. Animal Husbandry has obvious relevance in all its different facets including Animal Behaviour, in which students learn that animals are complex systems, not just a biological mechanism. To be familiar with an animal's requirements and needs, it helps to understand what external and internal factors contribute to an animal's motivation, the function of specific behaviours, what behaviours are normal, and how abnormal behaviour can be interpreted. The effect of genetic and environmental factors on learning and development, and the significance of different stages in development are also mentioned. This background can enrich our understanding when observing animals in the field or under natural conditions. Humans have a natural tendency to project their own priorities on other animals, but it might not always be in the animal's best interest that they do so.

Research studies are described which yield the kind of information useful for enriching environments or for providing more favourable conditions for animals.

The practical application of this type of research is illustrated by the setting up of economically viable and humane livestock units such as John Webster's calf-rearing system at Bristol (Webster and Saville, 1981) and Wood-Gush and Stolba's family pig unit in Edinburgh (Stolba: UFAW).

The Handling and Restraint classes emphasise that welfare ultimately comes down to the well-being of individual animals. Students learn to handle animals in ways which will cause minimum anxiety and stress (and hopefully give reassurance) as well as to ensure the safety of both the animals and the humans involved. Having these classes early on in the course helps students to identify with living animals and serves as a reminder that academic theory is not enough: observing, handling and interacting with animals are all essential for a good understanding of them.

Throughout the husbandry course, welfare aspects are addressed, whether discussing pros and cons of different management systems, or the economic implications of animal production, when visiting the zoo, the SPCA animal shelter, the PDSA clinic, the slaughter-house and various farms, as well as during lectures on such subjects such as housing, environment, nutrition, transportation, etc.

The subject actually called <u>Welfare</u> is usually part of <u>Animal Husbandry</u>. This will be described after pointing out the specific relevance of paraclinical and clinical subjects which deal in theory and practice with the detection, prevention and treatment of disease, illness and injury, and which are intimately concerned with the alleviation of pain and prevention of suffering. We are responsible for a great variety of species held in a wide range of environments and circumstances - the amount of information to be learned is vast, and is steadily increasing.

## Specific welfare course work

The following summary describes the basics as taught at one veterinary school, with contributions from visiting lecturers (Roger Ewbank of UFAW and Alastair Lawrence, from the East of Scotland Agricultural School). It takes place for the most part in the first year, in order to provide an early familiarity with the subject, which can be used throughout the following years.

Students are taught:

1. The different definitions of welfare, and the biological basis for such consideration (e.g. though a machine can have immense sophistication it can have no welfare).

2. The integrated approach to measurement of welfare, by assessment of health and appearance of well-being, by productivity, by physiological and biochemical parameters, by assessment of behaviour (whether normal, abnormal or altered), and by the recognition of pain and suffering as expressed by different species. It is pointed out that it can be misleading to look at one factor in isolation, for example productivity can be high and yet the welfare still be poor.

3. Bad welfare is described, and how ill treatment (from abuse, neglect or ignorance) is an unfortunate, unacceptable, but undisputed problem. Whereas bad welfare due to deprivation is both more difficult to assess and far more emotive in its implications.

4. Legislation. The early legislation for the protection of animals is described before discussing recent reforms. Specific reference is made to the impact of Ruth Harrison´s book "Animal Machines" (1964), which resulted in a general awakening towards what was happening in our intensive animal production

systems: how this led to the formation of the Brambell Committee. The implications of recent changes in legislation on experimental procedures is also mentioned.

For every way in which we keep, protect, or exploit domestic, captive, or wild animals, there is some sort of legislation involved. The students are made aware of the type of legislation and the authorities which are responsible for different groups or categories of animal. They are also told of the rôles of different groups, charities, trusts, etc. (such as UFAW, BVA Animal Welfare Foundation and the RSPCA) which act as advisors, educators, sponsors of research, conferences, workshops, etc., and of the many animal-orientated groups and charities involved with general and specific issues. Veterinarians should be aware of the presence of rescue organisations and charity clinics, and the importance of their supportive rôle.

The students are told of the growing public concern about animal welfare, and that as veterinarians, having sworn the welfare oath, they should take responsibility to keep informed on these issues.

## Humane Ethics

The scientific, veterinary and ethological approach can be taught and quantified, but it must be balanced by a consideration of the Humane Ethic, which is not so clear-cut. In the ethics class, assisted by a philosopher with an interest in animal affairs, we discuss the variations in human attitudes towards animals, how cultures differ and how individuals within cultures differ.

The students are asked to examine their own attitudes towards some of the most common areas of public concern, and to identify if possible what might have influenced their own opinions. We encourage them to share their ideas and to look at the implications of different ethical dilemmas. There is not time for lengthy philosophical debate but the purpose of this class is to make students aware that throughout their professional life they will need to make ethical decisions, like it or not. They should make sure that they make these decisions with integrity based on informed, aware and compassionate judgements.

So much of their course is being lectured at - but in this class we encourage them to think for themselves, and to exchange ideas.

They are warned that something often happens to medical and veterinary students, most of whom start out with altruistic ideals of helping, whether humans or animals. The increasing pressure of the course, the intense workload, and finally the sheer challenge of clinical work and exams sometimes results in students forgetting that the "pancreas in the next bed" or the "fractured pelvis in the end kennel" is a living creature whose overall well-being should always be kept in mind. This does not necessarily mean a great time commitment; it does mean a constant awareness and a sustained sensitivity. Leo Bustad (1983), the past Dean of Pullman Veterinary School (who still teaches a "Reverence for Life" course), quoted from one of Nixon´s colleagues who said (while waiting for sentence at the Watergate trials) "Somewhere between my ambitions and my ideals I lost my ethical compass". Leo reminds his students that they had "better have an ethical compass that always works and is never lost".

Hopefully our students will be reminded throughout their course to be aware of the implications of their decision-making, their actions and non-actions. As veterinarians with great power over life and death, they should take care not to kill thoughtlessly or carelessly.

As educators we should consider not only what and how we teach but to whom. Changes in public awareness also affect veterinary students, who are starting off their professional training with a very different ethical baseline than was prevalent when a lot of the teaching staff began theirs.

It is gratifying and very encouraging that students are taking the initiative towards a more active student participation in the welfare area, such as organising debates, planning and carrying out research projects, and considering the formation of a student welfare group to liaise with all the veterinary schools in the U.K.

A study of American veterinary students carried out by Robert Shurtliff et al. in 1981 showed that the majority were "proponents of animal welfare". From a similar study now being carried out in the U.K., it appears that the students do have strong opinions and feel that veterinarians have an ongoing obligation to work towards better conditions for animals. Most students feel that there is a need to include humane ethics as a standard part of veterinary training, and would appreciate more discussion of such issues as animal rights, at the same time as being critical of the more extreme and violent faction which often gives the animal rights movement a bad and even dangerous image.

Just as medical education is giving more prominence to medical ethics, the same is starting to take place in the veterinary schools and was "pioneered" by the philosopher Bernie Rollin who initiated a course in humane ethics at Colorado State Veterinary School. To quote Andrew Rowan of Tufts Veterinary School in Boston:

> "We must study the role of the veterinarian within his or her profession and within society and evaluate the changing moral and legal status of animals. Such studies may not produce many easy answers, but at

least they should show us how to reach reasoned and reasonable conclusions".

Professor Anderson at Liverpool Veterinary School gave the 1986 Weipers lecture in which he suggested that "Animal welfare issues generate a puzzling lack of interest among academic members of the veterinary profession" (Anderson, 1987).

An interesting statement - since in the schools we encourage students to keep abreast of new developments and changes which affect the profession. Actually welfare is getting a higher profile, with Donald Broom in the Chair of Animal Welfare at Cambridge, "new blood" posts of welfare lecturers, and the establishment of the BVA Animal Welfare Foundation. Things are looking up for welfare in our veterinary schools with the help of UFAW, and with the contribution of ethologists and philosophers. Professor Anderson said "veterinarians should not shy away from discussions on welfare issues because of extreme opinions often expressed on the subject". He suggests that the "veterinarian is uniquely placed because of his/her training to recognise and interpret normal behaviour and quantify welfare parameters". As for the "extreme opinions", this is a hard one. There is a saying "He who walks in the middle of the road gets hit by chariots from both directions". There is surely a danger of this happening to veterinarians who try to make dialogue with both sides over complex welfare issues. Moderates are rarely popular.

About the second statement - made at a Farm Animal Welfare meeting in Newcastle University the suggestion (anon: 1986) was made that veterinarians might not always be the best judge of animal welfare because by being exposed to so much suffering, they might become hardened or insensitive. This may still be so in some cases, but a number of factors which support Anderson's views include:

1. The increasing range and depth of present-day training.

2. Greater emphasis on practical clinical experience.

3. The greater prominence given to welfare and behaviour.

4. The current climate of opinion among many students.

Most of the veterinary students choose veterinary training because they like to work with and help animals. They should come out in a strong position to do so as long as they learn their skills well and do not lose their sensitivity and "ethical compass" somewhere along the way.

# References and Bibliography

Anderson, RA. (1987) Veterinary Record 4 July.

Anon (1986). Farm Animal Welfare Meeting. University of Newcastle-on-Tyne.

Anon (1987). Teaching of Animal Welfare (UFAW Symposium).

Appleby, MC. Farm Animal Welfare in Northern Europe. The influence of education. (1986, Winston Churchill Memorial Fellowship).

Bustad, L. Dean's Responsibilities and Bioethics. (1983) California Veterinarian. Spring , p97.

Harrison, R. Animal Machines. (London: Vincent Stuart, 1964).

Rowan, A. Centre for Animals Information leaflet.

Shurtliff, RS: Grant, P: Zeglen, ME: McCulloch, WF: Bustad, LK. (1983) Journal of Veterinary Medical Education 9 p3.

Stolba, A. "Family System of Pig Housing" p52. in Alternatives to Intensive Husbandry Systems. UFAW Symposium. London.

Webster, AJF: Saville, C. "Rearing of Veal Calves" Alternatives to Intensive Husbandry Systems. (London: UFAW Symposium, 1981, p86).

# PART SEVEN

ANIMALS AND THE MEDIA

Jeffery Boswall

## ANIMAL STARS : Considerations in the use of Animals in Film and Television

(This paper has been adapted from a lecture given at the 3rd International Wildlife Film-makers´ Symposium held at Bath University, U.K., in September 1985 under the title "The Moral Pivots of Wildlife Film-making". The author was a producer in the BBC´s Natural History Unit at Bristol, 1957-1987; he is now Head of Film and Video at the Royal Society for the Protection of Birds. The views expressed here are his own.)

There are two main moral pivots of wildlife programme-making and they are, I submit to you, firstly the obligation to the audience, and, secondly, the obligation to the animals. It could be said that there is the obligation to those who pay, and the obligation to those who are **not paid**. I can think of no important moral issues in wildlife film-making that do not fall under one of those two main headings. I will therefore venture to translate them into two commandments for your consideration: Thou shalt not deceive the audience; Thou shalt not harm the animals.

To anyone outside the wildlife film-making movement, these must appear so self-evident that it would be difficult to imagine that two hundred professionals could spend two hours talking about them. But they did. The point is that these nifty admonitions are easier to coin than they are to apply. Before I discuss how to apply them, may I mention that I exclude from this paper the question of the ethics of animal involvement in fiction films: an interesting and important, but different, issue. I approach this matter of ethics in natural history broadcasting intellectually - academically - because that way we can generate light rather than heat; we can more easily consider the matter rationally. Bertrand Russell (if I recall correctly) defined rationality as the selection of the best means for the achievement of an end. The idea of gut feeling which currently has some currency as a means of choice I profoundly mistrust as a form of mental laziness. Don´t get me wrong, I am not averse to passion, I am not against fire in the belly; I´m not opposed to fire in other places either, but I think that gut reaction is the fuel that you use in the car once you have rationally decided where to go.

## Thou shalt not deceive the audience

Now here I want to clear out of the way from the start what seems to me to be a red herring. Some people try to shelter behind the idea that films are all false anyway: the colours aren´t true, film time isn´t real time, we don´t see life through a 4 x 3 frame, etc. Where should we draw the line? Well, I´ll tell you where I think we

should draw the line. Between the three things I have
just specified plus any others which are also established,
ascertainable conventions of film-making and, therefore,
inescapable parts of our art; and - on the other hand -
those residual matters which are legitimate fodder for
moral evaluation. It is the legitimate moral fodder we
are chewing over here.

"Thou shalt not deceive the audience". Deceive them as to
what? The facts of nature? How the film was made? Well,
certainly we should not deceive viewers as to the facts of
nature; and perchaps not as to how the film was made.

"Thou shalt not deceive the audience as to the facts of
nature". If we ought not to do this, why ought we not to
do it? What is the reason for not deceiving people as to
the facts of nature? The reason is that they trust us.
The reason is that the audience takes the film to be fact
and not fiction, documentary and not story. They take it
to be true to life and not to be in part or whole the
result of somebody's imagination. If we are anxious to
discharge this obligation, then there are only four areas
where we can go wrong. We can deceive them with the
pictures, with the words, with the effects, and I shall
even suggest we could actually deceive them with the music
- yes, deceive them.

Let's take the pictures first. Against what do we have to
be on our guard? Against showing pictures of animals
behaving in ways in which they would not behave in nature,
against depicting them in a natural history film, un-
naturally. It has not been unknown for two species to be
introduced to one another for the purpose of a film, two
species which would not normally meet in nature. It might
be possible to bait an animal in such a way as to make it
behave un-naturally, or indeed to depict an animal eating
food it does not normally eat because it was provided by
us. It could easily happen that our presence causes the
animals to behave differently from how they would behave
in our absence. Move a hide up too fast to a bird's nest
and the wader may return to its eggs but it doesn't
actually sit on its eggs, it half sits on them because it
is torn between being frightened of the hide and wanting
to sit properly on its eggs.

Slow motion is by definition un-natural, as are fast
motion and other forms of time warp. These too can
deceive unless the shots concerned are self-evidently
"wrong" or unless we are told in the commentary that a
liberty has been taken with reality. Shots taken not at
the normal speed of 25 frames per second, but at 32 or
50, or even 75 frames per second, shall we say, of a
flying bird, merely give the impression that the bird is
bigger than it is because it is flapping its wings more
slowly, and so on. Some film-makers regard this as a
trivial moral issue; others give it more weight.

We can also deceive people as to the sound by tape-
recording it at the wrong speed! I well recall England's

New Forest resounding to the song of the nightingale one octave down and each phrase exactly twice its true length. But such events are, of course, unwitting errors, and not strictly relevant. Morality involves conscious choice. So what does the director do if he has superb visuals of, say, Eleanora´s falcon calling, but no sound? Is he justified in accepting the sound library´s offer of the voice of the closely related peregrine? I well know the temptation! And Oscar Wilde, as we know, said that he could resist anything except temptation. And we may find ourselves tempted to use not merely a real recording which is the wrong one, but an entirely artificial recording. Can such a choice be justified? For example, would you, my audience, use a recording of an umbrella being flapped to represent the noise made by a bird´s wings? At all? If it was virtually indistinguishable from the real thing?

Can I digress at this point to say that because I instance a moral point, it doesn´t mean to say that I approve or disapprove of it myself. I´ve tried very hard to cast myself in a quasi-judicial role and to hide from my listeners how I actually feel about each of these issues. Hence the title, "The moral pivots of wildlife film-making" I do know on which side I would come down off each fence, but the purpose of this talk is to place the listener in the position of the film director.

After the pictures and sound effects fences, a third fence at which we could fall is to deceive people with the words. The temptations here are to exaggerate, to melodramatise, to sentimentalise, to humanise. The word "humanise" has been proposed by Mary Midgley in her book "Why Animals are Important", as a replacement for the word "anthropomorphise", an ugly word at best. Let´s talk in the future about humanising, and not about anthropomorphising. Humanising is, of course, attributing to animals human characteristics that they don´t have. It´s a kind of lying.

Dare I suggest to you that anthropomorphic music is also a kind of lying? If you put music to a piece of animal behaviour that suggests that that animal is more human than it is, then you are deceiving the people who are experiencing the film.

So much then for the ways it is possible to deceive the audience as to what happens in nature. If we succeed in not doing so, we´ll be showing the audience what they could see and hear in nature if they were lucky enough to be in the right place at the right time; and secondly we would be telling them in the commentary only what is factually true. A narration may also include the currently respectable scientific interpretations of those facts, aesthetic appreciation, personal anecdotes and even a quotation or two. But these are artistic matters beyond the subject of this paper.

We come now to a more subtle problem: can we "deceive" the audience as to how the film was made? Well, if what we´re considering is rights and wrongs, rights and wrongs can only be assessed in the minds of human beings; and perhaps it is the audience´s minds that are the most important ones here. We need to know whether or not the audience would feel cheated if they knew how the film was made. It would not cost very much money to find out the answer to that question. If the answer was that a consensus of viewers did feel cheated, then I think it could only follow that we are doing something wrong.

In the wildlife film-making business we film tame animals: we tame wild animals for this purpose. We bring other wild animals temporarily into controlled conditions. We use captive animals from zoos. We husband animals for quite long periods of time. And we usually present all these animals as if they were wild - and go to a lot of trouble to create this illusion. Obviously, if we were to present captive animals as captive animals there would be no case to answer. But the words that go over those shots of "wild" animals require very careful consideration. They require what might be described as a "slight of the larynx". They may mislead. And again, if the audience assumes, and I´m sure that most among them do, that most if not at all of the footage is of truly wild animals, would the viewers feel conned if they knew it were otherwise? Would their admiration for the director-cameramen have been misplaced? And their trust in their presenters dented? There are director-cameramen who do not wish to receive credit that is not their due.

The question of wildlife film-making ethics is becoming - well, I was going to say - a "public issue", but that is an exaggeration. But certainly with "The Making of The Living Planet", a book by Andrew Langley (a writer from outside the wildlife film-making community), we had explained how much of the material in The Living Planet was secured. The book´s commendable honesty about the use of captive animals was picked up by a Sunday paper in Britain, surprisingly I think by only one Sunday newspaper. The headline was "Secrets of the Not so Wildlife - Attenborough Defends the Use of Captive Animals". When The Living Planet was repeated, Andrew Langley wrote a page in Radio Times which included the sentence, "You may be surprised, even outraged, to learn that the happy looking armadillo on your screen was in fact fresh out of a zoo". Now that man is a writer and he owes his obligation to his audience and he is anticipating and assessing how he thinks people would feel about the use of captive animals if they knew.

In 1985, the Canadian Broadcasting Corporation made a whole hour film and a team of investigative journalists, not from the Nature of Things Unit but from the Current Affairs department, made a film in their investigative series Fifth Estate, called Cruel Camera. Half of it was concerned with so-called "staging" in wildlife films.

The September 1985 issue of Discover magazine, Time Incorporated´s superb popular science monthly with a

circulation of 800,000 copies, carried an article about
wildlife film-making ethics by a highly responsible
reporter called Jamie James. The article is called "Art
and Artifice in Wildlife Films". James like Langley is
an outsider and I will just quote a bit to give you the
impression that he gets of the wildlife programme-making
industry because I think it´s a matter of concern:

> "Ask a wildlife film maker about ethical
> irregularities and he´ll usually have plenty to say -
> about his competitors. The prevailing mood in this
> field isn´t exactly one of fraternity; there´s a lot
> of tale telling, back stabbing, and finger pointing.
> Baker says that Marty Stouffer, the producer and on-
> camera host of the PBS series <u>Wild America</u>, has used
> unethical and environmentally risky tactics in
> shooting some of his programs, and he also accuses him
> of using tame animals - something Bayer himself does
> routinely.
>
> Stouffer accuses "Wild Kingdom" of using zoo animals:
> Jim Fowler, Marlin Perkin´s assistant on <u>Wild Kingdom</u>
> accuses the BBC of not having got their science quite
> right on a few points in a series about South America.
> The BBC and Oxford Scientific Films are feuding: at
> Oxford , they call the BBC arrogant and miserly, while
> BBC bigwigs say the Oxonians are "bloody
> unreasonable". The only thing upon which they all
> agree is that Walt Disney was guilty of every crime in
> the book - and he, of course, is no longer here to
> defend himself".

When I first read that, I chuckled all the way to the
cutting-room; but when I thought about it later I decided
it was really quite serious, because that is an outsider´s
view of what is happening in our industry. It may or may
not be accurate, it may or may not be justified, but is a
responsible reporter´s impression. The <u>Discover</u> story was
picked up by PCBS news and soon afterwards there was a 20-
minute item about natural history film-making.

To sum up on the first commandment: if you offer only
what the viewer could experience in nature, you´re okay.
If you were to have a disclaimer like the FCC disclaimer
at the end, and I would propose that we do that (I really
have come to that view myself), then you can only be okay
as regards the audience as well.


## Thou shalt not harm the animals

No: nor, for that matter, the flowers or the rocks
either. Define "harm"? Disturbance, distraction,
diversion, death. There are many different problems here.
Chasing creatures with cars or helicopters, or undue
disturbance of a bird´s nest by moving up a hide so fast
that the bird deserts; causing unnecessary suffering by

bad husbandry. There is incidentally an Act of Parliament that governs what we can and can´t do to an animal for the purpose of a film. It is sub-titled "An Act to prohibit the exhibition or distribution of cinematograph films in connection with the production of which suffering may have been caused to animals". Any person contravening the provisions of this Act shall be liable to imprisonment for a term not exceeding three months. It is, incidentally, the exhibitors who offend against the law and not the maker of the film.

The temptations are considerable. Time is money. Rising audience expectations demand better pictures, closer pictures, more detailed behaviour. The point that I think needs to be brought home is that morality is subjective. It´s up to each one of us to decide, for himself. In the lecture at Bath University I put it this way: "If you were asked how you would react in a particular moral situation you would not all agree. And I´d like to put that to the test. I´m going to offer you, if I may, a graded series of six moral problems and I´d like you to vote publicly on them:

(1)  How many of you, knowing that spiders do eat flies and therefore there´s no problem of scientific integrity, and knowing that you were doing it exclusively for the purpose  of a natural history film, how many of you would introduce a fly to a spider?

                    (yes:   ?  ; No:   ? ; Undecided:   ? ).

(2)  How many of you equally would introduce a worm to a frog?
                    (yes:   ?  ; No:   ? ; Undecided:   ? ).

(3)  How many of you would introduce a snake to a secretary bird?

                    (yes:   ?  ; No:   ? ; Undecided:   ? ).

(4)  How many would introduce a live small bird to a hawk?

                    (yes:   ?  ; No:   ? ; Undecided:   ? ).

(5)  How many of you would introduce a monkey to a boa constrictor for the purpose of a film, knowing that monkeys are normally the prey of boa constrictors?

                    (yes:   ?  ; No:   ? ; Undecided:   ? ).

(6)   Lastly, knowing that man is the normal prey of a crocodile, given that proper provision was made for his family, how many of you would introduce a man........

                    (yes:   ?  ; No   ? ; Undecided:   ? ).

The point about that exercise is that not everybody voted the same way everytime so therefore it <u>has</u> to be an individual choice.

213

To sum up on the second commandment, each of us has to decide what he or she is prepared to do. Morality <u>is</u> subjective; only when the law of the particular country where we are making or exhibiting a film lays something down are we given guidelines.

## Conclusion

To finish, human beings have free will; they are necessarily faced with the prospect of moral choice. Wildlife film-makers are human beings that often face difficult and complex choices. In making these choices we need to give to the audience and to the animals "due respect"; but except insofar as we are helped when the law lays it down on the line, each and every one of us has to decide what constitutes "due". Over to you.

**PART EIGHT**


**THE PLENARY SESSION**

Summaries and Questions

## PLENARY SESSION

### Summaries and Questions

**Clive Hollands**

We now come to the very last session of this conference on the Status of Animals.

In 1977, at the end of Animal Welfare Year, the first Conference of this kind was held at Trinity College, Cambridge. Organised by the RSPCA under the title of "Animal Rights, A Symposium", it looked at historical and social perspectives of our relationships with animals, including the religious, theological, philosophical, and political viewpoints. Three major areas of concern were studied - farming, wildlife and experimentation. At the end of the Conference, some 150 of those attending signed a Declaration Against Speciesism, drawn up by the then Chairman of the RSPCA, Richard Ryder.

In 1980, a second Conference was called, held at Sussex University under the auspices of the Humane Education Council, of which David Paterson was and is Chairman. This also looked at many of the aspects of a basis for social and moral responsibility in the way that we look at creation. But the emphasis at this conference was on the educational side of the problem. In introducing the it, David Paterson said: "So is true humane education more than ´teaching kindness´?" Certainly as we know it now it has become more, using disciplines such as ecology, biology, conservation, sociology, psychology, veterinary science and so on. Yet it transcends all of these, welding them together: it is larger than they. It embraces and is founded upon a sound philosophy, a thought-system: it is a responsible ethic. It is educative too: this ethic has to be seen in action.

I would suggest to you that the conference which we are concluding, has now brought action to the forefront. It has been designed to build upon those previous conferences. To look at attitudes, ethics and education "ten years on".

The prime purpose now is to take the whole concept of Humane Education into the next century, which some of us may not be here to see, but it is still important that our thoughts should continue.

The various chairmen will now give a digest of each session, prior to a brief general discussion.

## SUMMARIES & QUESTIONS

**1    J SOUTHEE, chairing "OUR MORAL OBLIGATION TO ANIMALS"**

The Symposium opened with a session in which we examined
our moral obligations towards animals. Professor Clark
identified the philosophical basis of what we mean by
"Animal Welfare", so setting the theme for all three days.
Are we in a position to decide.when an animal is or is not
"well-off"? What is our obligation to animals? How far
should we extend that responsibility?

Mary Midgley followed up by offering some practical
solutions to the problem of how we avoid stereotyping and
conflict within the animal welfare movement.

Finally, Andrew Linzey went further, giving the
theological point of view on animal rights and our
responsibilities towards them.

**2    G LANGLEY, chairing "EDUCATION"**

The common theme of the Education Session was that the
education system is a rather conventional and slow-moving
juggernaut, with considerable inertia which must be
overcome before we can expect it to change direction.

Education reflects the general standards of society, and
if we want to gain more than a toe-hold in the curriculum
we must plan our strategy carefully. We must, for
instance, ensure that we ourselves are informed about
children´s views on animals at different ages so that
effective educational material can be designed, building
on generally accepted duties towards animals and making
links with related issues such as pet-care and the
environment. We must also try to teach general values,
such as kindness, so that these will be applied to non-
human as well as human animals, and work to gain
credibility and respect for humane education as a valid
entity.

In general, the education session confirmed our belief
that all children and young people, at any level and
whatever syllabus they are following, should be taught to
respect animals as individuals with needs of their own.

**3a    CINDY MILBURN, chairing "FARMING"**

The first two speakers considered the ethical dilemmas in
animal usage. Their theme was that it is possible to
scientifically measure welfare to show how an animal is or
is not coping with its environment, but then a value-
judgement has to be made to determine what is and what is
not acceptable in terms of stress.

The use of animals falls into three main categories:

a)   The use of animals to help themselves
b) The use of animals to help others of the same
species
c)   The use of animals to help other animals of a
different species

The ethical problems in farming practice and consumer
education were then considered. Our "cheap food" is costly
to animals: organisations such as the Real Meat Company
can provide high welfare/low drug choice for the consumer.
One basic issue was whether we needed to eat animals at
all: children should be offered a vegetarian alternative.

Honesty in advertising food products was also discussed,
as was the welfare significance of ritual slaughter, where
it was felt that at least meat that had been pre-cut
stunned should be offered. This led to a discussion of
whether work in slaughter-houses had a de-humanising
effect.

### 3b    JOHN CALLAGHAN, chairing THE EDUCATION WORKSHOP

The format for this session was of course very different
to the others. There were no fixed speakers and the
session was open to all to give their own experiences
within the field of education. In fact, a high proportion
of those taking part were involved in education
themselves.

John Hoyt (President of the Humane Society of the United
States, and the World Society for the Protection of
Animals) gave the opening address, pointing out that we
must be prepared to learn from those whom we are teaching
- Humane Education is a two-way process.

The very term "education" means different things to
different people and covers a very wide field indeed,
although in the event we largely discussed practice in
British and American schools.

It was seen to be vital that animal welfare be seen to be
part of mainstream education. It is not a side-issue, but
part of the curriculum.

Some of the ways of ensuring this are obvious - through
the life sciences for instance. But the humanities and
particularly English were promising fields.

We have to take advantage of educational initiatives such
as TVEI, together with events such as Food and Farming
Year (1989), etc. We also have to be aware of inherent
restrictions in our educational system, such as pressure
brought about through the introduction of the National
Curriculum. But the issue which concerns us is
International.

We concluded that there was need for an international
umbrella organisation to provide a centralised resource

for educational publications which are already in existence, and to be a centre for receiving and disseminating research material as well as possibly funding educational research in this area and being a publishing agent for educational material.

## 4    CLIVE HOLLANDS, chairing "EXPERIMENTATION"

The whole emphasis of this session linked in very clearly with the perceived need for education. This may be seen as the education of those of us who work in the field of animal welfare so that we understand what we are talking about when discussing animal experimentation, rather than basing our discussion on emotive reasoning only. Or it may be thought that scientists need to be educated into examining the basis of their own feelings of guilt: only if they do this can they understand the feelings of those outside science who often look on what they do with horror. There needs to be a "coming together": education is the key to bringing this about.

The attitude of the Establishment towards research was also discussed - the government, the scientific community and the regulatory bodies. There was a great deal of inertia and lack of motivation to look at an increased use of "alternatives". Once again, education should play a large part here.

Ethical dilemmas cannot be solved solely by legislation. Legislation must be backed by education.

Some of the problems in Australia were used to exemplify and widen the issues being discussed. There is no consensus on the standing of animals in this field of human use.

Research, and the whole area of animal experimentation, touches a raw nerve more than any other area of animal use because of the empathy that we have with "the helpless innocent".

## 5    DAVID PATERSON, chairing "HUMAN/ANIMAL INTERACTION"

Dr Earl Strimple gave us an overview of pet-therapy programmes in prisons and nursing homes, though the question of "Who benefits most, humans or animals?" was rather difficult to answer in this situation. Undoubtedly, though, the people concerned gained very considerably and this seemed to be the main objective.

The paper had a parallel with that given in our previous symposium, where we looked at the use of animals in hospitals for the subnormal. Providing that the human/animal link was overviewed in a caring way, the animals also gained from these situations.

We then looked at attitudes to animals in areas of animal

usage ("exploitation"). The use of language is very important in determining our attitudes - for instance the terms game/vermin are used to discuss the same species in different situations. The scientist "sacrifices" an experimental animal, the vet "puts to sleep" an individual of the same species, using the same method.

Language is also used by people as a self-opiate, deadening an awakening conscience.

Nick Tucker gave a very amusing and yet thoughtful talk on the way in which animals are portrayed in children's literature - and we have seen throughout the conference the importance of background literature. The anthropomorphic (humanised) view of animals given to young children leads on to the naturalistic (animalised) view as children mature. The latter approach, though without too much overt cruelty, is more acceptable in present day children's literature.


6    DAVID MORTON, chairing "THE ROLE OF THE VETERINARIAN IN ANIMAL WELFARE"

Veterinarians were being put under the spotlight in this session: they were, as the guardians of animal welfare, being asked why they did not do more. But vets are an amorphous group with differing approaches to ethical issues, ranging from the newly-qualified, town-reared, anti-blood sports vet working for a charity, to the sixty-year-old self-employed horse practitioner working in the shires. This makes it very difficult to give "one view".

The first speaker, Alastair Porter, highlighted some of the legal difficulties in the veterinary surgeon/client/patient relationship. As far as the veterinary surgeon is concerned the owner, and not the animal, has legal rights. The animal is the owner's property. Inadequacies in the law have arisen because much of our legislation gets onto the statute book through Private Member's Bills.

Tackling the question of confidentiality, Mr Porter pointed out that breaching confidentiality might lead to a vet being in the same situation as are the parents of a battered child.

John Tandy outlined some of the practical difficulties faced by the general practitioner. Should, for instance, the veterinary surgeon dock puppy's tails - or should this be left to the owner who, on occasion, may do it badly, to the animal's detriment. Opting out by the veterinary surgeon may not always produce the best animal welfare. While all vets are involved in, and dedicated to, animal welfare, the way that they set about achieving it differs.

On the question of inherited defects such as progressive retinal atrophy in dogs, it has led to liaison between different "political" groups such as the Kennel Club, the

Breeders and the Veterinary Profession, in an effort to control and even eliminate disease.

This type of liaison was referred to again by Neal King in talking about the BVA/CRAE/FRAME grouping. By making an alliance the resultant broadening of the political base makes a much more effective political group. Mr King also discussed the question of a Farm Animal Welfare Inspectorate and how the State Veterinary Service was now actively taking on some of the rôles proposed for it.

His emphasis on education, both for the veterinary student and the veterinary surgeon in practice must also be stressed. The ethics of animal usage are changing and vets must be familiar with the arguments and issues involved. They should be leading more than they do.

Mary Stewart took up the point that the whole of a veterinarian´s education was geared to animal welfare. Before making welfare judgements one has to be familiar with an animal´s structure, how it functions, and how it behaves. This training enables a vet to make judgements in the future too, even over new issues such as genetic engineering.

The student movement for animal welfare is growing. Boycotting classes where animals are used unnecessarily has led directly to a reduction in animal usage, for instance.

We must remember that the veterinary students of today become the veterinary surgeons of tomorrow: there are marked differences at either end of the spectrum as regards veterinarian´s views and activities in the animal welfare field. Young vets are more welfare conscious than their predecessors. They are less certain of what is acceptable. They question "traditional practices".


7    MARY PALMER, chairing "ANIMALS AND THE MEDIA"

The session was built round Jeffery Boswall´s Paper on wildlife film-making. He gave us guidelines such as an obligation not to deceive the audience and not to harm the animals or their environment.

Temptations to break these two "commandments" are often great, as the audience´s expectations are often very high. Mr Boswall placed the audience in the position of a film-maker, and we found some decisions difficult to make.

There was a clear need for disclaimers when events were "staged", clear codes of practice, an animal-ombudsman, and covering legislation. But the most important thing, and the one which we must address, is to ensure that due respect is given to the animals.

**COMMENTS & QUESTIONS:** from various members of the audience and speakers. A resume of these is given here:


1) **TIME FOR QUESTIONS**

There is never time for sufficient discussion at these conferences. Perhaps we could pre-circulate papers another time, and thus allow conference time to be given to discussion in groups?


2) **COMMON GROUND**

A conference should be organised seeking common ground with the environmental movement. There are difficulties, and built-in conflicts such as the protection of the individual v the protection of the environment, but this "alliance for planet earth" (human/animal/plant/ environment) would appeal more to educationalists than a narrower concept of "humane education".


3) **STUDENTS**

Often need both moral support and information on issues such as the usage of animals. NICHE (Network of Independent Campaigns for Humane Education) exists to do this and to complement the work of other umbrella bodies.


4) **"ALTERNATIVES"**

These are now a viable concept - a reflection of the changing scene in the animal welfare field.


5) **ETHICS**

Those dealing with human issues have the advantage that there is much more general agreement as to the moral (ethical) status of human beings than there is of animals. Even now animals are seen as having differing moral status, depending upon their rôle - as pest, predator or experimental species, for instance: this is reflected in our use of language to describe them.


6) **THE KILLING OF ANIMALS**

This should be the subject of a separate conference, since it is a major issue. (It is: cf. BVA Animal Welfare Foundation Symposium No 7)


7) **USAGE OF ANIMALS**

This, also, should be the subject of a separate

222

conference. It has been too readily assumed that we have
the right to use animals, and not all who attended this
conference would agree with such a premise. We as
individuals have not moved far since the 1976 conference –
we are, for instance, still eating animals although we
speak of a violence-free life. At the least we should eat
"Real Meat".

## 8) THE MEDIA

Are vital in education. The ethical committees in
programme planning should not only consider _what_ is to be
shown but _how_ it is to be presented.

The Christian Consultative Council for the Welfare of
Animals has taken up this issue with both the BBC and the
IBA particularly over circuses – which always seem to be
shown on high Christian Festivals! There was no
satisfactory outcome.

WSPA undertakes to co-ordinate the laws of the U.K. on the
use of animals in the media with practices introduced into
New Zealand etc., and distribute these codes throughout
the world.

## 9) THE LAW

There should be more legal input at any future conference.

## 10) THE PROPOSED "HUMANE EDUCATION FOUNDATION"

Is not to be a fund-raising body, but an umbrella-body. If
we are to get into the field of humane education at all
levels of society this must be done by educationalists,
and not the animal welfare organisations. Proposals on
the new Foundation will be sent out with the published
Proceedings. Its name has not yet been decided, but it has
been suggested, and Lord Houghton has agreed, that we
could call it:

### "THE DOUGLAS HOUGHTON FOUNDATION FOR HUMANE EDUCATION"

## 11) THE CONFERENCE ITSELF

This conference has been hallmarked by the way that it has
been organised: every sort of view has been expressed
freely, the Chairmen have been independent, and people
with diverse views have been able to confront eachother.

We have dealt with two key issues: education and
entertainment. We must remember that education can be got
across through entertainment. We must also remember that,
not having a general moral consensus in our society on the
way to treat animals, education should be consciousness-
raising.

Philosophers have a lot to teach us in areas like "animal rights". More publications should set out to apply philosophy to the dilemmas which we have to deal with.

We are particularly grateful to the vets from BVA and would ask them most sincerely to "stay with us". The same applies to CRAE.

The public still has a rather superficial view of what is meant by animal welfare. Legislation has been brought in, each piece a step forward. The work of the Institute of Medical Ethics on using animals in medical experiments, etc.

## RESOLUTION

"This conference, being aware of the urgent need for humane education in its widest sense, calls upon individuals and organisations to make an educational contribution in whatever way they consider relevant to bring this subject to the attention of all levels of society".

## CONTRIBUTORS

Short biographical notes on contributors are given, where these are available at the time of going to press.

**Professor Stephen Clark**  Married, and with three children, Stephen Clark is Professor of Philosophy at Liverpool University: author of Aristotle's Man, The Moral Status of Animals, The Nature of the Beast, From Athens to Jerusalem, The Mysteries of Religion and Civil Peace and Sacred Order. Editor of Berkeley: Money, Obedience and Affection.

**Mary Midgley**  Born in 1919 and educated at Oxford, Mary Midgley is married to Geoffrey Midgley (also a philosopher), has three sons and now lives in Newcastle-on-Tyne. She is Chairman of the RSPCA's Animal Experimentation Advisory Committee and was formerly Senior Lecturer in Philosophy, at the University of Newcastle-on-Tyne. She is author of Beast and Man, Animals & Why They Matter, Evolution as a Religion etc.

**Rev Andrew Linzey BD AKC DPS PhD,** is Anglican Chaplain to the university of Essex, and Fellow and Director of Studies of the Centre for the Study of Theology in the University of Essex. He has written and broadcast extensively on aspects of Christian Ethics and has written or edited ten books, including: Animal Rights, A Christian Assessment, Heaven and Earth: Essex Essays in Theology and Ethics (co-ed Wexler), Christianity and the Rights of Animals, Research on the Rights of Animals, Research on Embryos: Politics, Theology and Law, (co-authored PAB Clarke), etc., and three books co-edited with Tom Regan: Song of Creation: An Anthology of Poems in Praise of Animals, Compassion for Animals: Prayers and Readings, and Animals and Christianity: A Book of Readings. Dr Linzey was a member of the Animals and Ethics working group, and was, for four years, a member of the RSPCA National Council.

**Professor Alan Bowd**  Alan Bowd is Professor of Educational Psychology and Special education at Lakehead University, Thunder Bay, Ontario (Canada). He received his MA in Psychology the University of Sydney, and his PhD from the University of Calgary was in Educational Psychology. He is the author of three books on educational psychology and numerous articles in scientific and professional journals. He is particularly interested in the development of children's beliefs about animals and the implications of this for humane education.

**David Paterson MA(Cantab) MPhil FRSH FLS MIBiol CBiol MBIM** Born in Inverness and educated at Ampleforth College and Cambridge University, David Paterson qualified (MA) to teach the Natural Sciences in 1960 and received a Masters Degree in Philosophy from Sussex University for a study of children´s attitudes to animals in 1986. He was Chief Education Officer of the RSPCA (1972-1978), Secretary to CRAE (1977-1979), Chairman of the Humane Education Council (1974ff) and has been (among other things) a teacher of biology and ethics and a headmaster. At the time of this conference he was Director of the British Veterinary Association´s Animal Welfare Foundation and is now a free-lance researcher working mainly for the BVA. He is a Fellow of the Linnaean Society and the Royal Society of Health, and a School Governor.

David was editor of the Humane Education Journal for five years, is co-editor of Animal Rights, a Symposium (1979), editor of Humane Education Symposium (1979), author of Children´s Attitudes to Animals (1986) and co-editor of numerous symposia, as well as of articles and scientific proceedings on animal welfare topics.

**Cindy Milburn BSc** Cindy has a degree in Zoology and a Certificate in Further Education. She joined the RSPCA´s Education Department in 1979, heading it from 1982 to early 1988, with responsibility for co-ordinating educational literature and films, and advising on educational policy.

During this period departmental strategy involved targeting policy makers and curriculum developers with the aim of securing a place for animal welfare within mainstream education. Success came with both major changes and reductions in the use of mammals for dissection at ´A´ level and, more positively, incorporation of animal welfare principles into the National Curriculum.

Committees include the Farm Animal Welfare Council, the Farm Animal Welfare Co-ordinating Executive, and the Animal and Theology Working Group.

Cindy is currently studying fifth generation computer principles and programming with a view to making use of Information Technology for the promotion of Humane Education.

**Professor Donald Broom MA(Cantab) PhD** Graduated at Cambridge University in Zoology in 1964 and received his Doctorate in Animal Behaviour there in 1967. He was first Lecturer and then Reader in the Department of Pure and Applied Zoology at Reading University, researching on behaviour development and motivation, particularly in farm animals. He is currently Colleen McLeod Professor of Animal Welfare at Cambridge and a Fellow of St. Catherine´s College.

Professor Broom´s research has covered areas such as grazing behaviour, the housing and management of calves, sows, piglets, pets and zoo animals, the transport of pigs, sheep and calves, and disease transmission in cattle. He is author of two books on animal behaviour and has co-edited another.

**Richard James Guy BSc** was born in Basingstoke in 1954, spending his formative years on his parent´s arable farm. He holds an honours degree in Chemistry from the University of Manchester.

He married in 1985 and his wife Gilly realised that her own working experience with pigs, combined with her new husband´s hobby (rearing pigs without growth promoters and under more "old-fashioned" conditions) had commercial promise. From their combined interests grew the welfare-orientated "Real Meat Company".

**Judith Hampson MA PhD** Read for her First Degree at Leicester University, specialising in ecology and the history of biology. Her Doctorate thesis, _Animal Experimentation 1876-1976_, was subsequently written in the History of Science Department at Leicester University.

From 1978-1980 Judith worked as a freelance journalist, researcher and broadcaster on animal welfare topics. From 1980-1987 she was Head of the RSPCA´s Department dealing with Laboratory Animals and has since worked in this field on a freelance basis. She is a member of the Home Office´s Advisory Committee on Animal Experimentation, and of CRAE.

**Michael Balls MA DPhil** Read Zoology at Oxford, and carried out research at the Universities of Geneva, California and Reed. He lectured for nine years at the University of East Anglia until he moved to Nottingham University to take up a Readership in Medical Cell Biology.

His research interests include the evolution of cancer, cell fusion, cell differentiation and alternatives to animal experimentation, particularly the development of valid cell and organ culture methods for use in evaluating the desired effects of drugs and the potential toxicity of drugs and other chemicals.

He became Trustee of FRAME (The Fund for the Replacement of Animals in Medical Experiments) in 1979, and Chairman of the Trustees and Director of their Research Programme in 1981.

He was adviser to the British Government during the passage of the _Animals (Scientific Procedures) Act 1986_ and was principal author of _The Use of Non-Human Primates as Laboratory Animals_.

**Jacqueline Southee BSc DPhil** is Scientific Executive to FRAME, with special responsibilities in the areas of

227

toxicity testing and publications. She joined FRAME in 1987 from a research post at the University of Nottingham School of Agriculture, with a degree in Agricultural Science and Animal Physiology.

Dr Southee has a particular interest in keeping science students adequately but realistically informed on the rôle of alternatives in scientific research at all levels and in provoking both ethical and technical enquiry in schools and colleges into the limitations of animal experiments.

**Gill Langley MA(Cantab) PhD MIBiol** Gill Langley´s early experiences as a scientist were entirely orthodox, her first Degree at Cambridge University being followed by a PhD in Neurochemistry.

She did, however, have increasing doubts about animal experiments, particularly as used in University teaching. She became a vegan and a proponent of animal rights in 1978, spending a year at Nottingham University Medical School as a research associate in cell culture work. In 1979 she took a job as research officer with the British Union for the Abolition of Vivisection. She became General Secretary of the Dr Hadwen Trust for Humane Research in 1980, and is now scientific adviser to this Trust as well as to Animal Aid and a number of related organisations. She is convinced of the need for criticism of experiments to be accurate and reliable, and of the need for humane research.

**James Serpell MA PhD** Graduated in Zoology at University College London, in 1974 and received a PhD in Animal Behaviour at the University of Liverpool in 1980. James Serpell is currently Research Associate in Animal Behaviour at the University of Cambridge and Director of the Cambridge Companion Animal Research Group. He is author of In the Company of Animals and numerous articles and papers on animal behaviour and human attitudes to animals.

**Nicholas Tucker** taught English in a London Comprehensive School before qualifying as an Educational Psychologist in the Inner London Education Area. He is now lecturer in Developmental Psychology at the University of Sussex, with a special interest in children´s relationships with literature. He has written four books for children themselves as well as other works to do with literature and children, including The Child and the Book. He is a frequent broadcaster and has lectured widely both in Britain and in America and Canada. He has three children and lives in Lewes, Sussex.

**Alastair Porter CBE MA Hon Assoc RCVS** has been Secretary and Registrar of the Royal College of Veterinary Surgeons for almost twenty-two years. He is not himself a

228

veterinary surgeon, but an Oxford Law graduate and barrister. Prior to joining the College he was permanent Secretary in the Ministry of Justice for the Republic of Zambia. He is keenly interested in European affairs, and was Secretary-General of the Federation of Veterinarians of the EC from 1973-1979, and Chairman of the EC´s Advisory Committee on Veterinary Education from 1986-1987. He was made a CBE in 1985.

**John Tandy BVSc MRCVS**     Qualified as a veterinary surgeon at Liverpool University in 1957. He spent three years in farm practice before "setting up his plate" in St. Helens, Lancashire. He is now Senior Partner of a six-man small-animal practice centred on the Rutland house Veterinary Hospital.

John has held various offices in the veterinary profession, including the presidencies of the BVA, the British Veterinary Hospitals Association, and the Society of Practising Veterinary Surgeons. He is currently chairman of the BVA Animal Welfare Committee and a Trustee of the BVA Animal Welfare Foundation.

**Neal King BVSc MRCVS**     qualified at Bristol Veterinary School in 1963 and has since been in general mixed practice with a small animal bias. Neal first became involved in veterinary political work as a representative of his local veterinary Division on the Council of the BVA. He was subsequently elected President of the BVA (1982-1983) and President of the Society of Practising Veterinary Surgeons (SPVS) from 1986-1987.

Neal chaired the BVA´s Animal Welfare Committee from 1979-1981 and was founder-chairman of the BVA Animal Welfare Foundation from 1983-1988. His interest in animal welfare emerged from considering the mutually beneficial rôle of the veterinary profession and the animal welfare movement.

**Marianne Stewart DVM MRCVS**     graduated from Cornell Veterinary School in 1949 and subsequently qualified as MRCVS from Glasgow University Veterinary School in 1951.

Mary is now Lecturer in Animal Husbandry at Glasgow, with a special remit for the teaching of animal welfare. Her main interests are in animal welfare and in human/animal inter-actions and inter-relationships.

**Jeffery Boswall**     is a professional wildlife film-maker and an amateur ornithologist. He taught himself moral philosophy, mainly through the writings of Bertrand Russell, and has written and lectured about the ethics of wildlife film-making for thirty years. He is currently self-employed and works mainly for the Royal Society for the Protection of Birds, as Head of their Film and Video Unit.

# WORD-INDEX

AALAS, 159
Abattoirs, 189
Abnormal; Abnormalities, 82, 84, 107, 187, 188, 201, 202
Absolutism; Absolutist, 16, 22
Academic, 20, 52, 55, 73, 122, 148, 152, 192, 201, 205
Academically, 208
ACCART, 131
Accommodation, 91
Accreditation, 130, 159
Activists, 107
ACUC; ACUCs, 105, 106
ACUs, 101
Additive-free, 88
Adler, 122
Adrenal, 82
Age, 1, 18, 26, 54, 59, 60, 61, 62, 71, 78, 91, 157, 162,
    169, 170, 171, 187
Age-appropriate, 71
Age-groups, 60
Aged; Ageing, 8, 10, 60
Agius, 30, 47
Agricultural, 77, 123, 196, 200, 202, 228
Agriculture, 89, 117, 179, 186, 192, 228
Aids, 67
Altman, 57
Altruism; Altruistic, 74, 116, 203
America, 53, 58, 63, 64, 99, 130, 138, 140, 141, 147, 212,
    228
American, 53, 57, 59, 60, 61, 64, 97, 138, 141, 148, 159,
    171, 204, 218
Ames, 140, 141, 142, 147
Amoebocyte, 147
Anaesthesia; Anaesthetic, 90, 165
Anaesthetised, 97
Anal, 187
Analgesic, 82
Anderson, 192, 205, 206
Anglia, 227
Anglican, 48, 225
Animal, 1, 2, 5, 6, 7, 8, 9, 11, 12, 13, 15, 17, 18, 20,
    21, 22, 24, 25, 29, 30, 31, 35, 36, 37, 39, 42, 43,
    44, 45, 46, 47, 48, 49, 50, 52, 53, 54, 56, 57, 58,
    61, 62, 63, 64, 65, 68, 69, 70, 71, 72, 73, 74, 75,
    76, 77, 80, 82, 83, 84, 85, 86, 87, 89, 91, 92, 93,
    96, 97, 98, 99, 100, 101, 102, 103, 104, 105, 106,
    107, 108, 109, 110, 111, 112, 113, 114, 115, 116,
    117, 118, 119, 120, 121, 123, 124, 126, 127, 128,
    129, 130, 131, 132, 133, 134, 135, 136, 137, 138,
    139, 140, 141, 142, 143, 145, 146, 147, 149, 150,
    151, 152, 154, 158, 159, 160, 162, 163, 165, 166,
    168, 169, 170, 171, 173, 174, 175, 176, 177, 178,
    180, 181, 182, 183, 184, 185, 186, 187, 188, 189,
    190, 191, 192, 193, 194, 195, 196, 197, 198, 199,
    200, 201, 202, 203, 204, 205, 206, 208, 209, 210,
    213, 216, 217, 218, 219, 220, 221, 222, 223, 224,
    225, 226, 227, 228, 229

Animal's, 8, 74, 165, 175, 176, 179, 182, 201, 220, 221
Animal-based, 62, 96, 124, 146, 148
Animal-control, 99
Animal-facilitated, 157
Animal-human, 32
Animal-ombudsman, 221
Animal-orientated, 61, 203
Animal-ownership, 13
Animal-related, 73
Animal-rights, 97
Animal-tested, 104
Animal-welfare, 99
Animalised, 220
Animals, 1, 2, 3, 4, 7, 8, 9, 10, 12, 13, 16, 17, 18, 20,
     24, 25, 27, 28, 29, 30, 31, 32, 33, 34, 35, 36, 37,
     38, 39, 41, 42, 44, 45, 46, 47, 48, 49, 52, 53, 54,
     55, 56, 57, 58, 59, 60, 61, 62, 63, 64, 65, 66, 68,
     69, 72, 73, 74, 75, 76, 77, 78, 80, 81, 82, 83, 84,
     85, 86, 87, 88, 89, 92, 96, 97, 98, 99, 100, 101,
     102, 103, 104, 105, 106, 107, 109, 110, 111, 112,
     113, 114, 115, 116, 117, 118, 119, 120, 121, 122,
     123, 124, 125, 126, 127, 129, 131, 132, 133, 134,
     137, 138, 140, 141, 143, 145, 146, 147, 148, 149,
     150, 151, 152, 157, 158, 159, 160, 161, 162, 163,
     164, 165, 166, 167, 168, 169, 170, 171, 172, 174,
     176, 178, 179, 180, 181, 182, 184, 186, 187, 188,
     189, 190, 191, 192, 194, 196, 199, 200, 201, 202,
     203, 204, 205, 206, 207, 208, 209, 210, 211, 212,
     213, 214, 216, 217, 218, 219, 220, 221, 222, 223,
     224, 225, 226, 227, 228
Anthropocentrism, 39, 46
Anthropomorphic, 59, 60, 61, 62, 163, 168, 169, 210, 220
Anthropomorphise, 210
Anthropomorphised, 172
Anthropomorphising, 210
Anthropomorphism, 61, 168, 183
Anti-scientific, 18
Anti-vivisection, 22, 136, 138, 139, 141, 147
Anti-vivisectionists, 150
Antibiotics, 88
Antidote, 64
Antitoxin, 147
Apes, 13
Appleby, 200, 206
Aquarium, 158, 159
Aquinas, 28, 29, 30, 31, 32, 33, 34, 35, 43, 48
Arable, 227
Aristotelian, 34
Aristotle, 29, 33, 34, 35, 49
Aristotle's, 34, 225
Armadillo, 211
Armour, 108
Ass, 45
ATB, 194
Athanasius, 25, 26, 27
Atheism, 33
Athens, 225
Atherosclerosis, 108
ATLA, 110, 111, 112, 121

Atrophy, 188, 220
Attenborough, 211
Attfield, 34, 47
Attitude, 16, 17, 18, 22, 56, 58, 61, 63, 76, 84, 124,
     144, 146, 151, 167, 191, 192, 200, 219
Attitudes, 18, 50, 54, 55, 56, 58, 60, 62, 63, 64, 74, 75,
     76, 80, 86, 124, 142, 151, 162, 163, 164, 165, 166,
     167, 169, 171, 190, 203, 216, 219, 220, 226, 228
Attitudinal, 73, 75, 77
Attwater, 28, 47
Austin, 72
Australia, 100, 101, 105, 123, 124, 127, 128, 129, 130,
     131, 132, 133, 219
Australian, 56, 123, 127, 130, 131, 133, 134

Baboon; Baboons, 8, 116
Bacon, 94
Baconers, 90
Bacteria; Bacterial, 84, 140, 141, 142
Badger-baiters, 169
Badgers, 169, 180
Bagnold's, 169
Bahamas, 12
Balliere, 86
Balls, 103, 110, 111, 114, 117, 121, 122, 227
Balthasar, 38
Baltimore, 149
Bankowski, 134
Barrister, 229
Bartells, 128, 134
Barth, 20, 23, 24, 25, 27, 28, 38, 39, 40, 44, 47, 48, 49
Barth's, 23, 24, 25, 27
Barthian, 26
Basil, 47, 48, 166
Basingstoke, 227
Bateson, 106, 110
Battery, 56, 74, 87, 185, 193
Bayer, 212
BBC; BBC's, 59, 60, 61, 62, 63, 208, 212, 223
Beak, 92
Beast, 25, 32, 33, 34, 39, 65, 87, 91, 170, 225
Beasts, 34, 45
Beecham, 148
Beef, 91, 92, 94
Behaviour, 55, 56, 57, 74, 75, 76, 77, 81, 82, 84, 86, 99,
     100, 110, 158, 167, 171, 185, 198, 200, 201, 202,
     205, 210, 213, 226, 227, 228
Behavioural, 75, 77, 82, 84, 89, 103, 121, 164, 182, 201
Behaviours, 63, 75, 201
Benziger, 48
Benzodiazapine; Benzodiazepines, 98, 108
Berkeley, 225
Berthold, 26, 48
Bessis, 116, 121
Bethge, 38, 48
BIBRA, 148
Bio-medical, 131
Bioassays, 140
Biochemical, 202

232

Biochemistry, 152, 201
Bioethics, 206
Biological, 25, 81, 117, 120, 137, 144, 148, 149, 150,
      153, 201, 202
Biologists, 58, 76
Biology, 54, 56, 57, 58, 77, 216, 226, 227
Biology-based, 193
Biomaterials, 112
Biomedical, 96, 107, 108, 114, 121, 134, 152, 164
Bitch; Bitches, 170, 175, 188
Boa, 213
Boarding, 178
Boswall, 208, 221, 229
Brabazon, 22, 48
Braithwaite, 130, 134
Brambell, 187, 203
Breeders; Breeding, 178, 188, 221
Breeds, 148, 187, 188
Breland, 171
Bristol, 92, 94, 192, 201, 208, 229
Britain, 12, 17, 58, 59, 66, 92, 93, 108, 147, 148, 150,
      162, 211, 228
British, 2, 10, 58, 60, 61, 73, 86, 105, 106, 112, 115,
      117, 122, 137, 138, 139, 140, 148, 149, 151, 152,
      174, 187, 200, 218, 226, 227, 228, 229
Britt, 125, 134
Bromiley, 24, 25, 40, 44, 48
Bronowski, 126, 134
Broom, 80, 82, 86, 205, 226
Broome, 35
Brown, 32
Brownley, 57
Bruce, 141
Brucellosis, 196
Brusick, 141, 146, 152
BSC, 110, 226, 227
BTS, 138
Bucket-reared, 91
Bull; Bulls, 11, 91, 134
Bullying, 182
Bustad, 204, 206
BVA, 2, 3, 179, 184, 186, 191, 192, 194, 195, 197, 203,
      205, 221, 222, 224, 226, 229

Caesarean, 188
Cage; Caged; Cages, 76, 160, 161, 168, 185, 193, 194
Calf, 69, 85, 195
Calf-rearing, 201
Calfhood, 8
Calgary, 225
California, 134, 206, 227
Callaghan, 2, 218
Calves, 65, 86, 87, 91, 206, 226, 227
Cambridge, 50, 198, 205, 216, 225, 226, 228
Canada, 101, 121, 129, 132, 133, 225, 228
Canadian, 53, 57, 112, 130, 133, 211
Canberra, 133, 134
Cancer, 108, 115, 136, 137, 141, 227
Canine, 8

Cannibalism, 10, 89, 90, 168, 169
Cannibalistic, 92
Captive; Captivity, 124, 133, 203, 211
Carcass; Carcasses, 189
Carcinogenic, 141
Carcinogenicity, 140, 141, 147
Carcinogens, 140, 141
Cardiovascular, 108
Carnivore, 176
Carrion, 168
Cart-horse, 171
Castrated; Castration, 8, 90, 91, 188
Cat, 60, 61, 158, 168, 170, 175, 176, 178, 186, 187
Catalysts, 2
Catapult, 167
Cattle, 7, 9, 10, 37, 66, 91, 227
Cell, 138, 140, 141, 143, 144, 145, 147, 151, 152, 153,
    160, 227, 228
Cell-based, 136
Cells, 117, 140, 141, 143, 144, 145, 151
Cetacea, 124
Charitable, 3, 32, 184
Charities, 146, 148, 196, 199, 203
Charity, 30, 137, 184, 198, 203, 220
Cheese, 167
Chemical, 140, 147, 148, 149
Chemicals, 117, 141, 142, 148, 152, 227
Chemistry, 152, 227
Cheshire, 137
Cheshunt, 137
Chicken; Chickens, 53, 56, 84, 88, 89, 92, 93, 94, 182
Chicks, 169
Child, 52, 54, 57, 61, 64, 68, 70, 71, 93, 144, 167, 168,
    171, 175, 181, 220, 228
Child-centred, 65
Childbirth, 107
Childhood, 55, 56, 168
Children, 6, 10, 13, 36, 52, 53, 54, 57, 58, 59, 60, 61,
    62, 63, 66, 67, 68, 69, 71, 72, 76, 86, 105, 106,
    107, 159, 167, 168, 169, 170, 181, 217, 218, 220,
    225, 228
Children´s, 13, 54, 55, 56, 58, 62, 63, 65, 68, 167, 168,
    169, 170, 184, 217, 220, 225, 226, 228
Chimp; Chimp´s, 11, 98
Chimpanzee; Chimpanzees, 60, 98, 99, 116
Christ, 25, 26, 27, 33, 34
Christ-centred, 27
Christian, 17, 20, 27, 28, 33, 34, 35, 36, 37, 38, 39, 41,
    42, 43, 44, 45, 47, 48, 49, 223, 225
Christianity, 33, 35, 38, 48, 49, 225
Christians, 35, 37, 44
Christological, 25, 27, 33, 46
Christology, 27, 44
Christopher, 131
Chrysostom, 28, 47
CIO, 48
CIOMS, 134
Circulation, 212
Circumcised, 45

Circus; Circuses, 85, 168, 194, 223
CIWF, 89
Clackston, 67
Clarendon, 48, 50, 166
Clark, 5, 25, 36, 39, 48, 49, 217, 225
Clarke, 49, 225
Class, 10, 16, 53, 56, 62, 119, 171, 203
Class-time, 59
Classes, 57, 58, 147, 156, 201, 221
Classroom; Classrooms, 54, 56, 65, 70, 71
Claws, 187
Client, 157, 174, 175, 179, 180, 186, 220
Client´s, 180, 186
Clients, 12, 13, 179, 180, 186, 187
Clinic; Clinics, 202, 203
Clinical, 182, 202, 203, 205
Clinicians, 143
Cobb, 168
Coccidiosis, 88, 90, 94
Coccidiostat; Coccidiostats, 88, 94
Cockrane, 200
Cockroach, 61
Code, 23, 89, 90, 92, 123, 127, 130, 133, 157, 186, 194,
    196
Codes, 76, 77, 87, 89, 90, 91, 92, 196, 197, 198, 201,
    221, 223
Colgate-Palmolive, 138
Colorado, 204
Colour; Colouring; Colours, 32, 89, 93, 94, 97, 208
Colourants, 89
Columbia, 98
Coma, 7
Comfort; Comfortable, 74, 83, 87, 90, 178, 185
Commerce; Commercial, 3, 92, 104, 108, 112, 148, 158, 227
Commission, 2, 100, 150, 155, 196
Commissioner, 67
Committee, 2, 99, 102, 104, 105, 106, 112, 117, 124, 127,
    129, 130, 131, 133, 138, 139, 145, 146, 148, 149,
    151, 152, 158, 159, 183, 184, 194, 203, 225, 227, 229
Committees, 101, 105, 127, 128, 129, 130, 131, 132, 134,
    145, 223, 226
Commonwealth, 123, 130, 133
Communist; Communists, 7, 16
Companion, 56, 61, 85, 174, 175, 176, 178, 179, 182, 187,
    188, 200, 228
Computer, 12, 117, 147, 226
Computerised, 149
Congenital, 187
Congress, 67, 111, 121, 192, 193
Conscious, 5, 25, 54, 124, 163, 165, 210, 221
Consciously, 41, 73, 77
Consciousness, 18, 23, 25, 36, 67, 102, 109
Conservation; Conservational, 1, 9, 10, 69, 74, 81, 166,
    216
Conservationist; Conservationists, 7, 9, 60, 114
Control, 2, 17, 25, 72, 82, 92, 96, 100, 101, 104, 113,
    131, 138, 142, 144, 145, 148, 158, 163, 191, 221
Controlled, 163, 189, 211
Controlling, 100, 105, 178

Controls, 113, 119, 145
Corn-fed, 92, 93
Cornell, 229
Cosmetic; Cosmetics, 102, 104, 113, 139, 140, 147, 187
Cost-benefit, 118, 120
Cost-effective, 108
Cow; Cows, 8, 178
Coyote, 69
CRAE, 2, 194, 195, 221, 224, 226, 227
Crated, 69, 87
Crates; Crating, 65, 86, 90
Creation, 17, 20, 25, 26, 27, 31, 33, 34, 35, 36, 37, 38,
    39, 40, 41, 42, 43, 44, 45, 46, 47, 48, 49, 65, 216,
    225
Creative, 33, 38
Creator; Creator´s, 26, 28, 31, 35, 38, 39, 40, 42
Creature, 7, 10, 24, 25, 31, 32, 33, 36, 38, 40, 49, 93,
    204
Creatures, 8, 9, 10, 11, 17, 26, 27, 28, 30, 31, 33, 35,
    36, 38, 40, 41, 43, 49, 52, 63, 106, 212
Crime; Crimes, 11, 68, 155, 196, 212
Criminal; Criminals, 68, 163, 166, 183, 192
Crocodile, 60, 213
Cruel, 61, 62, 166, 189, 211
Cruelties, 169
Cruelty, 2, 3, 31, 32, 33, 49, 52, 54, 55, 56, 64, 66, 85,
    89, 113, 123, 124, 133, 150, 167, 168, 220
Cruelty-free, 104
CSIRO, 123, 130, 131
Cultural, 52, 127
Culture, 17, 18, 64, 138, 140, 141, 143, 144, 145, 147,
    149, 152, 227, 228
Curricula, 57, 60, 71
Curriculum, 1, 67, 69, 70, 71, 201, 217, 218, 226
Cytotoxic, 112

Dalkeith, 149
Darton, 49
Darwinian, 18
Data, 58, 138, 141, 143, 146, 147, 148, 162
Database, 149
De-beaking, 89
De-horning, 91
De-humanise, 71, 84, 170, 218
De-personalise, 84, 164
De-voice, 178
Dead; Deadly, 8, 9, 21
Deakin, 133, 134
Death, 8, 29, 52, 53, 83, 104, 105, 106, 117, 163, 166,
    168, 170, 204, 212
Deaths, 7, 8
Declaw; Declawed, 178, 186, 187
Deer, 8, 194
Deer-stalking, 162
Defaecation, 98
Dekker, 120
Deprivation, 85, 102, 114, 202
Deprive; Deprived; Depriving, 7, 28, 98
Desensitises, 54

Desensitising, 69
DHSS, 108, 142
Diagnosed; Diagnoses, 16, 188
Diagnosing; Diagnosis, 143, 185
Diagnostic, 147, 184
Diets, 158
Digitalis, 137
Diploid, 144, 145
Disease, 61, 83, 85, 88, 94, 96, 98, 107, 108, 115, 141,
    142, 180, 185, 187, 188, 189, 193, 196, 199, 201,
    202, 221, 227
Disease-causing, 144
Disease-state, 83
Diseased, 8, 86, 189
Diseases, 86, 108, 110, 188
Disembowel, 42
Dissection; Dissections, 54, 61, 65, 69, 76, 77, 226
Dixon, 142, 145, 146, 152
Distress, 10, 97, 98, 101, 114, 136, 138, 175, 193, 200
Doctor; Doctors, 115, 175, 181
Doctrine, 6, 20, 24, 25, 27, 28, 31, 40, 43, 48, 49, 74
Dog, 2, 11, 24, 60, 61, 69, 83, 85, 170, 176, 177, 178,
    180, 181, 182, 186, 187, 188, 189
Dog´s, 174, 177, 189
Dog-fighting, 181, 194
Dog-fights, 181
Dogs, 7, 8, 9, 10, 13, 57, 62, 83, 113, 158, 163, 165,
    170, 180, 181, 184, 186, 187, 188, 220
Dolphin; Dolphins, 59, 60, 133
Dowding, 137
Draize, 112, 125, 137, 138, 139, 140, 148
Dresser, 105, 110, 129, 130, 134
Drug, 67, 88, 91, 102, 104, 108, 117, 122, 138, 152, 158,
    218
Drugs, 87, 88, 89, 97, 98, 106, 108, 110, 112, 115, 121,
    156, 184, 227
Dunn, 192
Dust-baths, 8
Duties, 12, 13, 28, 30, 35, 38, 124, 127, 132, 186, 190,
    217
Duty, 12, 13, 19, 31, 47, 49, 76, 93, 127, 184, 185

Ears, 32
Earth, 26, 27, 33, 41, 222, 225
Earthworm, 21
Ecological, 2, 49
Ecology, 2, 9, 168, 216, 227
Ecosystem, 9
Eddy, 66, 72
Edinburgh, 48, 49, 137, 201
Educate; Educating, 16, 67, 84, 86
Educated, 219, 225
Education, 1, 51, 52, 53, 54, 55, 57, 58, 59, 63, 64, 65,
    66, 67, 68, 69, 70, 71, 72, 73, 74, 75, 76, 77, 78,
    111, 113, 116, 117, 120, 121, 149, 151, 167, 191,
    193, 199, 204, 206, 216, 217, 218, 219, 221, 222,
    223, 224, 225, 226, 228, 229

Educational, 1, 52, 53, 54, 55, 58, 60, 65, 67, 68, 70,
    71, 74, 75, 76, 77, 116, 159, 216, 217, 218, 219,
    224, 225, 226, 228
Educationalist, 74
Educationalists, 73, 75, 76, 222, 223
Educative, 194, 216
Educator, 52, 56, 68
Educators, 53, 55, 56, 64, 65, 66, 67, 68, 69, 70, 71,
    203, 204
EEC, 89, 91, 93, 100, 101
EEC-approved, 88
Egg, 56, 89, 92, 93
Egg-producing, 56
Eggs, 56, 91, 92, 209
Electro-ejaculation, 194
Embryoplastic, 141
Embryos, 10, 225
Emotion; Emotional, 60, 61, 69, 83, 86, 97, 183, 195
Emotionally, 6
Emotions, 163, 168, 169, 184
Emotive; Emotively, 124, 179, 195, 198, 202, 219
Empathetic, 56
Empathy, 60, 68, 69, 96, 219
Endangered, 65, 69, 99, 114
Endorphin, 82
Enkephalin, 82
Environment, 1, 52, 53, 57, 63, 76, 82, 104, 109, 116,
    188, 200, 201, 202, 217, 221, 222
Environmental, 47, 69, 70, 101, 118, 201, 222
Environmentally, 212
Environments, 200, 201, 202
Environs, 158
Enzymes, 142
Equine, 168, 174
Essex, 225
Ethic, 22, 23, 24, 38, 57, 69, 203, 216
Ethical, 5, 20, 21, 22, 23, 24, 25, 57, 60, 63, 76, 80,
    87, 88, 93, 96, 97, 99, 100, 101, 102, 104, 105, 106,
    107, 109, 111, 114, 117, 120, 124, 125, 128, 129,
    130, 134, 135, 136, 138, 142, 146, 148, 151, 174,
    179, 186, 191, 200, 203, 204, 205, 212, 217, 218,
    219, 220, 222, 223, 228
Ethically, 23, 52, 126
Ethics, 4, 20, 21, 22, 24, 27, 35, 38, 47, 48, 49, 50, 77,
    87, 99, 101, 105, 125, 127, 128, 129, 130, 131, 132,
    134, 189, 200, 203, 204, 208, 211, 212, 216, 221,
    222, 224, 225, 226, 229
Ethological, 203
Ethologists, 205
Europe, 2, 53, 99, 100, 117, 123, 138, 194, 206
European, 24, 100, 101, 117, 120, 122, 123, 151, 195, 200,
    229
Euthanased, 187
Euthanasia, 175, 176, 177, 178, 188, 189
Eventing, 62
Ewbank, 185, 202
Experiment, 46, 52, 85, 98, 105, 110, 117, 150, 151
Experimental, 10, 18, 101, 105, 110, 111, 118, 120, 123,
    133, 136, 142, 147, 151, 153, 178, 194, 203, 220, 222

Experimentation, 19, 22, 57, 71, 95, 96, 100, 101, 103,
    106, 109, 110, 111, 113, 114, 116, 117, 118, 119,
    120, 121, 124, 134, 135, 145, 216, 219, 225, 227
Experimenters, 96
Experiments, 18, 99, 102, 103, 107, 111, 113, 114, 115,
    116, 121, 136, 137, 140, 145, 146, 148, 149, 150,
    151, 152, 165, 224, 227, 228
Expert; Experts, 5, 158, 159, 197
Expertise, 5, 105, 115, 119, 148, 151, 158, 199
Eye, 112, 137, 138, 139, 140, 148, 156, 157
Eyelid, 188
Eyes, 34, 47, 61, 147, 148, 170, 178, 189

Factory-farm; Factory-farmed; Factory-farming, 87, 91, 92
Farm, 46, 77, 84, 85, 86, 89, 164, 171, 174, 178, 179,
    182, 184, 186, 189, 192, 194, 196, 197, 198, 199,
    200, 205, 206, 221, 226, 227, 229
Farm-animals, 18
Farm-lands, 69
Farmer, 87, 88, 91, 164, 169, 196, 197
Farmer's, 8, 167
Farmers, 9, 93, 131, 162, 163, 164
Farming, 56, 77, 79, 87, 89, 93, 163, 164, 216, 217, 218
Farms, 89, 92, 164, 202
Farmyard, 10
Farrowing, 90
FAWC, 190, 194
Fellow-creatures, 93
Femur, 182
Feral, 9, 13, 163
Fertilisation, 128
Fettman, 141
Filipino, 93
Fish; Fishes, 44, 45, 46, 53, 58, 59, 60, 63, 66, 158, 161
Fishing, 9
Flea, 158
Flesh, 27, 34, 36, 47, 53
Flies, 213
Flipper, 59
Flock; Flocks, 91, 171
Florida, 155
Flower, 21, 24
Flowers, 212
Fogle, 54, 57
Footprints, 24
Forensic, 157
Foster; Fostering, 55, 176
Fowl; Fowls, 35, 84, 89, 94
Fox, 56, 57, 61, 129, 134
Foxes, 45, 164, 168, 169
Foxhunting, 62
FRAME, 2, 103, 110, 111, 112, 117, 121, 137, 149, 150,
    194, 195, 208, 221, 227, 228
Frazer, 141, 152
Free-range, 88, 89, 92, 93, 185
Freud, 171
Frisby, 171
Frog; Frogs, 169, 213
Fry, 150, 151

High-welfare, 88
Hitchin, 137
Hitler, 44
HMSO, 120, 121, 152
Holborow, 126, 134
Holistic, 22, 108, 109
Hollands, 143, 192, 216, 219
Holmes, 40, 48
Hopkins, 139, 140, 149
Hormones, 147
Horse, 60, 69, 168, 170, 182, 220
Horse-racing, 169
Horse-riding, 62
Horses, 13, 168, 178, 194
Horsham, 152
Hospital; Hospitals, 96, 105, 143, 157, 160, 219, 229
Houghton (Lord), 1, 120, 149, 150, 195, 223
Hound, 15, 157
House-mouse, 85
Howard-Jones, 134
Hoyt, 218
Hugo, 47
Human, 1, 2, 7, 8, 10, 11, 12, 13, 17, 20, 21, 23, 24, 25,
       26, 27, 29, 30, 32, 33, 34, 35, 36, 37, 39, 40, 41,
       42, 43, 48, 49, 52, 53, 54, 57, 74, 80, 97, 98, 101,
       105, 109, 112, 114, 115, 116, 117, 119, 121, 124,
       128, 134, 140, 141, 142, 143, 144, 145, 146, 151,
       152, 154, 164, 166, 167, 168, 169, 170, 171, 172,
       175, 191, 203, 210, 211, 214, 217, 219, 222, 228, 229
Human-centred, 80, 168
Human-kind, 34
Human-to-human, 24
Humane, 17, 52, 53, 54, 55, 56, 57, 58, 63, 64, 65, 66,
       67, 68, 69, 70, 71, 72, 73, 74, 75, 101, 105, 112,
       136, 137, 138, 139, 140, 144, 145, 146, 148, 150,
       151, 153, 157, 160, 167, 171, 201, 203, 204, 216,
       217, 218, 222, 223, 224, 225, 226, 228
Humanely; Humaneness, 78, 163, 166
Humanise; Humanised, 71, 170, 220
Humanising, 160, 210
Humanism; Humanists, 17
Humanitarian, 17, 24, 34, 96
Humanitarianism, 17
Humanity, 72, 100, 106, 164
Humankind, 25, 26, 27, 34
Humanoid, 61
Humans, 8, 25, 28, 29, 31, 32, 33, 34, 35, 36, 39, 41, 42,
       43, 78, 87, 88, 97, 98, 99, 100, 101, 140, 141, 143,
       162, 172, 201, 203, 219
Hunter-gatherer, 87
Hunters, 162, 165
Hunting, 62, 162, 163
Hunting-gathering, 87
Husbandry, 74, 88, 90, 91, 94, 101, 102, 158, 184, 185,
       186, 192, 201, 202, 206, 213, 229
Hutches, 8
Hyde, 96
Hygiene, 196
Hyperactivity, 89

Hypertension, 108
Hypophysis, 82

IASP, 98
IBA, 223
ICI, 147
Idealist; Idealists, 15, 162
Illness, 91, 101, 193, 201, 202
Immoral, 103, 192
Immune, 142, 192
Immunobiological, 152
In-vitro, 117 (see vitro/vivo)
Incarnation, 25, 26, 27, 44, 46
Incontinence, 188
Indians, 11
Inhumane, 17, 145
Inject; Injection, 98, 143, 185
Injure, 11, 22, 166
Injured, 8, 157, 175, 177, 181, 186, 189, 194
Injuries, 11, 36, 177, 180, 181, 182, 187
Injury, 22, 46, 91, 105, 116, 117, 177, 185, 193, 201, 202
Inoculating, 143
Insensitive, 166, 205
Inspection; Inspections, 88, 101, 130
Inspector; Inspectors, 130, 190, 194, 197
Inspectorate, 101, 102, 196, 198, 221
Insulin, 116
Inter-vertebral, 182
Interbreeding, 11
Intravenous, 147
Invertebrates, 81
IRB; IRBs, 134, 105
Irenaeus, 27, 49
Isaacs, 52, 53, 57
Isaiah, 43, 81

Jacob, 170
Japan, 53, 113, 121
Japanese, 53, 112
Jeffery, 208, 221, 229
Jekyll, 96
Jerusalem, 45, 225
Jesus, 20, 26, 33, 34, 44, 45
Jew, 45
Judaeo-Christian, 46, 80

Kangaroo; Kangaroos, 124, 133
Kant, 38
Kantian, 97
Keepers, 198
Kegan, 57
Keller, 171
Kellert, 54, 57, 63
Kennel; Kennels, 90, 188, 204, 220
Keratitis, 188
Kerygma, 44
Kidney, 98, 143, 144
Kill, 13, 28, 29, 33, 53, 83, 96, 101, 108, 162, 163, 164,
    166, 177, 204

Killed, 7, 8, 11, 81, 99, 143, 144, 145, 156, 162, 165
Killing, 10, 28, 29, 30, 36, 84, 99, 138, 162, 163, 165,
     166, 222
Kind, 6, 7, 8, 9, 11, 16, 17, 18, 25, 29, 30, 31, 39, 40,
     42, 43, 44, 45, 46, 52, 55, 70, 72, 81, 99, 101, 164,
     167, 175, 201, 210, 216
Kindness, 27, 47, 52, 54, 66, 68, 216, 217
Kipling's, 167, 171
Kitten; Kittens, 160
Konrad, 78
Koreans, 10
Kuchel, 129, 134

Laboratories, 111, 138, 143, 145, 176
Laboratory, 9, 84, 85, 96, 102, 104, 107, 111, 113, 114,
     115, 119, 120, 121, 128, 130, 134, 138, 143, 144,
     145, 146, 149, 150, 151, 159, 160, 200, 227
Lambing, 91
Lambs, 89, 92
LAMC, 194
Lancashire, 229
Lancet, 108, 110
Langley, 110, 136, 211, 212, 217, 228
Larynx, 211
Latham, 157
Laurance, 108, 110
Law, 1, 5, 12, 13, 22, 23, 28, 29, 47, 101, 104, 105, 110,
     115, 117, 120, 125, 127, 129, 134, 174, 176, 178,
     179, 180, 190, 213, 214, 220, 223, 225, 229
Law-making, 1
Lawful, 45
Lawler, 36, 48
Lawrence, 202
Laws, 36, 100, 101, 102, 111, 113, 114, 115, 119, 126, 223
Lawson, 137, 150
Lawson-Tait, 137
Lawyers, 178
Layers, 193
Laying, 89, 92
Lecturer; Lecturers, 200, 202, 205, 225, 226, 228, 229
Lectures, 202
Leg, 177, 188
Legislate; Legislations, 178, 179, 196
Legislating, 174
Legislation, 1, 75, 89, 100, 101, 102, 103, 104, 105, 110,
     113, 123, 124, 125, 127, 129, 130, 131, 132, 134,
     151, 164, 174, 178, 179, 194, 195, 196, 197, 200,
     202, 203, 219, 220, 221, 224
Legislative, 100, 104, 123, 124, 125, 127, 130, 132, 150,
     174, 196
Legislator; Legislators, 86, 106, 131
Licence; Licences, 102, 104, 115, 143, 150, 151, 198
Licensed, 68, 108
Licensee; Licensees, 150, 151
Licensing, 68, 101, 102, 105, 123, 195, 198

Life, 1, 5, 7, 8, 11, 13, 20, 21, 22, 23, 24, 25, 27, 28,
    29, 30, 34, 37, 38, 39, 43, 44, 45, 46, 48, 53, 54,
    56, 57, 70, 71, 72, 80, 81, 83, 85, 86, 93, 97, 109,
    144, 157, 162, 163, 165, 167, 168, 169, 170, 172,
    176, 177, 178, 182, 188, 189, 193, 203, 204, 208,
    209, 218, 223
Linzey, 20, 25, 26, 27, 28, 31, 37, 38, 39, 41, 42, 43,
    45, 48, 49, 217, 225
Lion; Lions, 42, 43, 168
Literature, 56, 60, 61, 69, 167, 168, 169, 170, 171, 220,
    226, 228
Litigation, 112
Littlewood, 148, 149, 152
Liver; Livers, 142
Liverpool, 183, 192, 205, 225, 228, 229
Livestock, 87, 88, 89, 91, 92, 93, 163, 164, 179, 186,
    190, 194, 196, 197, 198, 201
Livestock-keeping, 87
London, 47, 48, 49, 50, 57, 66, 69, 72, 86, 92, 94, 110,
    120, 121, 122, 137, 143, 152, 153, 206, 228
Lorenz, 78
Lorton, 155, 156, 157, 158, 159, 160
Lyman, 168

MAFF, 89, 190, 196
Magel, 36
Maize, 93
Malcarne, 68
Male; Males, 11, 34, 45, 69
Malnutrition, 185
Mammal; Mammals, 11, 24, 25, 61, 76, 81, 165, 226
Mammary, 107, 110
Man, 6, 17, 21, 25, 26, 27, 29, 30, 31, 32, 33, 34, 35,
    36, 38, 39, 40, 41, 43, 45, 47, 50, 80, 81, 84, 87,
    114, 121, 126, 134, 142, 157, 166, 170, 187, 189,
    198, 211, 213, 225
Man's, 10, 20, 28, 30, 31, 32, 40, 47, 63, 80, 192
Manchester, 48, 227
Market, 53, 66, 71, 89, 92, 104, 108, 190, 196
Market-place, 71
Marketed, 172
Marketing, 85, 118, 200
Markets, 86, 91, 117, 190, 194, 195, 197
Marshall, 49
Martin, 141
Marx, 16
Massachusetts, 72
Matthew, 45
Mature, 128, 220
McCloskey, 131
McCulloch, 206
McGriffin, 57
McLeod, 226
Me-too, 108
Meat, 44, 54, 66, 87, 88, 89, 92, 93, 156, 164, 169, 176,
    196, 218, 223, 227
Meat-eating, 18, 164

Medical, 96, 97, 99, 103, 104, 106, 107, 108, 109, 110,
     117, 121, 122, 123, 125, 136, 143, 146, 149, 150,
     151, 181, 184, 188, 203, 204, 206, 224, 227, 228
Medically, 189
Medication; Medicinal, 88, 89, 91, 92
Medicine; Medicines, 103, 109, 137, 144, 148, 158
Melbourne, 133
Men, 6, 8, 9, 16, 32, 33, 36, 47, 155, 158, 159, 160
Messiah; Messianic, 43, 81
Metabolise; Metabolism, 142, 152
Metazoa, 140
Microbiological, 145
Microbiologists, 143
Microbiology, 143, 152
Microscopy, 152
Midgley, 15, 210, 217, 225
Milburn, 73, 217, 226
Mink, 164
Mirror-experiments, 99
Monkey, 143, 144, 213
Monkeys, 118, 143, 144, 145, 213
Moral, 4, 5, 10, 11, 16, 17, 21, 23, 24, 27, 28, 30, 31,
     33, 36, 38, 40, 42, 45, 48, 49, 52, 64, 65, 67, 68,
     69, 78, 80, 82, 84, 88, 97, 98, 99, 100, 103, 104,
     105, 109, 114, 125, 126, 127, 129, 132, 133, 162,
     185, 198, 204, 208, 209, 210, 213, 214, 216, 217,
     222, 223, 225, 229
Morality, 17, 23, 45, 50, 57, 73, 77, 168, 210, 213, 214
Morally, 25, 36, 39, 40, 42, 43, 46, 53, 80, 96, 97, 101,
     103, 105, 106, 125
Morals, 67
Mores, 17
Morris, 61
Morton; Morton´s, 117, 121, 220
Mosaic, 28, 29
Moslem, 159
Mosquito; Mosquitoes, 9, 60
Motivation; Motivated, 11, 116, 136, 137, 149, 192, 201,
     219, 226
Motivations, 148
Motive; Motives, 9, 10, 22
Mouse, 107, 121, 126, 134
Mutagenic; Mutagenicity, 140, 142
Mutagens, 140, 141
Mutation, 142
Mutilation, 89, 187, 194
Mutilations, 179, 186, 187, 195
Myelopathy, 188

NAAHE, 68, 70, 71, 72
Nathan´s, 10
Natural, 1, 9, 11, 13, 29, 30, 31, 33, 36, 37, 38, 40, 43,
     50, 54, 58, 74, 90, 91, 146, 163, 164, 166, 168, 169,
     170, 171, 185, 201, 208, 209, 212, 213, 226
Naturalistic, 24, 220
Nature, 1, 20, 23, 24, 26, 27, 29, 30, 31, 34, 37, 39, 40,
     43, 47, 49, 53, 72, 80, 96, 100, 109, 112, 117, 121,
     123, 126, 129, 131, 134, 168, 170, 171, 177, 209,
     210, 211, 212, 225

Nature's, 87, 170
Natures, 11, 13, 26
Needs, 9, 39, 42, 54, 68, 83, 86, 87, 100, 119, 123, 127,
    129, 158, 184, 196, 199, 201, 213, 217, 219
Neglect, 12, 16, 42, 75, 85, 181, 202
Neglected, 16, 38, 49, 86, 108, 115, 171, 181, 196
Negligence; Negligent, 168, 183
Nematode, 84
Nephritis, 144
Nerve; Nerves, 36, 96, 219
Netherlands, 113, 121
Neuro-surgery, 107
Neurochemistry, 228
Neurochemists, 98
Neurophysiology, 198
Neurosurgery, 110, 121
Neutered, 175
Newcastle-on-Tyne, 205, 206, 225
NFU, 194
NICHE, 222
Nobel, 88, 143
Non-agricultural, 87
Non-animal, 114, 119, 136, 146, 147, 148, 149, 150, 151,
    152
Non-farming, 91
Non-human, 16, 27, 30, 33, 34, 36, 37, 40, 42, 44, 49, 52,
    54, 113, 217, 227
Non-invasive, 151, 165
Non-medical, 107
Non-microscopic, 9
Non-rational, 35
Non-scientist; Non-scientists, 128, 129, 131
Non-sentient, 102
Non-sentimental, 10
Non-theological, 26
Nottingham, 48, 137, 227, 228
Nutrition, 158, 160, 200, 201, 202

O'Brien, 171
Oates, 49
Oath, 203
Objective, 54, 58, 61, 76, 82, 103, 115, 195, 198, 219
Objectives, 1, 53, 67, 77, 132, 198
Objectivity, 126, 133, 134
Obligation; Obligations, 4, 12, 13, 80, 180, 204, 208,
    209, 211, 217, 221
Octopus, 81
Ohio, 157
Oklahoma, 72
Ontario, 225
Opinion, 2, 75, 102, 126, 162, 189, 190, 193, 194, 195,
    197, 199, 205
Opinions, 5, 17, 59, 80, 129, 131, 192, 193, 194, 200,
    203, 204, 205
Orlans, 117, 121
Orwell, 171
OTA, 111, 117, 121
Ottawa, 121
Otter, 169

Owen, 69
Owned, 160, 187
Owner, 174, 175, 176, 177, 178, 179, 181, 185, 187, 189,
    220
Owner´s, 174, 176, 177, 178, 181, 188, 220
Owners, 12, 99, 175, 176, 180, 181, 188
Ownership, 13, 76, 158, 160, 180
Owning, 181
Ox; Oxen, 8, 28, 29, 30, 45
Oxford, 47, 48, 50, 121, 134, 166, 212, 225, 227, 229

Pagan, 17
Page, 59, 72, 160, 171, 211
Paid, 13, 192, 208
Pain; Pains, 7, 11, 12, 17, 32, 33, 36, 66, 83, 85, 91,
    97, 98, 101, 102, 114, 117, 136, 138, 164, 165, 175,
    182,   187, 188, 193, 200, 201, 202
Pain-free, 188
Pain-killing, 82
Painful; Painfully, 18, 91, 114, 115, 175, 188, 189
Painless; Painlessly, 83, 187
PAL, 155, 158, 159, 160
Palazzini, 31, 49
Palestine, 45
Palmer, 221
Pancreas, 204
Panda, 60
Papal, 28
Parasite; Parasites, 94, 108, 185
Parasitical, 31, 43
Parasitism, 201
Parent; Parent´s; Parental, 13, 61, 175, 181, 227
Parenting, 7
Parents, 5, 6, 10, 59, 67, 168, 220
Parliament, 1, 2, 3, 104, 120, 124, 133, 174, 178, 213
Parliamentarians, 1, 2, 150
Parliamentary, 1, 2, 3, 49, 148, 149, 151, 195
Parrots, 194
Parturition, 107, 110, 188
Paterson, 37, 49, 54, 57, 58, 60, 63, 216, 219, 225
PDSA, 202
Pekingese, 188
Pelvis, 188, 204
Pennsylvania, 116
Peptides, 82
Peregrine, 210
Perkins, 144, 145, 153
Pest, 85, 163, 222
Pest-controllers, 163
Pest-mammals, 84
Pest-species, 84
Pet, 12, 53, 54, 60, 62, 65, 76, 85, 99, 187
Pet-care, 217
Pet-therapy, 219
Peters, 74
Pets, 9, 10, 56, 57, 59, 61, 68, 76, 83, 84, 85, 99, 112,
    163, 165, 184, 226
Pharmaceutical; Pharmaceuticals, 108, 148, 196
Pharmacology, 117, 153

247

Pharmacy, 117
Philadelphia, 49, 69, 168
Philippine; Philippines, 13
Philosopher, 5, 6, 14, 29, 73, 203, 204, 225
Philosophers, 5, 6, 10, 23, 37, 129, 131, 205, 224
Philosophical; Philosophic, 5, 17, 20, 29, 53, 80, 100,
    203, 216, 217
Philosophy, 1, 5, 6, 17, 23, 24, 34, 47, 106, 168, 194,
    216, 224, 225, 226, 229
Phylogenetic, 146
Physicians, 98, 107
Physiological, 182, 188, 202
Physiologist; Physiologists, 18, 117
Physiology, 81, 110, 117, 201, 228
Pig; Pig's, 10, 61, 85, 87, 91, 107, 110, 143, 147, 169,
    182, 185, 194, 201, 206
Pig-keeping, 183
Pigeons, 45
Piglet; Piglets, 90, 91, 178, 226
Pigs, 87, 89, 90, 91, 93, 107, 143, 145, 158, 169, 171,
    183, 185, 227
Pitman-Moore, 158
Plant, 24, 25, 80, 83, 170, 222
Plants, 25, 28, 29, 37, 81, 83, 84
Police, 156, 157, 177, 180, 181, 196
Policeman; Policemen, 174, 180
Policing, 196
Polio; Poliomyelitis, 143, 144, 145, 147
Political, 74, 111, 114, 126, 128, 131, 190, 193, 194,
    195, 198, 199, 216, 220, 221, 229
Politically, 193, 195
Politicians, 194
Politics, 1, 2, 49, 74, 110, 112, 126, 133, 134, 196, 225
Polymers, 112
Pony, 62
Pope, 35
Poultry, 88, 183, 185, 194
Pound-animal; Pound-animals, 99
Pounds, 58, 99
Preclinical, 121
Predation; Predatory, 43, 185
Predator; Predators, 99, 168, 169, 222
Pregnancy; Pregnant, 145, 147, 160
Presbyterian, 98
Pre-schools, 71
Prescribing, 125
Prescription, 15, 52, 121
President, 158, 218, 229
Press, 48, 49, 50, 57, 63, 121, 122, 133, 134, 152, 166,
    195, 225
Prey; Preyed, 7, 168, 169, 213
Primatt, 31, 32, 33, 35, 36, 43, 49
Prison; Prisons, 7, 155, 157, 219
Prisoner; Prisoners, 7, 8, 12, 155, 159, 160
Pro-hunting, 69
Producer; Producers, 75, 92, 208, 212
Product, 94, 104, 118, 123
Production, 76, 77, 82, 85, 87, 91, 92, 120, 143, 144,
    147, 153, 164, 176, 194, 202, 213

Productivity, Productive, 156, 164, 202
Products, 53, 92, 93, 94, 103, 104, 108, 115, 118, 144,
    158, 218
Professor; Professors, 5, 64, 70, 71, 131, 146, 192, 205,
    217, 225, 226
Professorial, 198
Prophet; Prophets, 10, 15, 44
Prosecute, 196
Prosecuted, 178, 196
Prosecution; Prosecutions, 181, 196, 197
Protectionists, 70
Psychiatry, 57
Psychological, 15, 56
Psychologically, 105
Psychologist; Psychologists, 52, 57, 171, 228
Psychology, 52, 56, 110, 216, 225, 228
Psychopaths, 10
Puppies; Pups, 175, 178, 179, 187, 188, 220
Pyfield, 48
Pyrogenicity, 147

Quantifiable; Quantified, 182, 203
Quantify; Quantifying, 75, 182, 190, 205
Quarantine, 144
Quasi-judicial, 210
Questionnaire; Questionnaires, 59, 128

Rabbit, 8, 60, 63, 85, 147, 169
Rabbits, 8, 83, 138, 145, 147, 148, 158, 168, 170
Rabies, 147
Racism, 69
Radical, 191, 195, 199
Radically, 11, 18
Ramachanran, 107, 110
Rambaut, 27, 49
Ramifications, 21, 71
Randell, 126
Rashers, 164
Rat, 60, 61, 107, 142
Rats, 9, 107, 113, 140, 141, 142, 171
Receptor, 83, 152
Recidivism, 155
Recidivist; Recidivists, 155
Reduction, 111, 113, 117, 120, 138, 140, 152, 165, 188,
    221
Reductionist, 109
Reductions, 117, 226
Reed, 227
Rees, 136, 153
Refinement; Refinements, 111, 120, 138, 145
Regan, 20, 27, 30, 31, 35, 37, 45, 49, 97, 109, 110, 225
Region, 150
Regional; Regionally, 127, 151, 198
Regulation, 123, 126, 127, 131, 132, 134, 143
Regulations, 103, 105, 111, 112, 120, 123, 131, 179
Regulators, 112, 132, 133
Regulatory, 110, 112, 117, 118, 122, 130, 132, 138, 142,
    152, 219
Rehabilitation, 155

Reject; Rejected, 26, 42, 43, 91, 127
Rejecting, 31
Replacement, 99, 103, 111, 119, 120, 138, 145, 147, 149,
    151, 210, 227
Replacements, 136
Replacing, 136, 145, 147, 148
Reproduce; Reproduced, 31, 82, 193
Reproducible, 138
Research, 54, 55, 57, 59, 63, 70, 71, 73, 75, 85, 90, 96,
    97, 98, 99, 100, 102, 103, 105, 106, 107, 108, 110,
    111, 112, 113, 114, 116, 117, 118, 119, 120, 121,
    122, 123, 124, 125, 126, 127, 129, 130, 131, 132,
    133, 134, 136, 137, 138, 139, 140, 142, 146, 147,
    148, 149, 150, 151, 152, 153, 164, 165, 182, 189,
    199, 201, 203, 204, 219, 225, 226, 227, 228
Researched, 58
Researcher; Researcher´s, 52, 105, 106, 114, 165, 226, 227
Researchers, 52, 58, 60, 75, 102, 103, 106, 107, 140, 142,
    148
Researching, 226
Responsibilities, 34, 48, 73, 78, 119, 177, 184, 190, 196,
    206, 217, 227
Responsibility, 1, 20, 22, 24, 28, 31, 33, 34, 37, 39, 41,
    46, 48, 73, 74, 77, 102, 114, 118, 123, 125, 126,
    127, 130, 151, 163, 165, 166, 178, 186, 191, 193,
    196, 197, 198, 203, 216, 217, 226
Responsible, 35, 76, 100, 101, 113, 119, 164, 165, 202,
    203, 212, 216
Retailers, 92
Reverence, 20, 21, 22, 23, 24, 25, 27, 28, 39, 41, 46, 57,
    71, 109, 204
Reverence-in-practice, 21
Reverencing, 38
Riddell, 122
Ride, 46
Riding, 45, 61, 191
Rieser, 57
Rightists, 17
Rightless, 42
Rights, 2, 13, 20, 22, 31, 35, 36, 37, 38, 40, 41, 42, 43,
    44, 46, 47, 48, 49, 53, 54, 57, 63, 66, 73, 74, 83,
    103, 106, 107, 108, 109, 110, 112, 114, 124, 162,
    166, 167, 174, 178, 179, 204, 211, 216, 217, 220,
    224, 225, 226, 228
Roberts, 27, 49
Robinson, 169
Rockefeller, 139
Rodent; Rodents, 9, 140, 141, 165
Rodeo, 69
Rollin, 53, 57, 204
Roswell, 54, 57
Rothschild, 164, 166
Routledge, 57
Rowan, 96, 125, 126, 135, 204, 206
Rs (three Rs), 64, 74, 111, 113, 119, 206
RSPCA; RSPCA´s, 3, 7, 35, 73, 76, 89, 109, 110, 131, 152,
    179, 180, 181, 194, 203, 216, 225, 226, 227, 76, 225,
    226, 227
Runcie, 40, 41, 49

Russel, 54, 57
Russell, 136, 140, 145, 153, 208, 229
Russia; Russian, 171
Rutgers, 129, 134
Rutland, 229
Ryder, 37, 49, 63, 216

Safety, 103, 104, 112, 120, 122, 145, 152, 187, 201
Safety-testing, 107
Saki´s, 170
Salanda, 157
Salisbury, 81
Salk, 144
Salsburg, 141, 153
Santmire, 28, 49
SCAW, 117
Scholar; Scholars, 28, 34, 43
Scholarly, 70, 71
Scholastic, 28, 31, 42
School; School´s, 53, 54, 56, 57, 59, 61, 64, 66, 69, 76,
    117, 155, 167, 192, 198, 202, 204, 205, 226, 228, 229
School-children, 60
Schooling, 54
Schools, 53, 54, 58, 59, 62, 64, 65, 66, 69, 71, 72, 76,
    77, 198, 200, 201, 204, 205, 218, 228
Schopenhauer, 17
Schweitzer, 20, 21, 22, 23, 24, 25, 27, 28, 43, 46, 48,
    49, 109
Science, 15, 18, 49, 54, 56, 57, 73, 78, 86, 88, 100, 115,
    116, 117, 118, 119, 121, 124, 125, 126, 127, 129,
    131, 132, 133, 134, 136, 143, 145, 149, 152, 159,
    198, 211, 212, 216, 219, 227, 228
Sciences, 5, 103, 117, 121, 146, 152, 193, 218, 226
Scientific, 2, 18, 19, 74, 86, 88, 93, 96, 101, 102, 104,
    105, 106, 111, 112, 114, 115, 116, 118, 119, 120,
    121, 123, 125, 126, 127, 128, 129, 131, 132, 134,
    135, 136, 138, 142, 144, 146, 147, 148, 149, 151,
    152, 185, 191, 192, 195, 198, 203, 210, 212, 213,
    219, 225, 226, 227, 228
Scientifically, 182, 217
Scientist, 110, 119, 148, 165, 220, 228
Scientists, 19, 75, 96, 107, 111, 114, 115, 116, 118, 119,
    120, 124, 129, 130, 131, 136, 142, 143, 145, 146,
    148, 150, 151, 152, 162, 164, 165, 219
Sclerosis, 115, 116
Scotland, 202
Scriptural; Scripture, 20, 29, 34, 35, 37, 38. 40
Sea, 8, 45, 161
Seal; Seals, 7, 8, 9, 65, 69
Secondary, 20, 24, 47, 53, 70, 72, 117, 123
Self-awareness, 25, 39, 97, 99
Self-concept, 99
Self-narcosis, 82
Self-opiate, 220
Senate, 124, 130, 133
Senator, 131
Sensitive, 60, 62, 128, 140, 141, 143
Sensitivities, 132
Sensitivity, 60, 62, 140, 141, 204, 205

Sensory, 83
Sentience, 96, 97
Sentiency, 36, 37
Sentient, 36, 76, 106, 114
Sentiment, 10, 11, 66
Sentimental, 10, 12, 18, 22, 24, 62, 170
Sentimentalise, 176, 210
Sentimentality, 168
Sentiments, 10, 11, 65, 187, 195
Serpell, 162, 166, 228
Sharratt, 141, 152
Sheep, 9, 10, 13, 28, 45, 91, 124, 133, 168, 171, 194, 227
Sheep-worrying, 180
Shelter, 91, 163, 185, 202, 208
Shepherd; Shepherds, 171
Sherwood, 57
Shistosomiasis, 108
Sinclair, 29, 49
Singer, 23, 30, 37, 50, 52, 54, 55, 57, 97, 131
Slaughter, 85, 86, 164, 176, 189, 194, 197, 199, 200, 218
Slaughter-house, 189, 190, 196, 202, 218
Slaughtered, 164, 176, 189
Slaughtering, 84
Societal, 64, 65, 117, 124, 125, 127, 132
Societies, 1, 5, 9, 65, 112, 131, 137, 139, 196, 198
Society, 2, 7, 10, 12, 13, 34, 35, 53, 54, 58, 64, 65, 66,
        67, 68, 87, 89, 100, 101, 105, 106, 108, 109, 110,
        125, 126, 131, 133, 134, 136, 137, 138, 140, 141,
        146, 147, 151, 152, 153, 156, 157, 160, 161, 163,
        166, 167, 170, 176, 191, 193, 204, 208, 217, 218,
        223, 224, 226, 229
Socrates, 6
Sow, 74, 86, 90, 91, 182
Sowerby (Lord Houghton), 120
Sows, 86, 87, 90, 192, 226
Sparrows, 20, 37, 45
Spayed; Spaying, 175, 188
SPCA, 72, 202
SPCK, 48, 49
Species, 1, 9, 11, 13, 30, 33, 39, 43, 59, 65, 69, 80, 81,
        83, 84, 85, 110, 114, 137, 141, 142, 144, 162, 163,
        165, 171, 200, 202, 209, 218, 220, 222
Species-good, 8
Speciesism, 216
Spider; Spiders, 22, 60, 61, 213
Spinal, 188
SPVS, 229
Squid, 81
Squirrels, 9
Statistical, 59, 141, 145
Statistics, 69, 155
Stereotype; Stereotypes, 19, 54, 171
Stereotyping, 15, 217
Stewart, 200, 221, 229
Stockmanship, 86, 92, 183
Stolba, 201, 206
Stone, 11, 21, 132, 135
Stories, 7, 44, 61, 62, 168, 169, 170
Story, 38, 167, 170, 209, 212

Stouffer, 212
Straw, 86, 87, 90, 93
Straw-yard, 86, 89
Stray, 69, 112, 165, 177
Strayed, 21, 180
Stress; Stressed, 16, 82, 90, 91, 163, 165, 171, 182, 187,
    191, 201, 217, 221
Stresses, 106
Sub-mammalian, 141
Subconscious, 69
Suckled; Suckling, 91, 145
Suffering, 17, 21, 35, 37, 44, 66, 73, 74, 78, 88, 90, 93,
    96, 97, 98, 101, 102, 104, 105, 106, 111, 114, 115,
    118, 119, 138, 139, 140, 144, 145, 152, 165, 175,
    178, 193, 199, 200, 202, 205, 212, 213
Supermantis, 10
Surgery, 106, 175, 177, 181, 188
Surgical, 180, 184, 188
Surgically, 107, 189
Sussex, 54, 63, 216, 226, 228
Swedish, 150
Sydney, 134, 148, 225
Syllabus, 77, 159, 217
Symposium, 49, 54, 57, 63, 136, 152, 189, 191, 206, 208, 216,
    217, 219, 222, 226
Synod, 41, 48

T-shirts, 156
Table, 21, 60, 89, 92, 137, 139, 141
Table-chicken, 88
Tail; Tails, 167, 174, 178, 179, 182, 187, 220
Tail-biting, 84
Tail-cutting, 90, 91
Tail-docking, 187, 194
Tame, 165, 211, 212
Tandy, 178, 182, 193, 220, 229
Tannenbaum, 125, 126, 135
Taxonomic, 146
Taylor, 117, 121
TB, 143, 147, 196
Teacher, 53, 70, 71, 72, 226
Teacher-evaluation, 160
Teachers, 1, 53, 54, 56, 58, 66, 67, 69, 70, 71, 72, 183
Teaching, 54, 55, 56, 57, 64, 68, 69, 70, 74, 77, 85, 117,
    123, 127, 129, 131, 156, 159, 200, 204, 206, 216,
    218, 228, 229
Terata, 141
Teratogenic; Teratogens, 112
Terrestrial, 31
Tetanus, 147
Texas, 72
Theism, 43
Theocentric, 39
Theologian; Theologians, 17, 23, 27, 43, 44
Theological, 20, 24, 25, 27, 33, 34, 35, 36, 37, 39, 41,
    42, 43, 48, 216, 217
Theologically, 41, 42
Theology, 24, 27, 28, 31, 35, 39, 47, 48, 49, 225, 226
Theos-rights, 39, 41, 42, 46

Therapeutic, 89, 108
Therapy, 57
Thomas, 28, 31, 35, 45, 48, 50, 132, 170
Thomist, 29, 32, 35, 42
Thompson, 167
Thomson, 25, 50
Thrombosis, 108
Tindall, 86
Toads, 147
Torrance, 24, 25, 26, 40, 44, 48
Toxic, 141
Toxicities, 140
Toxicity, 112, 117, 118, 120, 122, 136, 137, 138, 140,
    141, 142, 146, 147, 148, 152, 227, 228
Toxicologic, 121
Toxicological, 138, 152
Toxicologist, 141, 146
Toxicologists, 118, 137, 138, 141, 142, 148, 151
Toxicology, 125, 136, 138, 140, 146, 148, 152
Traherne, 28
Treated, 7, 8, 17, 84, 90, 94, 165
Treating, 18, 168, 193
Treatment, 17, 33, 35, 36, 42, 45, 54, 55, 56, 57, 60, 66,
    80, 85, 94, 108, 119, 132, 162, 163, 166, 167, 168,
    175, 177, 180, 181, 184, 185, 186, 188, 191, 193,
    196, 199, 201, 202
Trinitarian, 40
Trinity, 216
Tryon, 35, 36
Tubercle, 152
Tuberculosis, 143
Tucker, 167, 220, 228
Tufts, 204
Tulsa, 72
Turkeys, 89, 94
TVEI, 218

UFAW, 137, 152, 179, 185, 200, 201, 202, 203, 205, 206
Umbrella-body, 223
Undergraduate; Undergraduates, 117, 183
Unethical, 179, 212
Unilever, 147, 148
Universities, 53, 72, 77, 136, 200, 227
University, 49, 54, 63, 72, 116, 121, 133, 134, 135, 139,
    147, 148, 183, 192, 205, 206, 208, 213, 216, 225,
    226, 227, 228, 229
Urban, 53
Urinary, 188
Urination, 98
USA, 17, 60, 105, 113, 117, 128, 139, 140
Usage, 36, 80, 83, 88, 217, 220, 221, 222
Utilitarian, 23, 27, 97, 104
Utilitarianism, 17

Vaccinate, 159, 185
Vaccination, 106, 144, 160
Vaccine, 143, 144, 145
Vaccines, 108, 144, 145, 147, 158
Value-commitment, 66

Value-free, 126
Value-hierarchy, 19
Value-judgement, 217
Value-laden, 127
Values, 52, 53, 64, 65, 66, 68, 70, 71, 72, 78, 100, 110,
    125, 126, 127, 128, 131, 133, 134, 137, 217
Vandalism, 2
Veal, 65, 69, 86, 87, 206
Vegan, 22, 44, 228
Vegetarian, 22, 44, 47, 168, 218
Vegetarians, 34, 165, 166, 176
Vermin, 162, 163, 220
Vertebrate; Vertebrates, 11, 81, 117
Vet: Vets, 18, 196, 197, 198, 220, 221, 224
Veterinarian, 142, 173, 174, 175, 176, 177, 178, 181, 182,
    189, 190, 191, 192, 200, 204, 205, 206, 220
Veterinarians, 7, 53, 76, 119, 159, 180, 181, 183, 184,
    186, 189, 192, 193, 195, 196, 197, 199, 203, 204,
    205, 220, 229
Veterinary, 12, 13, 86, 97, 108, 117, 174, 175, 176, 177,
    178, 179, 180, 181, 182, 183, 184, 185, 186, 187,
    188, 189, 190, 191, 192, 193, 194, 196, 197, 198,
    200, 201, 202, 203, 204, 205, 206, 216, 220, 221,
    226, 228, 229
Victoria, 123, 127, 130, 133, 134
Victorian, 123, 133
Violence; Violent, 12, 43, 55, 96, 100, 106, 169, 189, 204
Violence-free, 223
Virginia, 155
Virulent, 144
Virus, 143, 144, 145
Viruses, 143, 144, 145
Vitamin; Vitamins, 136, 145, 147
Vitro (in vitro), 128, 136, 139, 141, 142, 144, 146, 147,
    148, 149
Vivisection, 137, 228
Vivisectionists, 137
Vivo (in vivo), 139, 142, 146

Wader, 209
Wales, 123, 127, 130, 133, 134, 135
Ward, 41, 177
Warnock, 126, 135
Warwick, 192
Washington, 57, 121, 152, 155, 157
Webster, 185, 192, 201, 206
Welfare, 1, 5, 6, 7, 8, 9, 11, 12, 13, 15, 18, 31, 35, 47,
    58, 60, 65, 68, 73, 74, 75, 76, 77, 78, 80, 81, 82,
    83, 84, 85, 86, 87, 89, 90, 92, 93, 96, 102, 105,
    106, 111, 112, 116, 117, 120, 121, 123, 124, 127,
    129, 130, 131, 133, 136, 138, 139, 147, 162, 164,
    166, 173, 176, 178, 179, 180, 182, 184, 185, 186,
    187, 189, 190, 191, 192, 193, 194, 195, 196, 197,
    198, 199, 200, 201, 202, 203, 204, 205, 206, 216,
    217, 218, 219, 220, 221, 222, 223, 224, 226, 227, 229
Welfare-orientated, 227
Welfarist, 74
Welfarists, 7, 73, 75, 131, 137, 139

Well-being, 7, 8, 9, 10, 11, 13, 74, 91, 119, 124, 160,
    182, 184, 200, 201, 202, 204
Weller, 143, 144
Westerlund, 67, 72
Westerman, 34
Westervelt, 63
Westminster, 1
Whale: Whales, 59, 65, 69, 133
Wheat, 93
Wheathampstead, 49
Whitefang, 169
Whitehead, 55
Whitehouse, 35
Whitelaw, 2
Whitfield, 157, 158, 159
Whitlock, 67, 72
Wild, 8, 12, 45, 60, 62, 63, 85, 114, 144, 169, 170, 172,
    184, 203, 211, 212
Wild-caught, 143, 144
Wilde, 210
Wilderness, 45
Wildlife, 2, 58, 59, 60, 62, 63, 65, 163, 166, 208, 210,
    211, 212, 214, 216, 221, 229
Williamson, 169
Winston, 206
Wohlwill, 57
Wolf, 60, 61
Wolves, 168
Women, 17, 45, 69, 155, 158
Wood-Gush, 201
WSPA, 223
Wynn-Tyson, 44

X-ray, 177
Xenopus, 147

Yards, 90, 194
Yeasts, 141
York, 48, 49, 56, 57, 64, 72, 120, 121, 122, 125, 134,
    146, 152

Zambia, 229
Zbinden, 118, 122
Zealand, 131, 223
Zeglen, 206
Zollikon, 122
Zoo; Zoos, 9, 61, 84, 85, 178, 195, 202, 211, 212, 226
Zoology, 226, 227, 228

## STEERING COMMITTEE

Societies associated with setting up this
Symposium:

**BVA.AWF   (BVA Animal Welfare Foundation)**
          7 Mansfield Street, London   W1M 0AT

**Dr Hadwen Trust for Humane Research**
          6c Brand Street, Hitchin, Herts   SG5 1HX

**FRAME     (Fund for the Replacement of Animals in Medical
          Experiments)**
          34 Stoney Street, Nottingham   NG1 1NB

**Humane Education Foundation**
          2 Hancock Court, Chapel Break, Norwich NR5 9NN

**RSPCA     (Royal Society for the Prevention of Cruelty to
          Animals)**
          Causeway, Horsham, West Sussex   RH12 1HG

**St Andrew Animal Fund**
          10 Queensferry Street, Edinburgh   EH2 4PG

## ACKNOWLEDGEMENTS

Our grateful thanks go out to all the participants and speakers,
without whom this conference could never have taken place, but
must also extend to the following organisations, who assisted
us greatly by helping to subsidise the symposium...

C-Vet
Hoechst
Humane Society of the United States
International Fund for Animal Welfare
League Against Cruel Sports
National Committee for the Co-ordination of Animal Protection
Norden Laboratories
Pfizer
Scottish Society for the Prevention of Cruelty to Animals
Vygon
World Society for the Protection of Animals

257